Greta Bradman is a registered psychologist, researcher, writer, broadcaster and performing artist whose four solo classical albums have all hit #1 on the ARIA charts. She works in private psychology practice where she specialises in values coaching individuals and teams, coaching high performers, and the treatment of anxiety disorders. Greta regularly writes and talks about applying human values in the modern world, including their use for the individual, the organisation, and in the context of contemporary AI. She also maintains a connection with classical music by presenting *Weekend Brunch* and *Mindful Music* on ABC Classic.

WHAT MATTERS TO YOU

WHAT MATTERS TO YOU

GRETA J. BRADMAN

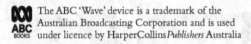 The ABC 'Wave' device is a trademark of the Australian Broadcasting Corporation and is used under licence by HarperCollins*Publishers* Australia

HarperCollins*Publishers*
Australia • Brazil • Canada • France • Germany • Holland • India
Italy • Japan • Mexico • New Zealand • Poland • Spain • Sweden
Switzerland • United Kingdom • United States of America

HarperCollins acknowledges the Traditional Custodians
of the lands upon which we live and work, and pays respect
to Elders past and present.

First published on Gadigal Country in Australia in 2025
by HarperCollins*Publishers* Australia Pty Limited
ABN 36 009 913 517
harpercollins.com.au

Copyright © Greta J. Bradman 2025

The right of Greta J. Bradman to be identified as the author of this work has been asserted by her in accordance with the *Copyright Act 1968*.

All rights reserved. Apart from any use as permitted under the *Copyright Act 1968*, no part may be reproduced, copied, scanned, stored in a retrieval system, recorded, or transmitted, in any form or by any means, without the prior written permission of the publisher. Without limiting the exclusive rights of any author, contributor, or the publisher of this publication, any unauthorised use of this publication to train generative artificial intelligence (AI) technologies is expressly prohibited. HarperCollins also exercises its rights under Article 4(3) of the Digital Single Market Directive 2019/790 and expressly reserves this publication from the text and data-mining exception.

HarperCollins*Publishers*
Macken House, 39/40 Mayor Street Upper
Dublin 1, D01 C9W8, Ireland

A catalogue record for this book is available from the National Library of Australia

ISBN 978 0 7333 4357 5 (paperback)
ISBN 978 1 4607 1761 5 (ebook)

Cover design by Louisa Maggio, HarperCollins Design Studio
Cover image by istockphoto.com
Internal design and illustrations by Louisa Maggio, HarperCollins Design Studio
Typeset in Adobe Garamond Pro by Kirby Jones

Printed and bound in the United States

*To my family, who inspire me daily
to live with the courage of my convictions.*

Contents

Foreword	1
Preface	5
Introduction	9
Chapter 1. **Understanding Values**	19
The Nature of Values	23
Values as Schemas	28
Chapter 2. **Two Sets of Values**	41
Core Values	43
Threat-Based Values	51
Chapter 3. **Know Your Core Values**	69
Identifying Your Core Values	71
The Roles of Your Core Values	77
How Your Values Play Together	93
Values and Negotiation	96
Chapter 4. **Know Your Threat-Based Values**	105
Identifying Threat-Based Values	106
Overcoming Threat for Your Performance	116
Threat-Based Values and the Drama Triangle	122

Chapter 5. **The Power of Meaning in an Uncertain World**   131
Your Relationship with Your Thoughts   135
Values, Emotion, and Navigating Fear   137

Chapter 6. **'Shoulds', Being Enough, and the Impostor Experience**   157
The Impostor Experience   158
Normalise Don't Pathologise the Impostor Experience   168
Indicators of Core Values Misalignment   176

Chapter 7. **Values and the Client Experience with the Impostor Phenomenon**   181
Getting Personal and Practical with the Impostor Experience   183
Play and the Impostor Experience   191
A Practical Approach   196

Chapter 8. **Connecting with Your 'Why'**   211
Core Values vs. Threat-Based Values   217
The Role of the Comfort Zone   230

Chapter 9. **Values-Based Decision-Making**   239
The Power of Values-Based Decision-Making   240
The Importance of 'Why' in Decision-Making   249
Values and Functional Fixedness   255
Applying Values to Small Choices   263

Chapter 10. **The Worthy Role of Values at Work**   275
Company Values Humanise the Organisation   275
The Problem with a Values Vacuum at Work   281
The Importance of Individual Values Diversity at Work   288

Chapter 11. **Conclusion**	293
Individual Values and Collective Impact	294
Values, Decision-Making 'Noise', and Predicting Human Behaviour	297
An Invitation	302
Acknowledgements	307
Appendix	309
Notes	313

Foreword

Didier Elzinga
Founder & CEO, Culture Amp

I've founded four companies, built a multi-billion-dollar software company, led and grown a Hollywood visual effects company, working on film series like *The Lord of the Rings* and *Harry Potter*, and spent my life fascinated by how you build an enduring company through the power of culture.

When I started my software company Culture Amp after 13 years working for Hollywood, I wanted to help create a better world of work. Today, thousands of companies turn to us to understand how to build a high-performance culture of impact. But back then the only person who believed in me – and my idea – was Greta. This book captures, in so many ways, the message she has been sharing with me for almost 25 years about what it takes to realise dreams and ambitions for oneself and one's impact.

What matters to you? It's such a simple question, and yet profoundly challenging to answer. In order to find clarity and an answer that stands the test of time and takes us where we want to go, we need a field guide – a framework to help us understand ourselves and each other.

After almost 30 years I keep coming back to one simple yet powerful framework as the foundation of everything I do: values. I've spent my working life thinking about how they work in an organisational context, but I've also spent my waking life trying to figure out what that means to me as a person and as a leader.

This book provides a field guide to how values actually work – what they are, why they impact us so much and, most importantly, how to figure out what yours are and how to live a life more attuned to them.

As Greta says at the beginning of the book, values are the way we start to answer that nagging feeling of 'there has to be more to life than this ...'

Through my life there have been several books that have fundamentally changed how I think about work, and life. *Man's Search for Meaning* by Viktor E. Frankl, *The Power of Full Engagement* by Jim Loehr and Tony Schwartz, and *Daring Greatly* by Brené Brown would be at the top of my list.

By bringing together all of her experience as a world-class performer, broadcaster and psychologist (Greta is also a highly sought-after coach for clients around high performance as well as anxiety) and as an AI researcher and practitioner (where she has been exploring how AI can be used to unlock these ideas at the next level), Greta has written the next book on that list. This is a book that will fundamentally change how I live the rest of my life.

In a way that only she can, Greta will take you on a journey that began grounded in deep and rigorous science, incorporates years of experience and practice, and is recounted with care and insight that will touch your soul.

FOREWORD

It has been my greatest joy in life to watch Greta wrestle with the ideas and build the framework that you get to enjoy when you read this book. May it be as powerful and important to you as it has been to me.

Preface

Human values are often spoken about these days – in the workplace, in society, in our personal lives. Yet we often fall short of using them to their full potential.

Your values can help illuminate and pave the path to your personal fulfilment and success, yet so often their full potential remains overlooked. Harnessing your values takes understanding of not just what your values *are*, but what a value *is* and how to use it.

Values represent a key to navigating life's greatest challenges and opportunities. More than just a guide, they can be your roadmap for navigating the complexity of what matters most to you. They can anchor and explain your convictions and beliefs. They motivate you to do things that serve your longer-term version of a successful, fulfilling life, rather than getting you caught in a cycle of prioritising short-term wins. Your values can help you make sense of your world and express yourself with authenticity and courage. They can enable you to be thoughtful and collectively minded while being unapologetically 'you'.

After years of practice and research, I believe in the profound utility of values and the benefit of better understanding what they 'are', for the sake of seeing what they can 'do' for us, which is why I've written this book. My goal is to provide some accessible insights into my thinking around values, suitable for anyone looking to dive deeper into understanding these fundamental drivers and how to apply them effectively in their lives.

Whether you're seeking to make better decisions, improve your relationships, or find more meaning in your work or beyond, understanding your values can be transformative. They can serve as an anchor to what matters to you in the long term and illuminate the choices that enable you to cut through the noise about what you 'should' do, have, or be. They can help you clear a path to the version of you that you strive to grow over time. They can help you make sense of life dissatisfaction, frustration and restlessness even when your life seems rosy from the outside looking in. And they can help you find fulfilment and satisfaction no matter the distance between how you spend your time and how you'd ideally like to do so. I fully believe values-in-action can elevate every life. They enable you to better understand others' motivations and unlock stronger relationships, too. Your values, then, help make sense of your experience and allow you to navigate decisions and relationships, and help you get to the crux of what matters to you in this one precious life of yours.

This book draws on my work as a psychologist, some research, and my time in various organisational contexts, but it's not a scientific tome. Instead, I'm offering a personal perspective on values – one shaped by countless interactions with clients, colleagues, academics, and my own journey. I've seen firsthand how understanding and applying values can transform lives, and it's these insights I'm eager to share. That journey for me was one of moving from struggling as a child with anxiety, sensory issues and school refusal, to reaching a point of being relatively comfortable in my own very imperfect skin.

The first inkling of using values as a way of moving forward (not that I had a word for them back then) – of trying to anchor my actions to what mattered most to me – happened when I was around 18 or 19 years old. I used to write a lot of poetry as well as journalling prolifically in an attempt to process events, and I found myself turning to taking 'little steps'. Little steps in the direction of a version of myself that was more than the sick girl, the weird girl, the 'not-enough' girl. I didn't exactly know what it meant to grow 'me' more intentionally, but I knew that I needed some guideposts (values) to help take me forward on this unknown journey. I started deploying values exploration and intentional actioning to gradually move myself out of an identity and direction fog and toward a clearer sense of self.

In *What Matters to You*, you'll get to explore your values more deeply and start actioning them in ways and situations you mightn't have thought of before, including in your decision-making and relationships. You'll learn about how each of us has not one but two sets of values that are relevant to our experience, and you'll discover how your values inform what's important to you, offer you courage, and help you navigate fear.

A caveat on the way in. This isn't about turning you into a perfectly values-aligned robot, nor is it about creating a life where you avoid the hard conversations, work, or regrets. It's about helping you build a navigational system that takes you where you want and need to go, where the destination is more about alignment with what matters to you, rather than a predetermined specific place. Further, you don't have to align every decision with your values to achieve satisfaction or make a difference to your life, work, family, community, or the world. Small, values-aligned moves toward where you wish to go are powerful enough. With small moves, great change is possible.

By the end of this book, I hope you'll have a deeper understanding of yourself and your values, along with the tools to make choices that align with what's most important to you. This can lead you to a life that feels more meaningful, fulfilling, and true to who you are becoming, on your own terms. You have this one precious life to make the most of – *What Matters to You* aims to support you in doing just that.

Introduction

Do you feel pressured to align your identity with society's version of 'normal' and 'enough'? You're not alone. From algorithms designed to stimulate our brain's reward system to the opinions of (ideally well-meaning) others, all the chatter of who you should be can drown out that version of yourself that might offer you satisfaction and fulfilment over the long term. The constant self-scrutiny that externally derived expectations – 'shoulds' – foist upon you can leave you questioning if you're good enough, successful enough, unique enough, conforming enough. This frustrating self-doubt and the actions that follow can take you off-track and lead you to pursue a life that doesn't ring true.

In psychology, I work with people who are suffering with anxiety disorders as well as people who are high performers in sports, the arts, business, and beyond. There is a commonality among those I've worked with, no matter whether it's on the clinical or coaching side of my practice, from folks you'd never have heard of, to names you'd likely know and associate with great success. A 'quiet voice' that holds a common musing. At times, it's expressed in a whisper, perhaps apologetically. Sometimes it comes with a question mark, it's been so frayed by experience. Other times, there's an exclamation mark that follows it and no whisper at all. It links to a desire to become more connected with what matters – whether the person knows what matters most to them yet, or not. If I had to sum up the musing, it's this:

'There's got to be more than this.'

This statement seems to have a universality to it, which can be both motivating and debilitating. No matter how little or much we've done, or have, or have achieved, we each have this quiet voice. Values provide direction to that desire for 'more', which I find, in the long term, tends to focus on alignment with what matters rather than simply acquiring trappings of success. 'More' can include resources to support ourselves and our families, the quality of our relationships and intimacy, the recognition and respect we receive, our personal growth, and our ability to contribute to the world.

There is much in life we cannot control, and if we wait until we have 'enough' in certain areas before pursuing other needs, we may find ourselves waiting indefinitely. Our values can serve as a guide, enabling us to work toward 'more than this', even when the horizon seems near, and we're unsure of what lies beyond it. The more we align our choices with our values, the more we can face the wind and move toward life's challenges and opportunities with a sense of possibility and potential.

I have also noticed that when engaging in values coaching, two personas appear relevant to everyone at one point or another. I call them the 'lost' persona and the 'high performer.'

The 'lost' persona is characterised by questions of identity – 'Who am I?' When occupying this persona, we can experience a

INTRODUCTION

sense of decision paralysis, leading from a sense of distrust in our own judgement or a sense of not really knowing what is right for us, perhaps after a lifetime of being told by others, 'This is what you *should* care about, and this is what you *should* choose to do with your time and your life.'

The 'high performer' is characterised by questions of growth and unlocking potential given our strengths and what matters most to us. Without values as a guide, our high performer can become caught up in cycles of doing what they think we 'should' do, have, or be, rather than putting on the brakes long enough to reflect on what matters and where we might best focus our energy. High performance is elevated and enabled with values alignment as it unlocks motivation, meaning, and one's unique edge, as well as longer-term fulfilment.

It may appear that the 'lost' persona is undesirable and the 'high performer' is desirable. However, it's not as simple as that. Both personas are valuable and have a place in cultivating a fulfilling and curious life. We are all both 'lost' and 'high performers'. Some people will spend more time in one persona than the other, but both are relevant to everyone. No matter what we 'do' in life or how much we 'achieve', at times we all feel lost, and at times we all strive to perform.

The quiet voice I mentioned, emanating from a deeper part of ourselves that transcends our current experience, in some sense, appears as a response to the experience of these two personas. The implication of this quiet voice is that, as frustrated as we may feel either by our sense of being lost or wanting to perform better, we perceive some hope. We're holding on to a tiny glimmer of a possibility of 'more' in the darkest of days or from the highest peak where it would seem there is nowhere left to summit. This, I find both audacious and inspiring.

Throughout this book, you'll learn about the power of values to elevate your life and help explain challenges and conflicts. At their best, values provide the courage of conviction to grow your own version of a meaningful self and a life that fits like a glove. They offer a way to explore your unique identity without being sidetracked by 'shoulds', guiding you toward a future version of yourself that benefits both you, your family and the broader world.

By aligning more choices with your core values, you contribute meaningfully to the present moment and set a trajectory toward your own version of a fulfilling life. This personal growth, in turn, helps create a values-led future for us all. The more we align our choices with our core values, the better equipped we are collectively to tackle the greatest challenges facing our planet today.

Human Being and Human Doing

In aligning your choices with your core values, you enable your values to connect your human being with your human doing. Because beneath all the doing – all your actions and decisions – lies an aspirational version of 'you' who is shaped by, yet distinct from, your experiences – what you have done, bought, said, thought and felt.

For so many people, constant 'doing' blurs a sense of who they are and what they really want. Whether climbing mountains, buying a coffee, or avoiding making decisions, your actions – intentional or not – accumulate to help define your current sense of self and where you are. Whether you mean them to or not, your actions guide you in a certain direction. This book provides you with an opportunity to reflect on how your 'doing' aligns with your sense of being, and where you want to go in life given your values. It gives you the opportunity to consider how aligned your choices are with what

INTRODUCTION

truly matters to you, and how you might improve this alignment for longer-term success.

Short-Term Wins vs. Long-Term Alignment

As a psychologist, I've had quite a number of clients who have enjoyed considerable success, who have come to me with some sense of dismay and lack of connection between the life they inhabit and what matters to them. It's not to say they are totally disconnected from what matters, but they sense a misalignment, which is beginning to add up. For a time, their misaligned 'doing' brought momentum and a perception of being productive, yet at some point they've woken to a widening divide between where they are and where they would like to be.

We can mistake productivity and hard work for success, rather than stopping to ask whether it's the sort of success we're after. Misaligned doing might manifest as people-pleasing, doing a 'good job' without pausing to think whether it's the right job, or buying hoards of stuff today rather than investing in a longer-term, larger return (be it health, finances, relationships, or beyond). We can find ourselves 'doing' in ways that inadvertently take us further away from where we seek to grow.

(Re)Connecting with Your Values

Without awareness of your most important values, 'doing' can gradually become misdirected, hollow, and lacking in meaning. We lose touch with how our actions connect to something bigger than the present moment – something longer term and larger than our present selves. We can even begin to deploy a string of momentary pleasures, avoidances, or distractions to numb us from or sidestep that suffering or lack of alignment I mentioned. I have encountered many folks from all walks of life who have lost touch with their values-aligned 'human being' through a relentless pursuit of 'doing'. Often, there is no realisation of this disconnect until it is so patently obvious it becomes exquisitely unsettling.

I have come to the conclusion that our times of life-crises – be it the stereotypical 'midlife' crisis or indeed the quarter-life or third act crisis – usually come about when we suddenly realise we're off course – maybe a little, maybe a lot. The 'aha' that can come at such times invariably follows lengthy bouts of misaligned 'doing', which is akin to aiming to climb a mountain and taking small steps in the wrong direction. As small as those steps can feel, each one contributes to us winding up further away from the summit.

Making Small Changes for Big Impact

Making small, values-aligned choices can have a big impact on where you end up. Rather than waiting for the struggle of misalignment to become unbearable, start making small, daily choices that better align with your values today. Seemingly minor decisions can significantly impact your life's direction over time. And you never know which 'small' choices are big ones in disguise. Many years ago, I said yes to having a peppermint tea with a young man I was sceptical about. Well, in fairness to him I was sceptical about all young men at the time. What made me say 'yes' was an inkling of values alignment between us (and it didn't hurt that he was tall, dark and handsome). There was a resonance that increasingly I understand as an important signal of relational potential, be it in intimate relationships or friendships.[1] At the time, I experienced this values alignment as something about him that I was drawn to, and while I turned down a dinner invitation (and lunch), peppermint tea seemed manageable. I didn't identify this as a values-aligned choice but rather, simply something that felt okay and that I was curious about. Fast forward to now, we're happily married and have two children together.

By connecting deeply with your values, you'll gain more clarity on what truly matters to you. This process involves others and requires regular reflection on your desired future self. Be wary of FOMO (fear of missing out) pushing you to pursue incompatible futures. Instead, focus on choices that align with your core values and long-term aspirations.

I hope that by connecting more deeply with your values, you can reach the end of this book and feel more confident about your answers to questions like, 'What really matters to me?', 'How is it that certain things push my buttons?', 'What is success to me?', and 'How can I improve the alignment between what matters to me and my actions?' As we don't live in a vacuum, these questions invariably involve others around us and perhaps the planet or beyond as a whole. You will have the time and space to explore these questions for yourself, both solo and with those who are important to you.

The Gap Between What Is and What Could Be

The gap or distance between where you currently see yourself and where you want to be can bring feelings of frustration and discomfort. The experience can be energising and provide motivational impetus for change or debilitating and lead to a sense of hopelessness and further inaction. When your aspirations are values-aligned and (while potentially audacious) you see them as feasible, the gap, though painful, can inspire you to make choices that bring you closer to your aspirational self. However, when your desired self doesn't align with your values or what really matters most to you, or when you feel that your desired self is impossible to work toward, suffering can ensue. The gap becomes wider, fuelled by the frustrations of focusing on an illusory 'should' that either doesn't align with what's important to you, or doesn't feel achievable.

For me as a young woman, the illusion of physical perfection occupied my mind at the expense of what mattered most – forging meaningful relationships, thinking deeply about what I was capable of and where I wanted to go in the longer term. Rather than fuelling my body with what I needed to focus on growing forward, I sat with a level of physical hunger in which food occupied a large enough proportion of my attention that I couldn't focus on other things for large swathes of the day.

Especially in this hyperconnected age of social media, I see many people who are preoccupied by momentary physical perfection, in one way or another. I see them seeking diffuse social approval that in many ways is unachievable or, at best, fleeting, rather than catering to the needs of their body and mind such that they can focus in on what matters most to them. As for why that matters, the longer-term results from making small choices in the direction of what matters to you are huge, even when it doesn't feel like that at the time.[2]

This book advocates for making values-aligned choices and for relinquishing expectations or 'shoulds' that don't resonate with your authentic self. An authentic self, mind you, which is built up over time and understood as such thanks to consistency and alignment of your values-based actions. Indeed there is more to 'authenticity' than momentary truth telling, and we will delve deeper into how to cultivate an authentic self a little later. Your values play a crucial part in establishing not just what really matters to you, but who you become and who you are known to be over time. Your task is to pursue choices that align with your personal manifestation of authenticity.

Each choice you make widens or reduces the gap between your current sense of self and your desired state. Bridging this gap requires two key elements: clarity about what matters to you and a practical means of progress. Your values can assist with both. When a future desired state does not align with what's important to you, it's not values-aligned and it's best to *in*action moves toward it; such misaligned actions (however epic or enjoyable in the short term) will take you in the wrong direction. Of course, you can't have total clarity around which choices move you toward or away from that future self you desire to cultivate – twists and turns in your journey are inevitable and fun! But there are some moves you know are just distractions or don't align with that self you wish to grow. Identify those moves and inaction any inclination toward them. Easier said than done, I know! When a future desired state aligns with your values – with what's important to you – then you can take steps to reduce the gap, by making small, manageable, values-aligned choices in the direction that matters.

What Matters to You aims to help you gain insight into your values as fundamental drivers impacting your experience and life trajectory. It provides practical activities to help you identify, refine and use your values to grow your version of a meaningful life, including the broader contribution you seek to make. I hope that it offers a pathway to deeper self-understanding and more intentional living. Not only that, I sincerely hope it offers you some resources and insights to help you navigate life's challenges, for yourself and for your relationships, and that by embracing values-aligned opportunities you find longer-term fulfilment, both in the life that you lead and the contribution that you make.

CHAPTER 1
Understanding Values

When discussing values, the focus is often on what they 'do' rather than what they 'are'. What they 'are' is taken as a given and when I ask folks about what values *are* to them – how they define them – the answer often circles back to what they 'do'. For instance, you might have heard them described as offering a 'North Star' or a 'compass' for moving toward your version of a life well lived. These descriptions aren't wrong, but to fully harness the power of values, we need to explore their nature more deeply. This exploration helps inform how we can harness their potential and put them to best use in our lives.

At their core, values are deeply embedded concepts or drivers that impact us whether we're aware of them or not. For us humans, concepts are everything – we begin forming them from our earliest days.¹ Concepts help us make sense of our world and as concepts, values integrate three interconnected elements:

1. Our *beliefs* based on our past experiences and learning.
2. Our current *needs*.
3. Our *goals* – including our aspirations and desires for the future.

This unique combination gives values remarkable power: they can form a motivational bridge between our thoughts and our behaviours.² Values help us cross the often treacherous 'knowledge-action' gap – that frustrating chasm between knowing what's good for us and actually doing it. Values reflect what matters to us and help supercharge our actions – from the mundane to the profound – with a personalised 'why' that offers us courage under fire.

Values are highly motivational, too.³ When a value is activated, it triggers an emotional response.⁴ Moreover, your values provide an evaluative framework through which you perceive and interpret the world. Whether or not you consciously act in line with your values, they influence how you understand, assess and respond to your experiences (and how you feel about your actions). There are many drivers influencing our choices at any one time, and just because you have certain values that are especially important to you, it doesn't mean that you will necessarily align your actions with them. But you probably will feel better if you do.

Here's an interesting thought experiment. The next time you see someone acting out of alignment with what they claim are their values, rather than thinking, 'Aha, what a hypocrite!' consider this alternative: 'Wow, they're so out of sync with their values, they must be feeling quite miserable.' More often than not, you'd probably be right. We're going to get into this more when exploring 'shoulds' in Chapter Six. I describe the size of the gap as representing the magnitude of your suffering. The larger the gap between how things 'are' and how you think things 'should' be, the greater your suffering.

Now, let's delve a bit deeper into how values work in practice. When you encounter something in your environment that aligns with a value important to you, you'll likely experience a positive or pleasurable emotional response. Say you've just spent time with your family being present and patient with them. All being well, and despite some minor frustrations, on balance you may have a sense of satisfaction and pleasure from aligning what means a lot to you (your family) with an action (spending time with them).

Increasingly, I've started paying more attention to how movies and TV shows use a string of values-activating instances to move us emotionally and motivate us to keep watching. If you've watched the movie *Jurassic Park*, you might have experienced a warm, glowy feeling when the protagonist, Dr Alan Grant, saves the two kids from the t-rex. That glowy feeling is likely thanks to the release of two neurotransmitters: oxytocin, the bonding hormone; and dopamine, a pleasure hormone.[5]

But what promotes the release of these neurochemicals in the first place? It may be thanks to the impact of values activation on your reward system.[6] Further, because the viewer understands, by that scene in the movie, that Dr Alan is uncomfortable around children – he's not a natural with children or a 'lovey dovey' kind of person – his display of committed action in line with loyalty to children is likely to be especially resonant. He is maintaining alignment with important values even under duress and with people he doesn't naturally warm to. We recognise this, and it can be incredibly pleasurable for us to see him prioritise the kids' needs over his own safety in that moment.

Conversely, when you perceive something that conflicts with your values, you'll likely feel uncomfortable or negative emotions – frustration, disdain, even anger. We experience values conflicts particularly strongly, and it's the time at which our values are most likely to be activated and to elicit an emotional response.[7]

Back to *Jurassic Park* and the scene where Dennis Nedry, the computer programmer, attempts to smuggle dinosaur embryos out of the park in a modified can of shaving cream right when the kids (among others) are in the park and in danger. We perceive this behaviour as self-serving and in conflict with values we would hope to see prioritised at such a time. Our evaluation and the emotion activation that follows helps prime us to not care so much about what happens to Dennis a little later in the movie. Indeed, when you perceive a values conflict, this is when it's essential to be careful about your choices. At such times, we can feel justified in abandoning values alignment in our behaviour. Yet abandoning our own core values prioritisation can contribute to a potential spiral of increasingly poor behaviour and can erode our sense of self over time. After all, your values reflect the version of yourself that you aspire to grow into over time. That takes effort. When we make choices that contradict our values-led self, we steer ourselves in a direction away from that aspirational version of self.

If we act incongruently with our *own* values, this can trigger an especially uncomfortable state of values conflict.[8] Say you lose your temper with someone you care about. You raise your voice and use language that doesn't reflect you at your best. When the initial flush of anger abates, you may feel a sense of shame or even anger toward yourself for your behaviour. Perhaps you try to justify or downplay your response, but there's still a lingering discomfort. What's happening here? This event may have activated values around Respect and perhaps Family or Relationships for you. You may feel you've acted incongruently – out of alignment – with these values. You're experiencing the emotional aftermath of an internal values conflict.[9]

In such situations, rather than explaining away your behaviour, it can be more productive to acknowledge the values misalignment and take steps both to make up for it (for instance, with an apology if that's appropriate) and to plan for how you're going to show up better next time. The solution lies in taking small, consistent steps toward values alignment. We will get into that more in Chapter Nine around values-based decision-making.

As we progress through the current chapter, we'll explore how to identify your core values, understand their impact on your decision-making, and learn strategies for living more in keeping with what truly matters to you. Remember, this journey isn't about perfection – it's about progress and growing awareness of the guiding principles that can shape you and your life.

The Nature of Values

It's not uncommon for me to get halfway through a conversation with someone about values only to realise they assume I'm talking about moral principles that are aligned with a 'right' and 'wrong' that we all can agree on – and individual values simply aren't that. It's worth emphasising, then, that personal values are distinct from societal morals or shared principles, although admittedly there can be overlap. Socially agreed-upon values serve as morals,[10] but that's not the topic of this book. I'm focused on how a person's individual-level values – those values that vary greatly between people – impact one's life as an individual and help that individual contribute to the collective. The impact of individual values on one's life trajectory is nuanced, personalised, and different from the impact of adhering to broad moral codes.[11]

In essence, individual-level or personal values are best approached as *amoral* – not immoral, mind you, but separate from overarching societal notions of right and wrong. Individual values represent guiding principles for behaviour and decision-making and are not tied to broadly applicable moral judgements. When we introduce morality into discussing values, we are probably discussing social principles or falling into the trap of 'shoulds.' These 'should' values can emerge in one of several ways.

First, 'should' values can develop from internalised assumptions about which values you *should* hold as most important when in fact you don't. Perhaps you internalised a sense of their importance from external sources like family, friends, social media, or beyond. And while there's nothing wrong with these values, they're simply not really a top priority for you, relative to other values you may wish to prioritise in a moment of choice. For instance, say you're someone who has learned to prioritise Harmony at all costs including in situations where you wish to prioritise Achievement or Growth. Or you've learned to prioritise the value of Likeability above Competence in a work context, even at the expense of the best outcome or your own career.

In such cases, you may even find you are holding two opposing thoughts at once: 'You shouldn't be such a people pleaser! Stick up for yourself and take credit!' as well as the opposite, 'You should always present as likeable over competent in moments like this one.' 'Should' values can be exhausting to maintain. They can add another layer of priorities you're trying to balance when making a decision, rendering the process even harder and more cognitively taxing.

Another way that 'shoulds' can emerge is from among your own values framework. For instance, you may over-prioritise or overuse one of your values to the detriment of your experience and your whole self – we'll hear more about that in Chapter Three. In short, it's my hope that this book provides insights into what your *personal* values are, what they have to offer, and how they impact your experience.

Your personal values are just that – personal. Just as you're not obligated to abide by my values, I'm not compelled to live by yours. This holds true even when we share a society with common principles or social values. Our personal values are ours alone, and additionally the interactions between my values and yours offer synergistic properties that are valuable for our collective experience. The way you prioritise your personal values helps make sense of how you interpret and respond to others' behaviour, too, and informs what you choose to do when making decisions. For instance, when thinking about working late, whether you prioritise Family over Achievement will help inform what you decide to do.

I refer to your most important personal values as your 'core values' – not because they're unchanging but because they're most important for now. Our respective personal values explain some of the variation in how we choose to spend our time and contribute to the world. In knowing each other's values, we can have a greater understanding of each other's motivations and aspirations, too. Chances are, even when someone else's most important values are quite different from yours, you can still appreciate some if not all of theirs, even if you wouldn't prioritise them as highly as they do.

Time for a thought that might surprise you: if we all lived more in line with our most important personal values, I believe the world would be a better place. There's an underlying humanity that sits behind our diversity of core values. We have our nature as social beings to thank for that – once our fundamental needs for survival and security are met, we tend toward growth needs, including to contribute to something larger than ourselves. The diversity of our contribution enriches our collective experience and fosters innovation, empathy and resilience in the face of challenges.

Given the potential benefits of personal values diversity for the collective, there is a broader implication: when we (and millions of others) align our actions with our personal, goal-oriented values – those that reflect us at our best – it can have a profound impact. The tendency of values to be outward-looking and collaborative, combined with the diversity of individual values, can contribute to building a more cooperative society. This, in turn, could enhance our collective ability to address some of the most pressing issues of our time, including existential threats to our planet. Collective, values-based decision-making is required to tackle the greatest issues of our time. And it starts with people, including you and me, thinking more deeply about what matters to us, connecting that with our personal, core values, and actioning them more often.

Identifying Your Values

Identifying your values involves pinpointing those that mean the most to you – not to me, your best friend, colleague or grandmother. There will be other values you see as important, too, but we're looking to work with the top of your list. I generally advocate focusing on your top five core values that are most important to you at this stage in your life. This number is manageable to work with in decision-making and is applicable to a variety of life domains and circumstances. It is not such a long list that it's unwieldy or paralysing, nor is it so short as to be unnaturally constraining with what you may wish to prioritise.

In Chapter Three we get into how to identify and flesh out your values. That is, how to name and clearly define them on your terms, and understand what choices, actions and goals flow from them. Once you know your values, you can use them better to build toward the future you aspire to, both in how you frame the world and in the actions you take. Choices are central to this. Your life is abundant with choices, although many of them remain unseen. Some of the most impactful choices of your life will only reveal themselves long after the choice was made.

When you make choices led by your values – choices about where you direct your attention, which version of events you choose to engage with, and the actions you take in the world – you cultivate a sense of fulfilment. That is, values-led choices help you grow eudaimonic happiness[12] – a form of profound satisfaction that emerges over time from more consistently making the 'right action' where 'right' is determined by the level of values alignment for you.

Now, let's be clear: the 'right action' mightn't provide the largest short-term payoff. In fact, sometimes the 'right action' can be downright uncomfortable or challenging in the moment. The question to ask yourself is: 'What action can I take right now that aligns with my values and moves me toward my version of personal success?' It's about building a life where you can look back and say, 'I lived aligned with what was important to me. I achieved success on my own terms.'

As we move forward, remember that working with your values isn't about achieving perfection or seeking total values alignment – that's impossible. Nor is it about imagining a life where more basic needs are met in order to prioritise your values. It's about progress, about gradually aligning more of your choices and actions with what truly matters to you.

Values as Schemas

To deepen our understanding of values, it's helpful to explore the concept of 'schemas' – a term with rich history and application in psychology and cognitive science. While I will go on to refer to values as 'complex concepts', the notion of schemas offers additional insights into how values function in our minds. If you wish to focus more on how to use your values, however, without getting this deeper dive, that's quite all right and I'll catch you at the start of the next chapter when we dive into your not one but two sets of values.

The word 'schema' comes from the Greek 'σχήμα' (skhēma), meaning shape or plan. I think of schemas, and indeed values, as being a bit like islands in an ocean, where each island is in fact the peak of a vast, interconnected mountain range that is only visible deep below the surface. Each island, while connected to the rest, has distinctive characteristics as it's grown on and experienced.

In cognitive sciences, schemas explain how our brains organise thoughts, knowledge, and new information.[13] A schema, much like a complex concept, represents a bundle of interrelated knowledge, containing both 'declarative' (what something is) and 'procedural' (how it works) information.[14] This efficient packaging helps us make predictions and decisions without overwhelming our cognitive load. In essence, schemas provide an interpretive lens through which we view and make sense of the world. We constantly use our schemas to make predictions about how the world around us is unfolding, and our schemas are adjusted accordingly depending on the new information coming in.

There are several primary proposed functions of schemas.[15,16] They help us organise information into manageable chunks, making it easier to understand and retrieve. They help guide our perception and attention by influencing what we pay attention to and how we interpret new information. They help facilitate memory by enabling information to be added to existing schemas, making remembering and recalling easier than when the information is entirely new or intelligible as its own chunk. They also allow us to make sense of new situations based on experience and help us predict outcomes.

The four main types of schemas are those of the self that guide the processing of self-relevant information; social schemas or representations of general knowledge about social processes and relationships; event schemas (scripts), where we can form and follow sequences of actions in certain contexts, easing our cognitive load and freeing up attentional processes; and object schemas whereby we understand inanimate objects and their properties and functions.[17,18]

Understanding schemas is crucial to our discussion of values because values can be conceptualised as a type of schema – specifically, as positive, goal-directed schemas (or complex concepts) that guide our behaviour and decision-making. In the next section, we'll explore how this understanding of schemas from cognitive psychology can inform our approach to working with core values.

The Power of Story in Remembering

The notion of a schema was introduced to psychology by British psychologist Sir Frederic Bartlett in the 1930s through his groundbreaking research on memory and recall.[19] Bartlett was intrigued by the mechanisms of memory storage and what is going on when people retell events after they occur. He wanted to understand how we store memories and how those memories change over time when we access and share them. His hunch was that we remember things through story and reconstruct a memory by bringing together fragments during the instance or moment of retelling.

To test this hunch, Bartlett used a Native American folktale called 'The War of the Ghosts', a story of a young man who joins a war party and encounters supernatural elements including ghosts. Bartlett chose the story partly because it was unfamiliar to his British participants and partly because it is a story ripe for adaptation over multiple tellings. In his experiment, a participant read the story and was then instructed to verbally tell it to another person, who would then pass it on, similar to the children's game of 'telephone' or 'whispers'.

What Bartlett discovered was fascinating: the story subtly changed with each retelling. This led him to conclude that our recollections are more akin to reconstructions than to simply pressing 'play' on a recorded video. Bartlett introduced the concept of 'schema' to explain this phenomenon of story retelling and memory recall. He thought of schemas as mental frameworks or templates that help us organise and interpret information. He held that our personal beliefs, experiences, cultural background, and the context in which we're trying to recall the memory, all influence what we remember. This finding was revolutionary at the time because it challenged the prevailing idea that memory was static and unchanging.

Bartlett demonstrated that memory is dynamic, creative, and profoundly influenced by our personal context. Even when we believe we're remembering accurately, our 'cognitive filter' or evaluative framework – composed of our schemas – influences how we interpret, evaluate and respond to information. I suggest that our values serve as an 'evaluative filter' through which we interpret and respond to information coming in from the world around us.

Schemas in Early Life

The notion of the schema was further developed and popularised in psychology by developmental psychologist Jean Piaget, who suggested that children organise their world into schemas – a series of abstract mental structures where cognitions and constructs are grouped by association.[20]

This association can occur through direct experience. For instance, encountering dogs helps a child build a schema of 'dog' that includes attributes like fur, four legs, ears, eyes, and a wet tongue. Association can also happen through indirect experience. A child might learn that a stove is hot and suitable for cooking but dangerous to touch, not through being burned but through instructions from parents or caregivers.

Piaget held that as children interact with their environment, they encounter new experiences that might not fit into their existing schemas. This discrepancy leads to cognitive dissonance, resolved through one of two processes: assimilation or accommodation.

Assimilation occurs when new information fits within an existing schema. For example, a child might assimilate the concept of a golden retriever into their existing 'dog' schema. Accommodation occurs when the new information doesn't seem to fit anywhere and requires you to alter an existing schema or create a new one. For instance, if a child knows 'dog' and then comes across a cat, they may initially assign the cat to the schema of 'dog'. However, over time, a new schema, 'cat', may be established as it becomes clear that a cat differs from a dog. Schemas are not constrained to objects like cats or dogs, however. Complex concepts like 'love' and 'fairness' are schemas, too. Indeed, psychologist Jeffrey Young, who founded Schema Therapy, makes the point that 'A schema can be thought of generally as any broad organising principle for making sense of one's life experience. [They] can be positive or negative, adaptive or maladaptive; schemas can be formed in childhood or later in life.'[21] The same can be said for values.

Modifying Schemas

You might be wondering why I'm bringing up the concept of 'schema' when it comes to values, instead of sticking with simpler terms like 'complex concept' (after all, schemas are forms of complex concepts). It's because psychology has done some fascinating work with schemas that can help us understand how our values help shape our world, whether we've consciously identified them or not. Schemas offer a structured way of thinking about how our minds organise and interpret the world, and values function as a special type of schema.

I won't delve deeper into the theory of schemas here (I've included some further insights in the notes for this chapter in case you're interested).[22] Rather, let's focus again on values themselves. After all, values help drive our interpretations, evaluations, and responses to the world, even when we aren't especially aware of them. One challenge of having low insight into our values is that without values insight, it's difficult to work out which actions and goals satisfy that inner voice saying, 'There has to be more than this.' We can find ourselves anchoring to generic ideas of what we should strive for or go after, rather than pursuing activities and goals that personally resonate and build lasting fulfilment.

One other comment to make, which flows from thinking about values as schemas, is that they aren't static — our values evolve based on how much we engage with them and the choices we make. With insight into our values, we can be more intentional about guiding our actions and decisions in ways that line up with what matters most to us. Through practices like mindfulness, attention training, and deliberate reflection, we can strengthen our values and bring them more actively into our lives. The choices we make reinforce our values, and in turn, our values shape who we are, who we're becoming, and how we're remembered.

Take a moment now to reflect on one of your values that you'd like to more intentionally nurture for longer-term growth. For example, if Family is one of your most important values, its influence isn't limited to when you choose to think about it. Your Family schema will enduringly impact how you evaluate events and actions in the world and how they make you feel, whether or not you intend for that to occur at the time. However, the strength of that influence may change based on how much you prioritise Family in a given moment.

Consider this scenario: it's Shar's birthday – a milestone one – and she's invited her closest friends, and her family, including siblings, for dinner. A week before the event, one of Shar's siblings tells her they can't make it due to a work trip. Shar understands their situation, but deep down feels they should have prioritised her birthday. This is experienced as feelings of mild hurt, disappointment and frustration. This emotional response stems from the value Shar places on Family and how she believes family members should prioritise one another in important moments.

With the insight that this response is linked to Shar's value of Family, she may still feel disappointed but is better equipped to understand why. By acknowledging her own feelings without judgement, she can make space for them rather than engaging in more and more thinking around 'why' she feels this way. Moreover, this awareness allows her to reflect on her sibling's decision. While Family holds the greatest importance to Shar in this context, her sibling prioritised their commitment to people in their fast-paced work life. They may not even realise the significance Shar is placing on the moment. Recognising this can help Shar see that her sibling's decision isn't necessarily about prioritising them over her; it might simply be about weighing up their commitments differently. From here, Shar is better placed either to have a conversation with her sibling to explain her priorities and how she's feeling about their decision, or to choose to breathe through it and remain committed to family – including to her sibling – in spite of their choice. In this way, insight into your values enables you to weigh up and make values-aligned choices that take you forward.

Now consider another situation that also involves Shar and her value of Family. Shar has a child in primary school and she's been invited to a coffee morning with other parents. Despite her work commitments, she has been trying to prioritise cultivating relationships within the school community as part of how she actions her value of Family as she sees it as important for their longer-term support at the school. The coffee meet-up happens a half hour before Shar has an important work meeting booked. Without hesitation, she sends her apology to the coffee morning. The decision doesn't trouble her and there's no internal conflict even though her value of Family extends to prioritising such events. Why? In this context, to Shar the value of Work Ethic takes priority over Family.

The ease with which Shar made this decision demonstrates how values prioritisation can shift depending on the situation. She's not abandoning her value of Family; instead, she's either drawn to or is consciously making the decision to prioritise work over family. By being clear about this prioritisation, you can avoid unnecessary guilt or second-guessing yourself.

I have one final scenario involving Shar who we have already seen place importance on Family as well as a value around Work Ethic.

Shar is an executive at her company and is due to present at a high-profile business event she and her team have spent months preparing for. It means a lot to her and her team, and has the promise of other opportunities if it goes well. On the morning of the event, however, Shar's child falls ill and needs to be taken to the doctor. Yes, there is another parent on the scene, but Shar's child prefers to have Shar around when he's feeling unwell.

Shar can feel herself being pulled in two directions at once – she wants to prioritise family and work because she has needs in both areas that she wants to meet. But it's a real challenge because Family versus Work leads to very different actions. One way or another, she will need to compromise and get intentional around how she prioritises family and work in this situation.

She pauses and reflects. Insight into her values enables her to understand that this isn't a 'right' or 'wrong' decision, but rather one that necessitates her making trade-offs and prioritising her way forward based on the context and her longer-term sense of self. She must ask herself what values-aligned actions best reflect who she wants to be in this moment and in the long term. The emotional turmoil caused by this values conflict can be understood as a natural response rather than evidence of overwhelm or life being 'too much'. Part of Shar's decision-making is to recognise that a perfect solution doesn't exist, that she can only do her best, and in intentionally choosing an action to move forward with, her values can help her make peace with her choice, and reduce the intensity of lingering guilt or regret. Her values can allow her to live in alignment with the person she wants to become, in a world where prioritisation, trade-offs, and hard decisions are inevitable.

At this juncture, you may wish to think about what you'd do if you were in Shar's position. What do your choices reflect about your values and beliefs, current needs, and future goals that influence what you prioritise?

So far, we've discussed how values are like positive schemas that influence how you show up in the world and perceive your experiences. By using Shar as an example, we've explored how this can work in practice.

In short, when one of your core values is activated, it triggers an emotional response. This response can be positive and feel good when the action is value-aligned (a sense of 'Yes, I'm on the right track') or negative and uncomfortable when it's activated because of a values conflict, where you are squarely out of alignment with it ('Something doesn't feel right about this'). Understanding your values can help you better understand these 'gut' reactions and adjust your choices for the onward journey.

Think of values as complex concepts that combine beliefs, needs and goals. Our current context includes *needs* related not just to what we want now but also to our future desires and aspirations. Our life circumstances impact what we prioritise. Our needs can shift with significant life events – the birth of a child, transitioning from study to work, or experiencing social upheavals like a recession or climate change. At pivotal times when our needs shift, this may lead to a reprioritisation of values. While it may seem like your top five values change, it's often a reprioritisation of a longer list of values rather than a complete overhaul (although that is also possible with intentional work).

The upshot of this is that when you experience a significant change in your life, it's worth revisiting your values to reconsider what you wish to prioritise and action. Certain values may remain constant through different life stages, such as Achieve Together for me in my working life. Others may emerge or change over time, illustrating how values can adapt as our priorities shift. For instance, new parents may prioritise family even if that wasn't a prioritised value in previous life stages.

Values research shows that the greatest utility of human values is in guiding behaviour and human decision-making.[23,24,25] Human values involve the active, goal-oriented expression of underlying needs or motivations. When a value is held as deeply important, its influence on behaviour and decision-making is related to whether it is driven by growth or survival needs, and socially or personally motivated. Over time, growth-oriented values yield the greatest rewards, especially when they include a mix of social motivations (e.g. Care for Others) and personal motivations (e.g. Achievement, or Curiosity).

The way that you prioritise values in a given situation not only impacts the choices you make but also how you evaluate others' behaviour.[26] We often expect others to prioritise values the same way we do and we can tend to assume our values are the 'right' ones.[27] Furthermore, our values shape more than our actions and how we feel about them; they impact how *valuable* we find objects, acts, people and events.[28] If I value sustainability and I'm taking actions to reduce my use of single-use plastic then I may be willing to pay more for biodegradable packaging. Our level of appreciation of the impact that values have on our decision-making, what feels right for us, and the way we value goods and services in the world, is still in its infancy. Apart from anything else, the impact our values have on our perception of what is right or the best thing to do explains why well-meaning advice from others might not resonate with you – it may simply be based on their values, not yours.

Understanding values as schemas gives us insight into why they activate the emotion system and explains why they're such powerful motivators. But what about those times when you feel motivated to act in ways that contradict your values? Does that mean your values are 'false' or that you're a fraud? Absolutely not. First, read about 'should' values in Chapter Six to ensure you're not merely trying to live up to externally imposed expectations as opposed to your own values. Second, if you're confident that the value is not a 'should' value, then no, you're not a fraud.

Many people I've worked with struggle with feelings of being a fraud with their values. They hold certain values as important but feel disconnected because they're not prioritising those values in daily life. If this experience rings true for you, rather than concluding your identified core values aren't truly yours, you can recognise this disconnect as a common, albeit painful, experience. By offering yourself compassion and intentional understanding in that moment, you can begin to bridge the gap between your values and your actions – beginning with compassionate understanding. You can focus on answering this question: 'What is one tiny thing I can do in this moment to better align myself with a value I hold as important?' Self-compassion means taking one tiny step toward a value you hold dear. In doing so, you reduce the tendency to engage in avoidance, which can take you further away from those values you care about.

In the next chapter, we'll explore how our values can shift depending on our circumstances, particularly when we feel threatened. This understanding will provide a foundation for learning how to navigate challenging situations while staying true to our core values.

KEY TAKEAWAYS OF THIS CHAPTER:

* Personal values are different from societal morals; they can vary significantly from person to person.
* Think of values as schemas – deeply embedded drivers that bring together beliefs from past experiences, current needs, and future goals.
* Your core values help create a motivational bridge between knowledge and action; they anchor you to your 'why'.
* Values activation brings an emotional response.
* Values provide an evaluative lens through which you experience the world.
* Values can help guide your decision-making and influence your behaviour.
* Your core values are stable as a group within a life stage, but the way you prioritise your core values is dynamic and can vary between situations.
* Working with a short list of 'core values' (I like no more than five) makes it possible to prioritise them in useful and manageable ways.
* Aligning more of your actions with your values supports longer-term happiness, deep fulfilment and satisfaction.
* Values-aligned decisions for 'larger, later' gain can feel uncomfortable in the short term.
* Values conflicts are inevitable; recognising their role in your experience of difficult emotions can be helpful.

CHAPTER 2
Two Sets of Values

How do we make sense of times when we have seemingly acted totally out of line with our core values? Are values-incongruent behaviours evidence that the values we treasure are just aspirational, not truly reflective of our 'real self'? I've lost count of how many clients have come to me thinking of themselves (or someone else) as a 'fraud' for acting out of line with their values. More often than not, these incongruencies cause suffering to the person rather than reflecting an un-truth about them.

When I was younger, I mistakenly thought of the human psyche as being like an apple. I assumed that I had a metaphorical core with seeds of self that I was born with. I thought that my worst thoughts and behaviour reflected my deepest truth. These days, as I sit with

courageous souls who open themselves up to me as a psychologist, I've come to recognise how common this assumption is – that our worst actions, or even thoughts, reveal an unchangeable essence or core. Let me assure you that your worst actions do not reflect your truest self. Albeit it's up to you to be accountable for your actions. Values-incongruent actions do not mean your core values are 'lip service' to who you want to be. Change is always possible. It starts with knowing your values and finding small, manageable ways to action them. Each of us can reconnect with our highest values, even on or after the darkest days. The opportunity is here now, because the present moment is all we ever have to act in.

This raises an important question: Why do we sometimes choose actions that misalign with our core values? Does this mean that our values are merely 'fair weather friends' – useful in calm moments but sidelined in times of crisis? First and foremost, your core values are there for you even in turbulent times, and in fact, they can become even more vital during these moments. But in times of stress you may need to be especially intentional about prioritising them. Why? Because when we're stressed or feeling threatened, we can default to a second set of values. Our core values tend to surface more naturally when life feels stable and supportive – when conditions are relatively threat-free or 'permissive'.[1] When we perceive a threat to our safety or wellbeing, threat-based values (TBVs) or 'survival' values can take precedence. TBVs like Control, Security, Avoidance, and Perfectionism, which prioritise short-term survival over longer-term growth. Now, I am certainly not saying we should act in line with our TBVs – but at times we can very much feel inclined to do so. When we're feeling safe and our needs are being met, we can focus on growth and our contribution to others – for instance, by nurturing Family, Community, our Personal development, or our Achievement. Conversely, when we feel threatened, our priorities can shift toward protecting ourselves and minimising short-term risks.

In this chapter, we'll delve into our tendency toward these two sets of values – that is, the two values prioritisations we can find ourselves favouring depending on whether we're in a state of growth or survival. Most importantly, I will encourage you to get far more intentional about which mindset and values you choose to *act* on, rather than defaulting to what 'feels' right in the moment. How you respond to the activation of your values matters because many of us spend a lot of our time in a threat-based state. Yet, even when you feel under threat, it is often better to focus on actions that align with your core values.

Core Values

Core values are those values that are most important to you – as I've mentioned, I tend to suggest working with a top five as this provides flexibility in prioritising your values across different areas of life while being manageable to remember and work with. That said, there is no hard and fast rule around how many core values you can identify. Since they should be relevant across your life domains, I recommend having enough to avoid artificially limiting your decision-making but not so many that you feel overwhelmed. In practice, I find this means identifying four to five (with five being my preference for personal values work). Also, when I talk about the importance of a value to you, I mean whether it's consistently prioritised for you – perhaps not always in action, but at least in thought.

So, for instance, if Family is highly important to you, it's likely to strongly impact how you feel in situations where this value is activated, which may happen quite frequently. When a value is often prioritised as one of the most important in decision-making contexts (whether or not you act on it), it is a strong contender as one of your core values. Acting out of alignment with your core values doesn't mean they're not deeply important to you; however, it probably means you feel unfulfilled or even rather unhappy. If you consistently act out of alignment with your core values, no matter how good your life looks from the outside, chances are you feel miserable or disconnected from your life. We'll discuss that further in Chapter Three around values conflicts.

Your core values reflect the growth-oriented self you aspire to over the long term. You're most likely to prioritise them when you feel at ease and inspired to lean into the best version of yourself. But ideally, you want to be finding more and more opportunities to action your core values, even when it may initially feel unnatural or challenging to do so. Core values are typically outward-looking – that is, they reflect your interest in being part of the world around you and your thoughts around how you seek to contribute to this broader world, with the longer term in mind.

When we make choices and take action aligned with our core values, we're more likely to:

1. **Consider the bigger picture and long-term consequences.**
2. **Balance the needs of others alongside our own.**
3. **Make decisions that support personal growth and self-actualisation.**
4. **Act in ways that feel authentic and elicit trust from others.**

Core values serve as a guide that can help navigate both minor daily choices and significant life decisions – whether it's how you show up in relationships or choose between an electric or gas-powered car. They provide a framework for understanding what makes life meaningful and fulfilling for you personally.

Core Values and Personal Growth

Your core values offer a guide for personal growth. But growth doesn't just come from having some broad sense of what you're aspiring to. Personal growth comes from doing the hard thing in the moment, when many fibres of your being are calling out 'No! Do the easy / safe / pleasurable / numbing thing instead! You can worry about personal growth tomorrow!' But tomorrow never comes except in our imagination; today is always today. 'If onlys' – as in, 'If only I hadn't lost my patience' – are the yesterdays of tomorrow. Put simply, if you want to avoid tomorrow's 'if only', make the values-led choice today.

I've already talked about how values provide a motivational bridge across the knowledge-action gap, increasing our ability to do what we know is important or meaningful to us. This comes from the three roles of values as your anchor, wings and compass.

Core values as your anchor. Picture a boat on the ocean, not too far from the shore. There's a storm coming, the waves begin to grow, and the captain drops the sea anchor to avoid being pushed further toward land. The device quickly deploys, pulling the bow *into* the approaching weather, the wind and the waves. From this position, the boat rides out the storm without drifting into rocks or becoming beached on the shore.

An anchor does more than just hold you in place. During rough weather, it slows your drift and keeps you facing toward the storm to reduce its impact. Often, overcoming metaphorically inclement weather in life requires facing into the storm, rather than trying to escape it and ending up way off course. Knowing your values – what matters most to you – can serve as your anchor. They hold you steady, reminding you where you need to be and why. From this position, you can weather difficult times where the 'best', most values-aligned choice might feel tough because it comes with short-term discomfort, but it gets you through the storm. Sometimes, it's not about making the most audacious values-aligned choice; it's about making a small, manageable, values-aligned choice that is just enough to keep you from straying way off course as the storm rages.

Core values as your wings. Your core values can help unlock vulnerability and courage, and help define for you what it means to show up at your best in the present moment, balancing your needs now and your future aspirations. They give you wings that enable your potential to soar above what you thought possible. Rather than focusing on your skills or what you think you're capable of, you focus on what matters and your 'why'. From there, failure and success become measured less by achievement and outcome, and more by alignment with your values. Aligned actions take precedence when it comes to judging your performance, and you can become less knocked around by fears and worries about short-term performance.

Rather than being discouraged when things don't go as planned, you focus on growth and learning. When something doesn't work out, you can hold the conviction that it's okay, bolstered by your connection to what matters. From here, there's no need to play small in your life, or beat others to the punch of 'Who does she think she is?' You are set free, vulnerably and with values as your wings, to soar. Because, at the end of the day, you showed up and aligned your actions with what's most important to you, which nourishes who you seek to grow into over time, and that is precisely enough. Even when others try to push you off course, staying true to your values makes it harder for them to succeed.

Your values provide wings to rise above discomfort in pursuit of something greater. Whether in sport, the arts, trades, with family, friends, in business, medicine, or beyond – your values help you grow beyond what you thought possible. Core values give you wings that help you transcend success and failure in the now for something better – the sort of growth that enables the scaling of higher mountains, and the sort of long-term fulfilment that comes from reaching the summit.

Values as your compass. In psychology, values are frequently described as a compass.[2] Values help you navigate life's immediate challenges and discomforts in ways that align with what is truly important to you. But they're more than just a litmus test for what to do right now. Your values provide a compass – a navigational device for the minor adjustments *and* the big leaps of courage that accumulate and define the person you'll look back on at the end of your life. When you align your actions with your most important values, you're heading in the direction of your own personal True North.

This dual function of values – guiding you in the short term while also steering you toward the longer-term future you seek – makes them uniquely powerful. They enable your deepest convictions and aspirations to come to the fore, rather than letting short-term needs dominate. This matters because your longer-term trajectory matters. Your compass helps you check in around whether your decisions and actions today align with the future you want to create.

Values don't just inform how to act in the moment in the same way that social rules or norms do. They guide where you want your actions to lead you. Values help colour in the details of the life you aim to live, based on what matters most to you. The beauty of values diversity is that when I align with what matters most to me, and you align with what matters most to you, we each contribute uniquely to a broader tapestry that benefits everyone. Values alignment isn't about selfishly prioritising yourself at the expense of others. When we align with our core values, we bring our unique contributions to the collective, enhancing creativity, problem-solving, and avoiding the pitfalls of groupthink.[3]

The Importance of Core Values Diversity

It's worth remembering that core values can vary significantly from person to person. Assuming that everyone has the same values can cause frustration, interpersonal conflict, and may reduce the potential for understanding, empathy and co-creation of value. What one individual holds as a core value (one of their top five most important values) might be far less important to another person. This diversity in values is part of what makes human interactions so rich and complex. It contributes to our vibrancy and potential for innovation while also requiring that we seek to understand each other's core values so we can consider each other's vantage points as best we can.

Core values diversity is inevitable and makes the sum of our values greater than their respective parts. Values diversity can positively impact decision-making and interpersonal contexts.[4] We can offer each other a variety of perspectives when problem-solving. It's crucial that we find common ground between the perspectives our values provide us, given values diversity is inevitable, and given it comes with benefits.

When you know your own values and those of others, you can gain greater awareness about the assumptions you make about people. Often, for instance, we assume that others will, or should, have and prioritise the same values that we do when making decisions. That is, we make a value judgement about what matters and assume it holds for everyone. But even in cases where two people have the same values, it doesn't mean they'll prioritise them the same way. Let's say you and I have named the same core values, including Achievement and Curiosity, and we're deciding where to go for a holiday. As I've discussed, we will never have exactly the same values, even if they look the same on paper, because your interpretation of 'curiosity' and 'achievement' and mine will differ. Additionally, we may choose different holiday destinations if you prioritise curiosity as most important and I prioritise achievement (for instance, due to differing needs and goals).

Let's say curiosity is your top priority, and you choose a destination you've never been to that is rich in cultural heritage with opportunities for learning and exploration. Conversely, achievement is my top priority, and I prefer a holiday that enables me to accomplish specific goals, such as climbing a mountain or completing a bike ride. Even though you and I share very similar values (with the same names) in this example, the way we prioritise them helps lead to different choices. Recognising this allows us to appreciate that when people make divergent choices, it doesn't necessarily reflect conflicting values. Instead, it stems from a different values prioritisation for that particular situation.

Understanding that values prioritisation affects our choices can help reduce misunderstandings and judgements between people. In reality, it is impossible and unnecessary to identify every difference in values prioritisation. The most important thing is to recognise that values prioritisation impacts our choices and to remember to make generous assumptions that another person is doing the best they can. Additionally, it is counterproductive to judge others for not prioritising values as we do. Just as we have had well-meaning others tell us what we 'should' value, we risk telling others what they 'should' value rather than making space for their experiences.

Knowing your core values and those of people closest to you reduces the likelihood of you judging others negatively when they prioritise things differently. You can 'occupy their heart' *and* walk in their shoes, better understanding things from their perspective, and, ideally, finding common ground. This opens the door to examining the possibility that others are making considered choices, even when those choices run counter to your opinions.

Understanding others' perspectives as values-based doesn't mean you stop lobbying for your position or, where appropriate, trying to change someone's mind. For the most part, values insight enables people to locate common ground and respect one another's viewpoints. Understanding someone's values can help us make sense of their thinking, enhancing our respect and empathy for them, even when we disagree with their choices. Values provide part of the panacea to polarisation where 'shoulds' run rampant and we seek too swiftly to cancel others when they hold a different perspective. That is, insight into core values promotes understanding and respect, and provides different vantage points when seeking to overcome positions of threat.

Your core values reflect your beliefs and goals, which come to the fore when your basic needs are met, allowing you to focus on growth, contribution, and self-actualisation. But what happens when we feel threatened? As I've mentioned, the values we prioritise can differ from our core values. This doesn't mean our core values are any less real, but while the objective is to better align our actions with our core values more, the typical aim with threat-based values is to action them less.

Threat-Based Values

Identifying your most relevant threat-based values helps you understand what's going on when you feel you're letting yourself down and failing to prioritise what matters most to you. Yet, TBVs are often overlooked in values work.[5,6,7] Just as core values reflect the best of our beliefs and goals when our basic needs are met and we can focus on growth, threat-based values tend to take precedence when we feel threatened, or when our more fundamental needs seem unmet and demand attention.

When we feel threatened, we naturally prioritise immediate survival over long-term thriving. The challenge is that, in today's world, many of us operate in a state of chronic threat, unnecessarily responding to the world from this reactive stance. Acting from a threat-based mindset can counteract long-term growth and be unnecessary for the short term even though we can find ourselves justifying assuming a survival stance. When this happens, we might begin prioritising TBVs such as Control, Avoidance, Self-focus, Perfectionism, Blame Deflection and Security, seeking short-term relief at the expense of longer-term growth.

The purpose of acting in line with TBVs is survival, growing toward the best version of yourself. If you consistently operate from a threat-based state, you may have internalised these responses as safety mechanisms. This reinforcement loop keeps TBV-related behaviours going at the expense of personal growth. I see this in some professions, such as in law, where individuals function regularly under pressure and conflict. I have had clients whose modus operandi involves being vigilant to threats, lacking vulnerability, and finding it difficult to let go of minor errors or 'mistakes' made by others. This can lead to a prioritisation of Control for instance over and above Family and Connection, even when the person in question loves their family dearly. Moreover, this values prioritisation can be taken as a personality trait rather than a dynamic values prioritisation stemming from perceived threat.

The good news is that it's never too late to start consciously making choices around what you prioritise in action and why.

Identifying Threat-Based Values

When it comes to identifying threat-based values, I recommend focusing on one to three TBVs that you've noticed emerging when you're under threat. (See Chapter Four for an in-depth look at how to identify TBVs.) Your TBVs are the ones you lean toward to keep yourself safe in the short term, often at the expense of longer-term growth. TBVs relate to our mind as an incredible judgement machine whose primary job is to assess for threats in order to keep us alive. Growth and future direction don't matter if we don't survive the next five minutes. The challenge is that many of today's threats exist more in our mind's eye than in the physical world. We can feel deeply threatened when it's not our physical survival that's at risk, but our identity, reputation, competence, social status, autonomy, control, finances, privacy or health. Fear of failure, loss, humiliation, among other things, can trigger these responses. And when we don't know what matters to us – what really matters in among all the inevitable slings and arrows of life – we can start to respond to a bevy of threats as though they were especially threatening to us. We can take them as warranting a response that focuses our energy on survival over growth.

Our threat response system doesn't distinguish between physical and psychological threat, and threat-based values can be activated even at relatively low levels of perceived threat. Without awareness, we can find ourselves over-indexing on short-term survival tactics at the expense of our longer-term trajectory. During times of extreme threat, by all means, prioritise acting in alignment with threat-based values; after all, that's what they're there for – to keep you alive. Most of the time, however, when threat-based values are activated it is about recognising the pull to act on them rather than your core values. In these moments, thank your mind for trying to protect you, and make a conscious effort to refocus on what core values are relevant and how they would have you act. The task here is to *in*action your threat-based values and action your core values, even when prioritising your TBVs in ways that don't leave space for your core values appears necessary.

Regularly operating from a threat-based stance can erode your sense of self, life fulfilment and growth. Moreover, when we react from this place of threat, we reinforce for ourselves a false belief that it was the threat-based response that kept us safe. More often than not, we survive *despite* our threat-based actions, and we've cost ourselves growth longer term. But our autonomic nervous system doesn't know that. All it knows is, 'I'm alive!' Why does this matter? Because the next time a similar perceived threat arises, your body will send a stronger signal that translates to, 'You're under threat! Do what worked last time!' Our sympathetic nervous system or 'fight-or-flight' response will be triggered, prompting you to 'do the thing' you think kept you safe last time. You may feel highly motivated to 'do the thing' and if you go ahead and do it and things work out, this will further reinforce that when you were under threat you performed certain actions and stayed safe, and so on. These behaviours, often called 'safety behaviours' in anxiety work, are actions we engage in to prevent or reduce perceived threats or an anxiety response in the short term. Unfortunately, safety behaviours inadvertently reinforce fear, control and avoidance in the longer term.

Practical Exercise: Move Toward Your Core Values, Away from Your Threat-Based Values

Consider a time when a TBV comes to the fore for you. Try to get really clear on the context – ideally there's even a specific scenario you've experienced that you can bring to mind.

Where are you? What are you doing? Who else is there? What was your 'inner dialogue' telling you? How did you know you were under threat? Now, in this present moment, while reading this book and not under any immediate physical threat, ask yourself: 'Which of my core values would I like to bring into that moment?'

Don't worry about how you'll do it – just think about what those values are and why they're relevant. How does actioning them help you grow further into the version of 'you' you want to develop over time?

Now, take some deep breaths, perhaps in through your nose and out through your mouth:

Inhale over 4
Pause for 4
Exhale over 6
Pause for 4
Repeat this 2 more times.

Allow your breath to return to its natural rhythm.

Guide your attention to your breath. And each time your mind wanders, gently bring yourself back to the present moment by refocusing on your breath. Get really curious about how the air feels as it moves in through your nostrils, down into your lungs, and back out again. Notice the temperature of the air as it moves in versus out of your nostrils. And when your mind wanders, which it will again and again, simply notice where it has taken you, thank your mind for doing what it does best (after all it is an incredible thought machine) and guide your attention back to your breath. There is power and beauty in the repetition of this exercise. Each time you guide your attention back to where you intend it to be, that is a 'rep' of your 'attention muscle'. You don't have to be good at keeping your attention somewhere. You just need to get in the reps of shifting your attention. You can start with the breath, and then open it up to other elements of your present experience.

* * *

Your breath and five senses (sight, hearing, taste, touch, smell) offer you resources to help bring yourself back into the present moment. When you're deeply immersed in some experience of the present moment, the past and future fall by the wayside and it's more possible to unhook from the 'if onlys' and 'what ifs' rattling around your mind. Slower, controlled breathing can help activate your parasympathetic nervous system, promoting a 'rest and digest' state. This is ideal for values work, as it promotes blood flow to areas of the brain associated with strategic and reflective thinking.[8]

In promoting this internal state of 'rest and digest', you're in a better position to consider which of your core values are most relevant to the current situation. What choices will best support your core values for long-term growth? And what threat-based value might be activated, tempting you to act from a place of fear or control?

It's worth remembering that this preparation isn't about stopping threat-based values from being triggered. It's expected, normal and natural for them to arise. Instead, this preparation helps you set the intention to *in*action those threat-based values and act in alignment with your core values instead.

When you notice that TBVs are in play, name them. Thank your mind for trying to keep you safe by prioritising these values – after all, that's what it's doing! Your mind is doing its best to keep you safe. Acknowledge this, and then remind yourself that you don't need to act on these values unless you consciously decide it is absolutely necessary.

Reflecting on how threat-based values have shown up in your life can help you make some simple, practical preparations for the future. When TBVs are being triggered, this is not the best time

TWO SETS OF VALUES

to have to marshal your resources to think differently and devise an alternative, core values-aligned solution. It's more beneficial to scenario plan in advance. For instance, when my kids leave their dirty cereal bowls on the kitchen counter rather than putting them in the dishwasher, this triggers a values conflict in me around Respect, which then leads to a desire in me to align what I do with Control and Moral Vigilance. In practice, this sounds like me lecturing them for not cleaning up 'again', branding this as 'lazy' and saying in my you're-in-trouble voice, 'Come back right now and put them in the dishwasher, I mean come on boys?!'

This behaviour from them is a repeated occurrence in our house, and I absolutely know it has a small but detrimental impact when I speak to them that way (and it's not like it's worked!), so it's paid for me to do two things. First, commit to acting directly from Respect and a desire to maintain a good connection with my kids – that is, to now allow what I see as their misalignment with my value of Respect to lead me to also misalign my behaviour with respect. Second, to tie this to a 'why.' My 'why' in this case is: 'To ask my kids clearly and kindly to come back and put their dishes away, so that we stay well-connected – they'll learn what's expected eventually!' Preparing a simple 'why' statement for these times is useful. Devising a 'why' for a specific type of situation can help you anchor to core values alignment.

Let's look at an example from a few years back. Clara, Henry's mum,[9] was seeing me for help around decision-making and transitioning back into full-time work. She identified Control and Perfectionism as values she tends to prioritise when feeling threatened, and her core values as Curiosity, Collaboration, Family, Health, and Work Ethic. Clara had been reflecting on how her TBVs showed up at work in her tendency to micromanage her direct reports. The conversation shifted to how those same TBVs might be influencing her interactions with Henry, particularly when helping him with his homework.

Clara shared that the night before, when she was reviewing Henry's middle-school history paper, she'd had a strong urge to dive in and make corrections to improve the work. She also reflected, however, that Henry had become increasingly reluctant to show her his assignments. Knowing that she and I were catching up the next day, she'd paused on offering much help until we talked it through.

Clara did most of the reflecting and hit the nail on the head around the issues at play. She wondered if she felt under threat not just because she cared deeply about Henry's progress, but also because of how his progress reflected on her as a parent. She was aware of her insecurities around how she was doing as a single parent, especially now that she was going back into full-time work. She further reflected, however, that in the long term what she truly wanted for Henry was for the lines of communication between them to remain open. She knew that consistently acting on her TBVs of Control and Perfectionism might improve his short-term assignment performance but that it could damage his willingness to be open with her in the future.

Clara realised she could call on her core values of Curiosity and Collaboration to navigate these homework moments with Henry. Instead of jumping in to fix things, she could remain focused on communicating with a spirit of curiosity and collaboration, not judgement and a fix-it mentality. The 'why' she came up with around this was 'To support Henry with curiosity and collaboration, so that we can remain connected and close and I can continue to support him in the long run.' At times when she felt her resolve wavering, she would say to herself, 'Curiosity over judgement, Clara! Curiosity over judgement.'

Henry is now at university and still shares insights with his mum. She has doubled down on her 'curiosity over judgement' approach and credits insight into her core values and TBVs as enabling her to notice what's going on for her and how she needs to be intentional. With preparation, you can notice activation of your threat-based values in all sorts of situations. Rather than focusing in on them, consider what you might do to intentionally act in a way that aligns with one or more of your core values. And at times when you still find yourself reacting from a place of threat, learn from the experience to do better next time.

As to why I am suggesting that threat-based values might be in play in the case of a parent helping their child with homework, it's because such moments can challenge the parent's identity or sense of what being a 'good parent' means. It can challenge the parent's internalised sense of being 'good enough,' creating a space for threat-based values to dominate without intentional reflection and realignment. And there are times when we don't even realise the role of TBVs in our experience. One of my challenges is calling people, including on their birthday, because I am so worried I will call at an inopportune moment. This concern leads me to prioritise avoidance, even though I know that if I don't speak to them I'll feel more awkward and disconnected in the longer term.

I have already explained that when values (core or threat-based) are activated, they trigger an emotional response, making them highly motivational. When TBVs are activated, then, you feel motivated to act on them. Rather than doing so, take a deep breath (or several), pause and reflect. Ask yourself, 'What matters most right now?' and 'What would my core values have me do?' This is important because when a TBV is in play we can feel strongly about acting on it. Any type of values alignment feels good and in the short term, if you act in line with a TBV, it, too, can feel good and 'right' or at least justified. When there's congruency or alignment between what you value and what you do, you might experience it as a 'feeling of rightness' that helps drive direction and momentum over time. The effect on your emotions is why using your core values to navigate your life can feel satisfying. When you listen to your values and establish what you want, you're unstoppable. It provides you with a position from which you can change your life and make a meaningful difference to the world in ways that are right for you.

During threat-based values activation, however, the associated 'felt sense' of values alignment is not necessarily something to rely on. Because it is prioritising, for instance, a sense of wanting to control, a justification for avoidance, an inclination towards moral vigilance where you are channelling an energy associated with fear, hurt, even anger. It doesn't reflect behaviour that aligns with your core values and help grow the version of you that you seek to build over the longer term. A sidenote, at this point, about what I'm generally referring to when I speak of 'values alignment'. Typically, when I talk about values alignment, I'm referring to alignment over the *long* term – alignment with core values that supports longer-term growth and satisfaction, rather than just 'Oh, I feel aligned in the present moment.'

Your mindset, and specifically whether you're feeling under threat, impacts your priorities and your ability to respond with longer-term growth in mind. So, at times when you feel under threat, and you know that the actions you're compelled to take are not aligned with your core values, stop. Breathe. Acknowledge the desire to prioritise a threat-based response over your core values. Intentionally guide your focus back to, 'Which of my core values are most relevant here? How can I act in line with them instead?'

So far, we've discussed values activation as an emotional response, but that's only half the story. Over time, values activation means aligning more of your actions with your values, more often. The way we prioritise our values changes depending on the situation and the beliefs, needs and goals that are relevant at the time. This makes values activation a dynamic process. Striving for values alignment often involves balancing our (short-term) survival needs and goals and our (longer-term) growth-oriented needs and goals.

If you're thinking, 'But there are times when prioritising threat-based values is useful,' you're right. It's not that TBVs should never be prioritised. It's that, more often than not, we tend to prioritise these values automatically, far more than is necessary. This needs to be a more conscious process, where you choose to make this prioritisation, fully aware of the ramifications. Aligning your response with values you naturally prioritise when under threat might not take you where you want to go in life. So, make sure you really need to prioritise them before you act on the emotional pull.

What's interesting about threat-based values is that they vary far less between people. While threat-free – aka 'growth,' aka 'core' – values can vary greatly between people and be quite nuanced and individual, there are only a small number of TBVs that apply to most people. This is because threat motivates us more similarly than growth does. I might want to grow my life as a baker and have a small shopfront in a country town. You might want to grow your life as a parent and focus on doing what you can to raise three happy kids. A friend of mine is growing their life in the direction of raising happy kids while having an incredible career as a business leader. But we all want to survive and stay safe when we're under threat. That is, when we're under threat our needs and goals, and the values that support them, tend to shrink in number, be more similar, and be grounded in short-term survival.

Humans and Chickens

Imagine a flock of chickens in their run on a pleasant summer morning. One chicken might be under a leafy tree enjoying a dust bath – the perfect remedy for removing mites and cooling off. Another might have just laid an egg and is proudly squawking about it. Meanwhile, a few others are scratching at the damp, loose earth, heads bobbing as they eagerly search for juicy grubs.

All these behaviours reflect how chickens can act when they are relatively carefree. Note how there can be a lot of variation in how the chickens spend their time.

Now imagine Mr Fox arrives. He sneaks through a weak spot in the fence and launches himself at one of the hens! What happens next? In your mind, you can probably picture it – chaos! They are now *all* squawking, running around frantically, trying to escape or evade the attacker. Suddenly, all of the chickens are acting the same way. They're responding to a threat, focusing on survival. Other needs – like dust bathing or finding food – no longer matter because none of that is important if they become a snack for Mr Fox.

If the chickens spent all their days running around frantically, squawking, and expending large amounts of energy, this wouldn't be a productive use of their time at all. It won't help them eliminate mites, cool off, find food, socialise, or reproduce. In other words, within the chicken universe it wouldn't help them grow or live their best life. But when survival is on the line, frantically running and squawking is their best shot at survival so they can live to grow another day.

I'm not suggesting that chickens have values. But they do have needs associated with surviving and growing, which, like our values, shift based on whether the situation is threatening or threat-free. Unlike chickens, humans have values, and those values – bringing together our current needs with beliefs and goals – enable us to maintain greater agency and choice over what we *do* next when we perceive threat. This is most fortunate, given that for us, our 'fox' is most likely in our mind's eye. That is, rather than a baddie chasing us or our very survival being at stake, we're more likely to perceive and be tempted to act on a threat to our identity, reputation, sense of self or relationships.

So what happens when a metaphorical fox enters our world – even one associated with our reputation or identity? The same threat response system kicks in that we would use were a tiger chasing us. We shift into survival mode, and our responses – metaphorically at least – start to resemble those of the chickens. We focus on self-preservation, including the preservation of our very nearest and dearest. The issue for us, when so many of our threats exist in our mind's eye, is that it's difficult to resolve them through fighting or fleeing. So, they can accumulate until we're living in a chronic state of threat and stress. The chickens' guardian dog or the farmer can't come and scare our fox away, repair the fence and minimise our greatest fears.

For most of us, then, our greatest battles are waged inside our minds, not in the world around us. Yet as I've mentioned our physiological response is the same either way: activation of our sympathetic nervous system, triggering us to fight, take flight, or freeze. In this threat-based state, without our own intentional intervention, we're likely to prioritise survival responses. If we are inclined toward a 'fight' response, then perhaps Control, Moral Vigilance, or Blame Deflection are the threat-based values we prioritise. Alternatively, Avoidance might be our style when we are inclined toward taking flight or freezing. Acting on these inclinations, however, is not inevitable. In a world filled with perceived threats, becoming intentional about which values we act on – why, when and how – is vital.

Intentional Values Prioritisation is Key

To recap. Core values can come to the fore more naturally when we're not under threat. We can more easily prioritise and act in line with them. Under threat, however, safety- and security-oriented values can take precedence. These self-serving values focus on our survival in the short term, even if this comes at the expense of longer-term growth. The problem is that for many, whether due to environmental, relational, or psychological factors (such as anxiety, living with trauma, or conditioning), we can find ourselves living in a threat-based state much of the time, even when there is no imminent danger outside of our own mind. Over time, we become so accustomed to acting from this state that we don't question it. Our threat-based actions can create a self-fulfilling prophecy: we project the very threat we're trying to avoid. In turn, we perpetuate and expand threatening circumstances in our lives while simultaneously reducing the sort of longer-term growth that provides us personal fulfilment. We can become increasingly disconnected from the version of ourselves we seek to develop and grow into over time.

Am I advocating that you push aside your internal worries to try to control them or eliminate them? No! Please don't do that – and especially, please don't try to control away your thoughts and feelings. If you try to push away or control thoughts and feelings, they are likely to rebound with twice the force.[10] That said, there are times when you will need to intentionally and consciously lean into responding to threats in ways that are challenging for you because they run counter to your core values. Sometimes, standing your ground requires a firm response that acknowledges the conditions you're enduring as pressing. However, what I am advocating for is a different way of dealing with habitual threat-based activation.

First, become aware that you perceive a threat. Notice it non-judgementally, and remember: whether or not the threat is 'real' or justifies your level of perceived threat, your body and mind are responding in a (potentially misguided) effort to keep you safe – and that is something to be grateful for. Next, actively choose not to respond based on threat. Intentionally decide to *in*action the threat you perceive. Then, guide your attention back to actions that align with your core values. How can you lean into your core values during these moments? What would that look like? Which of your values are relevant right now?

At times when your mind takes you to a place of perceived threat, but your fundamental safety – such as your physical safety – is not at risk, then make room for the experience without acting on it. Notice the suffering that comes with feelings of being in danger. Reflect on the universality of this experience from thoughts around 'what if' and 'if only.' Even though it may feel isolating and unique to you, remember that others have experienced similar suffering. Next, mindfully lean toward this experience of threat, with acceptance and openness. Guide your attention to the present moment and look inward. Notice the feelings and sensations associated with the perceived threat. See if you can locate them in your body – where are they strongest? Breathe in and around these sensations, making space for them without trying to change them – just observe.

It's important not to try to push away these feelings. Instead, recognise the value in having this threat response mechanism when it's needed. You can express gratitude for how this system has protected you and countless generations before you, paving the way for your existence. There is nothing wrong with the threat-based infrastructure or system, and it's helpful to remember that it's universal. However, in the modern world, we need to be especially selective about prioritising actions that flow from its activation. That is where getting more familiar with your core values comes in. Doing so enables you to scenario plan around what to do in certain contexts, even when you feel under threat.

Furthermore, once you better understand the impact of your values on how you interact with the world, you can start to take control and focus on becoming more intentional about prioritising and acting in line with values that mean the most to you.

The process of intentional values work involves reflecting on what actions and thought processes align with which values. From there, it's about intentionally choosing behaviours that match the values you want to prioritise in a given situation, and guiding your focus toward thoughts that support them.

Mindfulness helps us observe our thoughts without immediately reacting to them, such that we can make room for all thoughts without feeling we need to engage with them or do anything about them. We can either hook into them if they serve us, or observe them non-judgementally and let them pass if they don't align with our desired direction in life.

While you can't control the thoughts you have, you can influence how you engage with them, and this skill improves with practice.[11] Mindfulness and attention training can help you focus on growth-related values that serve you in the long term, by guiding your attention toward thoughts that support these values. Over time, this can also help reduce the pull on your attention of threat-based values that don't serve you well.

Mindfulness and attention training provide you with an observational pause in which you can notice your thoughts and make a choice as to what to do next. For example, you might say, 'I see that perfectionism is in play right now. I feel the need to get this perfect. Thanks, mind. This isn't a life-or-death situation, so I'm going to guide my attention to my value of Compassion, which I think will be useful in this scenario. Specifically, I'm going to move toward expressing self-compassion for imperfection ...' This is why scenario planning is so useful when it comes to values-based decision-making. In moments of stress, it's useful to have a plan where you don't have to start from first principles with what you're going to do. You have already decided: 'In this situation, I'll set aside TBVs and act on my core values, and this is how.'

KEY TAKEAWAYS OF THIS CHAPTER:

* You have two sets of values, not one. Based on your current needs and whether you feel under threat, you're likely to prioritise one type or the other (thriving or surviving).

* It is helpful to be aware of your core *and* your threat-based values.

* Commit to actioning your core values, and *in*actioning your threat-based values (unless you're sure you are under imminent physical threat!).

* Notice and accept threat-based values activation as normal, natural, and to be expected. However, activation of values doesn't mean you need to action them. Noticing them prior to acting on them provides you the opportunity to change tack, and *in*action them.

* Use mindfulness meditation and breathing exercises to help reduce physiological arousal associated with being under threat, to make it easier to incline toward your core values.

* Give yourself a break. Recognise that feeling under threat is a form of suffering, and the first port of call is offering yourself compassion. Just because you *feel* like acting from a place of threat, it doesn't mean you need to or should do so.

CHAPTER 3
Know Your Core Values

Understanding your values is a critical part of self-development, which benefits your performance, success, satisfaction, relationships, and life trajectory. Whether you're aware of your values or not, they help shape your experiences and impact your forward journey.

Let's begin with three prompt areas I often use in group sessions and workshops.[1] Take some time to think about each of them. There's no rush. You might like to do this work with a partner, friend, or journal about it to reflect on later. You can muse on them in your mind, too, and come back to them again later. You can create dinner parties with friends and offsite sessions with teams around these questions (among others) to deepen conversations, connections, and leave people feeling seen and heard like never before. After some time (months or a year, even), circle back and see whether your answers have changed and how that might reflect changing priorities or life circumstances for you. There are no right or wrong answers to these prompts, and no need to overthink them.

- **Describe a time or place that brings you joy.**
  - Where is it?
  - Who (if anyone) are you with?
  - What is it about this place that brings you joy?
  - How do you feel in your body when you think of this place?
  - Where in your body do you feel any positive sensations?

- **Who is someone you admire, and why? This can be someone you know or a stranger, a historical or living person, even a fictional character.**
  - What is this person's name?
  - How would you describe their character?
  - What are the features of this person that are particularly admirable?
  - Can you describe a time when they've actioned these features?
  - What are the values words that come to mind when you think of this person?
  - How (if at all) are these values important to you in your own life?

- **What is a dealbreaker for you? An action that if you see it, you find it hard to walk past and difficult to retain respect for the person who took the action.**

- Can you describe the behaviour?
- What is the context?
- What is it about this behaviour that makes it a dealbreaker?
- Is there anyone in your life who has exhibited this behaviour?
- How have you gotten past it (if you have)?
- How does this behaviour make you feel in your body when you witness it?
- Where are these feelings in your body?

Having taken some time to think about your answers to some or all of the three questions, what are values themes that emerge for you? Are there certain words or principles that come up again and again?

Identifying Your Core Values

You can now make your way through the value identification process (via gretajbradman.com or use the values words and definitions in the Appendix, see page 309).

As you work toward identifying or refining your core values, think about what might be missing or standing out from your reflections. I recommend aiming toward five core values. Some of these might not always be front and centre in your life. They may be activated when others act incongruently with the value and it triggers a negative emotional response in you. This is handy to know. Similarly, it might be that there is a subset of your top five that tends to be prioritised during decision-making. Understanding this subset, and indeed understanding any especially dominant core values for you, can be useful to help you ensure they don't become overemphasised in ways that become counterproductive.

You'll notice that values names often start as adjectives like *adventurous* and *curious*, or as nouns like *courage*, *work ethic* and *wisdom*. But values are more than just generic labels. When you appreciate values as schemas that bring together your beliefs from past experience, current needs, and future goals and aspirations, it follows that their names should be personally relevant. It is important that your core values have names that are meaningful to you, and resonate with you emotionally. There is no right or wrong to the names you choose for your values. For a while one of mine – Persistence – was 'Little Red Engine' (capturing the Golden Book story of the engine that would puff up the hill – 'I think I can, I think I can'). My needs and goals changed, and now I have reverted to the word 'Persistence' as it has a straightforward quality to it that these days really works for me. As I say, there's no right or wrong!

Your Values Are a Work in Progress

Values discovery evolves over time and requires a leap of faith. You won't know if they're 'right' until you've tried them on for a while, and they continue to evolve as you learn and grow, given your beliefs, needs, and goals. At the level of the individual, values are there to help you take steps in the direction of your Mount Everest – your version of a brilliant life. There's no comparison to other people that can adequately stand in for intentional, ongoing values discovery work. All you can do is identify values that you think are among your top five and test them out in the real world.

Revisit the process at least once a year and spend some time actively checking in that your core values are working for you. And in the early days of values identification and refinement work it might be a case of doing this on a very regular basis – weekly, fortnightly, monthly and quarterly, at different levels of depth. Remember, the goal of values work is twofold: to make sense of your experience and your responses, and to help you align more of your actions with your most important values. Both of these goals are set to help you cultivate a life filled with more of what matters to you – and more of the satisfaction and aligned contribution that follows.

Personalising Your Core Values

Once you've identified what you think are your top five core values, it's time to personalise them. Think of this as an opportunity to make your values feel more real. To use myself as an example, my value 'Achieve Together' brings together Achievement and Collaboration. For me, Achieve Together works as a name – it resonates with me, evokes an emotional sense of what this value means to me, and I can envisage what it looks like in action in different scenarios.

Once you have a reasonable sense of a likely top five, you need to define your values – write a one-liner that's all your own. To be honest, half the benefit of defining personal core values is in the effort it takes, and the thinking time that is spent on them. This is a golden moment to imprint them more consciously. Moreover, oftentimes I find people second-guess their values names and definitions when they first come up with them. I suggest that when you find a contender, you write it down without overthinking it or judging yourself for coming up with something 'uninspired' and just let it percolate. Some of the most memorable, resonant, and sticky values started out as 'terrible ideas'.

Next, pen a longer description, perhaps two or three sentences in length. It needs to be broadly applicable and avoid 'should'-based language. This isn't the time to plan how you'll beat yourself up if you don't live up to your values perfectly. This longer description is really about joining your values with broad exemplar actions, to help ground them in reality. To aid this process, you might like to identify some actions that align with your values. For instance, Achieve Together involves including my team in decisions and actions. This serves as a helpful reminder for me, especially since I sometimes prefer to work alone and can find myself getting caught up in doing so, despite valuing teamwork.

Let's recap on those steps. For each of your core values:

- **Name it – what name resonates most with you?**
- **Define it (one line) – don't rely on a generic description, tweak it or change it completely to make it your own.**
- **Description (roughly a paragraph) – provide a longer description of your value to help you make sense of it at depth, and also to help those close to you understand it better, if you choose to share your values with them.**
- **Identify actions you *already* take that align with this value.**
- **Identify actions you *want to* take that align with this value.**
- **Identify actions that run *counter* to this value.**

You can also consider how each of your values show up. Consider how each of them emerges across the different domains of your life. Where 5 = extremely relevant, 1 = not relevant, and 3 = somewhat relevant. If you find a core value isn't showing up with some high ratings in at least some life domains, either get more intentional about it or accept that it's perhaps not a core value for you at this point in your life.

- **Which life domains is this value most relevant and important for?**

KNOW YOUR CORE VALUES

	Curiosity	Achieve Together	Contribution	Work Ethic	Persistence
Work and career	Place your score here				
Family and relationships					
Health and wellbeing					
Education and personal growth					
Leisure and recreation					
Spirituality and religion					
Community and social involvement					
Finances and material possessions					
Environment and sustainability					
Politics and social justice					
Creativity and self-expression					
Mindfulness and self-awareness					
Travel and adventure					
Philanthropy and service					

Strongly Disagree	Disagree	Neutral	Agree	Strongly Agree
1	2	3	4	5

- For each of your values, think of a short phrase or mantra you can use to call it to mind at times when you need the motivational oomph it can provide you to harness courage, conviction, and follow-through energy.

Life Domains

I've shared my thoughts on values as positive schemas, which can be prioritised in different orderings depending on context. We tend to broadly prioritise values based on level of threat, where threat-free values promote core values activation, whereas a threatened state promotes activation of threat-based values. But there's another key factor influencing how we likely prioritise core values: the life domain we're currently operating in. Quite often at work, for instance, I find I prioritise Achieve Together over Persistence, but when I'm running with my German shepherd I tend to fairly reliably prioritise Persistence over Achieve Together.

I have found it is quite common for people in a work context to prioritise values like Achievement and Work Ethic, whereas at home values related to Love or Relationships are prioritised more frequently. At first glance, this context-driven reshuffle of core values makes sense – different values come to the fore in different life domains. A sidenote is that when we view important values as fundamental drivers, their activation influences how you feel and interpret any situation. It's just that different life domains may surface different needs and goals and values that support them. But your mind isn't waiting for confirmation of what life domain you're in, and life domains are blurry, now more than ever. Trying to separate values strictly by life domain – for instance 'These are my work values, and these are my home values' – can be counterproductive. This is especially so given how values jostle for primacy at the messy intersections between life domains – those points of transition between work and home, or health and social connection, for instance.

My experience is that it is at times when life domains are pushing up against one another that you want clarity around how you are prioritising your values. This can help explain how you are feeling, how you *need* to prioritise your values to align with your values-led life, and what that means in action. That is one of the reasons I advocate for focusing on one values set that is applicable across all life domains, and then looking at which values from the set tend to dominate in one life domain versus another.

This suggestion of identifying one set of values – your top five – aligns with prominent values researcher and psychologist Shalom Schwartz who has found that we experience greater wellbeing and less internal conflict when our actions and decisions are consistent with our core values, regardless of context.[2] In addition to the evidence base, there are several compelling reasons for this stance, too.

I've already alluded to life domains overlapping. One of the key ways that values help you navigate life is managing your internal negotiation around allocating resources – your time, energy, finances – across multiple areas of your life. It is often at the inflection points between life contexts where values conflict and, therefore, where values negotiations reside. For instance, considering whether to work late or go home involves prioritising one life domain over another at a point where both are somewhat in play. Seemingly small decisions often shape the trajectory of our relationships and lives. We'll delve deeper into this in Chapter Nine on values-based decision-making. For now, let's take a closer look at the roles your values can play and how they affect your experience and decisions.

The Roles of Your Core Values

What active roles do your values play in how you show up in the world? How do your values inform what matters to you? To keep things simple, I'll focus on three roles, which I've used for around a decade now to help contextualise how values can show up and impact our experience: values as a motivating force, values conflict, and the shadow side of values.

Values serve as a motivating or driving force in your life, underpinning your 'why' and helping you complete actions that grow the version of yourself you aim to become. This is the so-called 'golden side' of your values – their ability to inspire and empower us. At times, however, values can conflict with one another and in moments of conflict this elicits a negative emotional response that is both uncomfortable and motivating. Understanding values conflicts can help you make sense of your experience both internally and interpersonally. Lastly, our values have a 'shadow side' – that is, a side that emerges when we overuse or over-prioritise our values, which can be counterproductive. Let's go deeper into each area of human values.

Your Core Values as a Motivating Force

Core values activation brings with it an emotional response. This is why values can be so powerfully motivating. When an action or event aligns with the value, it generates a positive emotional response; when there's misalignment, the response is negative. Values activation is most likely to happen when you view an action as conflicting with one of your values.[3] For instance, when *you* do something that goes against one of your values, or you see someone else act in ways that misalign with it. Unless you've done values work, you're unlikely to stop and think, 'Huh, I understand this feeling of unease or frustration is a motivational response to a values conflict I see going on.' Instead, you're likely to experience it as a negative emotional state (e.g. frustration, anger, shock, or sadness) and start searching for reasons why you feel that way, often based on 'right' or 'wrong' rather than perception. We will dive deeper into values conflicts soon, but for now let's turn to the *positive* side of values as a motivating force.

As you become more in tune with your values through intentional work, they increasingly serve as a powerful internal guide for your decisions and actions. Aligning your responses with your most important values can bring a sense of joy or conviction ('rightness') in having made the 'right choice' for you.[4]

Your values as a motivating force provide intrinsic motivation – the kind of drive that comes from within – that is often more sustainable and fulfilling long term than relying on external validation or rewards.[5] They can help stabilise your emotional responses by grounding you in purpose and direction, especially in choppy waters.[6] Relatedly, your values can bolster courage of your convictions, helping you bounce back after adversity or challenging circumstances. In so doing, they can provide a foundation for resilience and growth following setbacks.[7,8]

When your actions align with your values, you create a reinforcing loop of joy, happiness, satisfaction and fulfilment. This offsets short-term practices detrimental to longer-term growth, which are tied to hedonistic pleasure-seeking, comfort, or attempts to numb from discomfort such as risky or addictive behaviours or substance abuse. Because values connect to what matters most at a deeper level, they provide you energy and enthusiasm to help you aspire to grow beyond your current self. It's this deeper motivational power of values that enables them to guide us toward the sort of 'deathbed satisfaction' we might achieve at the end of our lives if we're lucky. And, in this context where deathbed satisfaction intersects with our relationships, our core values can also motivate us to work on our meaningful connections with others. Even in tough circumstances, we can use the power of our values to motivate us to show up for others in alignment with our better selves. In this way, values as a motivating force promote the development of an authentic 'you', on your own terms.

Practical Exercise: Values as a Motivating Force

Values are made real through action, and their motivational potential is expanded when we engage in values-aligned activities that give rise to the sort of positive reinforcement mentioned above. Take some time to think about how your values motivate you into action.

For each of your values:

- **How does this value help you show up at your best?**
- **What is the role this value can play in helping you be your best today?**
    - Some values are very useful daily, whereas others are prioritised less often but are nonetheless crucial to making choices that align with how you seek to grow yourself.
- **What is the role of this value in enabling you to make good choices?**
- **What is one teeny-tiny way you can action this value in the next hour?**
    - This question forces you to consider how small an action you can identify that aligns with this value.
- **Think of a time when you've prioritised this value:**
    - Where were you?
    - What was happening?
    - How did this value enable you to show up?
    - How did it make you feel at the time?
    - How do you feel about it now?
    - Where do you feel this in your body?

* * *

When Values Conflict

All values conflict with one another to some extent – some more than others. Have you ever found yourself in a dilemma, wanting to do two very different things that pull you in different directions? For instance, perhaps you feel that you have a work deadline to meet (Work Ethic) but also a dinner date with friends (Connection, Relationships) you need to get to? It's when you find yourself trying to prioritise two values that pull you in very different actionable directions that you can experience a values conflict. Probably the neatest way I have had a client describe this state to me is 'It's like being pulled by two equally strong magnets, making it hard to decide which way to go.'

One of the simplest ways to assess whether a values conflict is in play is to reflect on your emotion state. Where you perceive a sense of unease or indeed even outrage or disgust (or something in between), it is worth considering what values conflict is in play. This insight can give you a better understanding of the 'why' behind how you're feeling, which can help you observe your feelings and understand your emotions instead of seeking external explanations that add further fuel to the fire. Insight into values conflict can help you make sense of your experience in more constructive ways.

Values conflicts can happen within an individual, between individuals, or even between an individual and an organisation. A common occurrence is when two of your values are competing for priority, and the way they're prioritised leads to very different actions. For instance, some values conflicts I've seen in practice include Work versus Family, Connection versus Work Ethic, Tradition versus Curiosity, Humility versus Ambition. Some experiences of 'parental guilt' can be understood as examples of values conflicts, too. For instance, where a prioritisation of Work and Family appears to give rise to two different actions (focusing on work, being there more for one's child). Similarly, a busy worker who forgets their lunch and values efficiency as well as environmental sustainability faces a values conflict when considering actions associated with the convenience of buying lunch that involves single-use packaging, versus seeking out a lunch environment where they can opt for reusable items but it will eat into their work time.

Practical Exercise: Internal Values Conflicts

Take some time to explore values conflicts that exist in your own life, between two or more of your own core values. You can also apply these questions to values conflicts between one or more of your values and someone else's values (i.e. an 'external values conflict').

- **What is the context of the potential values conflict?**
- **Which of your values might be involved in this conflict?**
- **Thinking about the values involved, one at a time consider the different action each of the values would give rise to if you prioritised it.**
- **How are you feeling in your body? Where do you feel these sensations?**

    Breathe in and around these sensations. Allow them to be there. No need to push against them or try to get rid of them. Give them space to be there. Understand they're a sign that you care. But you don't need to act on them. They're a normal and natural response to a values conflict.

- **Given the information you have, which of these values do you intend to prioritise in this situation?**

* * *

Get intentional about how you prioritise your values. Understand that you can't hold them as equally important in a given moment. You will always need to make a trade-off and decide your priority. Where you find you wish to prioritise two values that in the current context are incongruent in terms of the action you would take, you are very likely to experience the discomfort of an internal values conflict. Don't try to push the discomfort away or resolve it. Make space for this experience – allow yourself to feel it. Instead of seeing it as a sign that you're not making the 'right' decision, understand it as a normal response to deprioritising a value that is really important to you. Remind yourself that you are being thoughtful and intentional in your decision-making. Follow through and reflect on how you feel afterwards, so you can learn from this experience for next time. In the current world, we are too quick to view discomfort as negative and avoidable, rather than understanding it as an inevitable part of the human experience. You cannot please your whole self at the same time, and that's okay.

External Values Conflicts
External values conflicts happen when one or more of your values clash with someone else's. This can occur with a complete stranger, a good friend or family member, a colleague, or with a public figure you see on socials, to name a few.

One of the objectives of values work is to recognise that we don't all prioritise the same values. Understanding this allows us to accept that people may reach different conclusions and make different choices based on their own values – and that's okay. By acknowledging values conflicts as just that – conflicts of values, rather than personal faults – we can improve our relationships and reduce the risk of polarisation or burnout caused by sitting with unspoken, ongoing values clashes.

Practical Exercise: Getting Granular with Values Conflict Exploration

When thinking about your core values, how do they conflict *with one another*?

- Values in conflict (i.e. the values names that conflict with one another)?
- How does the values conflict tend to show up?
- How does this values conflict make you feel?
- How do you handle the values conflict?
- For this specific values conflict, how can prioritising your values help as a remedy?

What are some common values conflicts between one (or more) of your values and someone else's value(s):

- Which of your values are involved in this conflict?
- Which external values are involved in this conflict?
- What is the values conflict you perceive?
- What is the generous assumption you can make about the values-based motivation of the other person?
- How can you intentionally incline toward this generous assumption, rather than going looking for further evidence about why you are 'right' and they are 'wrong'?

What is your remedy for overcoming this values conflict? Choose as many as are relevant:

- **Allow conflicted feelings to be present and make space for them. Guide your attention back to your core values and reflect on the actions they inspire.**
- **Recognise that this values conflict exists because you care. Celebrate your values while also allowing space for the emotions this conflict evokes.**
- **Remind yourself that even when someone else's values differ from yours, their perspective remains valid. Others may prioritise values differently in a given situation – and that's okay.**

* * *

When experiencing a values conflict, remember that you're seeing the world through the lens of your values and associated beliefs, needs, and goals, and that due to values activation the experience will be emotionally charged. Values help shape your emotional responses and influence your thoughts. Rather than channelling your energy toward another person with judgements like, 'This person is being so foolish,' reflect on how your own thoughts arise given your values. Your initial response – your thoughts and emotions (before you act) – reflects what is meaningful to you, but you get to choose what you do next, aligned with what is important to you in the longer term. Instead of focusing on the judgements your values might incline you toward making, step back and observe your experience. Notice how your values are shaping it.

Let's look at an example. Imagine you're at a family barbecue, and your cousin Dan announces they've quit their stable job to pursue their dream of becoming a full-time artist. Some family members express concern, quietly whispering about the decision being 'irresponsible'.

Others applaud the decision and Dan for their courage to follow their passion. If you zoom in on these family members, you'd likely notice their emotions are playing a role in the opinions they're expressing. In my practice, I often find that when you drill down, these feelings flow to beliefs and underneath these beliefs are activated values. Further, the beliefs seem to appear *after* both the values activation and the feelings. Beliefs are used, retrospectively, to justify and make sense of the emotional response. Someone who values Security and Conformity might see the decision as irresponsible, while others who value Creativity and Personal Freedom applaud the move.

Put yourself in this position at the barbecue. Are you concerned or applauding? What are the beliefs associated with this? How might this link to values that are important to you? And how would you respond to Dan's announcement if you were there? You may wish to ask yourself, 'Does my response help the situation or positively contribute to my experience or ability to engage constructively?' If not, rather than focusing energy on judging the decision or others' reactions, you have several choices. One is to get curious and muse on what values Dan might be prioritising in having made this decision. Sometimes understanding another's values can help reduce a values conflict. Alternatively, redirect your focus to other elements of your present experience. Observe the thoughts and feelings arising within you. Reflect on how your response demonstrates what you value, whether it's Security, Family, Creativity, Personal Freedom, or beyond. From here, you can genuinely thank your mind for bringing you this response; it's an indicator of what matters to you and that you care deeply about these issues.

Staying with this scenario a little longer, let's say you're deeply concerned with Dan's decision. You've seen it play out badly before and you don't want to see Dan making the same 'mistake' (as you see it). When you're at the family gathering, simply notice your thoughts and feelings, and understand that there is still a values conflict in play as much as you might consider yourself absolutely in the right about your opinion on this one. Resolve in your mind to find time later to talk with Dan about this and share your insights. But don't do so here. If you're serious about this as an issue, as opposed to simply expressing an incongruent perspective due to a values conflict, wait until the initial flush of emotion has subsided and then have the conversation. At the end of the day, Dan might still decide to follow through with his new career as an artist, and if that aligns with his values and he can make it work, who are we to argue?

Empathy and Perspective-Taking

Sometimes, we amplify our own suffering and strain relationships by not taking an empathetic, values-based perspective on others' choices. Imagine someone prioritises Work over Family again and again, and you think they should prioritise Family more. This difference in values prioritisation leads to different actions.

When you feel tempted to tell someone, 'You shouldn't prioritise that!' or 'You should do x not y!', before doing so, try this exercise. Ask: 'What do they value? How does this choice of theirs align with their values?' As simple as it sounds, this is an exercise in occupying someone else's heart via their values, rather than just walking a mile in their shoes while bringing your own values along for the ride. The goal is to make room for and respect the experience of others more often, and meet them where they are. You are not looking for 'right' and 'wrong' in this scenario but rather acceptance of different values prioritisations and the influence that has on choices made.

This approach can reduce your own suffering and foster healthier, more empathetic relationships. Even if you're genuinely concerned about the consequences of someone's choices, this balanced perspective allows you to approach them with curiosity rather than judgement. And this isn't simply about accepting others' choices all the time. Rather, it's about interrogating where your perspective comes from, and seeking first to understand the other better. Over time, you may gently influence their perspective and even change their mind, but in my experience you're more likely to avoid a defensive reaction or negative impact on your relationship this way. Values conflicts are inevitable and the key is to make space for them, as part of making space for other people's ways of doing life. This enables empathy, perspective-taking and relationship building beyond the surface level.

Practical Exercise: Sitting with the Discomfort of Values Conflict

Bring to mind a values conflict in your life – either between several of your core values, or between a value of yours and one belonging to a valued friend or associate. See if you can bring it to mind in some detail – what is it, how does it make you feel, where does it tend to be activated? Perhaps it's a values conflict you explored in the previous exercise.

Take three deep breaths, in through your nose and out through your mouth. Incline toward your breath as though you were a curious scientist, observing it for the very first time.

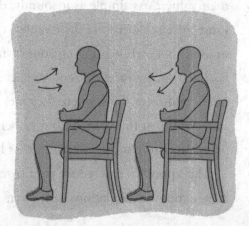

After your three deep breaths, allow your breathing to return to normal, although keep bringing your attention back to it. You may wonder whether it's still a little slower and more deliberate than usual; that's fine, no need to change it, just keep guiding your attention back to the breath.

I invite you now to go looking for any places of tension or discomfort in your body that might be associated with this values conflict that's in play. Notice it. Breathing in and around this sensation. If it had a colour, what would it be? Is it a gas, or a liquid, or a solid? What about its temperature? If you tried touching it, what would it feel like? Would it have a texture – rough, spiky, smooth, or something else entirely? There are no right or wrong answers. Breathe in and around this sensation associated with your values conflict. You don't have to do anything with it. Just allow it to be there. Make space for it.

Take another three deep breaths, in through your nose and out through your mouth. When you're ready, you can open your eyes and come back into the space.

In this state that you're now in, which is more reflective and open to observing with curiosity rather than judgement, take a moment to reflect on a core value of the other person, which might be driving their choice. What is it? How might you define it in a generous way? How does the choice they've made support this value of theirs?

In a similar situation, which of your values would you prioritise as important to action? And what choice flows from these value(s)? Notice the differences between the choice you have made, and the choice made by the other person. Take a moment to intentionally recognise that they flow from different values, but values that are equally valid and real – just to different people.

* * *

The Shadow Side of Your Values

When you overuse or over-prioritise your values, their shadow side emerges. Even the most wonderful values have a shadow side. This is normal and natural. It's just a matter of recognising and mitigating the impact of its shadow.

Imagine every value has two 'sides' – a golden side and a shadow side. Or perhaps, think of it more like parts of the day – day and night, to be specific – where dusk and dawn represent in-between zones where the pros and cons of a value are blended together. But really, we're focusing on high noon (golden!) and midnight (shadow) – the extremes of how values can be most productive and counterproductive.

The golden side of your values includes all the ways they can help you grow and be your best self. The shadow side shows up when a value is overused, misused, or over-prioritised, negatively impacting your experience. For example, if Accountability is one of your core values, its shadow side might involve taking more than 100 percent of your share of responsibility and accountability for a task. Let's talk this through, remembering the context in this example; you're over-prioritising Accountability and, in doing so, have unintentionally set up a dynamic where you're shouldering more than your fair share. How does this affect you? For starters, others might have grown accustomed to this, and even appreciate it (or take it for granted). But for you, it can lead to frustration – not only because others aren't showing the same level of accountability (creating a values conflict for you) but because you begin to feel exhausted and overwhelmed by the disproportionate burden. Further, there can be a snowball effect where increasingly, others fail to be accountable, and productivity and performance suffer. This experience can strain relationships and lead to chronic stress, even burnout. For the person over-prioritising

Accountability, it can culminate in threat-based values activation involving Avoidance, Control, and Perfectionism, further exacerbating their stress and exhaustion. One of the more delicate areas of coaching work is sensitively unpicking agency, where someone's overuse of one of their values is negatively impacting their experience or progress.

Practical Exercise: The Shadow Side
For each of your values:
    What characterises its shadow side?

- **Overuse**
- **Misuse**
- **Over-prioritisation**
- **Relentless fear of falling short of this value**
- **Assuming everyone prioritises this value as much as you do**
- **Believing others *should* prioritise this value as much as you do**

* * *

Sometimes, just becoming more aware of how you're over-prioritising your values can make a positive difference to your experience. For instance, say True to My Word is a value that is really important to you (i.e. a value that's akin to Accountability). It was one of Alison's values, who nicknamed it 'True'. What a terrific value! And yet, when overused, she found that far from merely being 'true to my word' for her actions, she was severely criticising herself for moments when she perceived she had not sufficiently lived up to this value. This self-criticism was leading to feelings of inadequacy, stress, and that she was letting other people down.

In fact, Alison was so concerned about following through on everything she promised people at work, she'd recently turned down a promotion. On talking it through, it became apparent that she knew she had the skills, but there were unknown areas of the role, which left her questioning whether she'd let the new team down. Rather than run the risk of falling short of being 'true to her word' (by taking up the role, thereby implying she was up to it), she declined.

In being aware of this tendency to over-prioritise and overuse True to My Word, Alison might have benefitted from extending self-compassion to her experience: 'Ah, I notice that I am overusing True to My Word just now, and it's leading me to feel like I'm going to let others down. I acknowledge this may happen, but this opportunity means a lot to me, and I'll make room for my experience around True and do it anyway.'

Another values domain that is often over-prioritised or overused is Achievement – encompassing values including Achievement and Work Ethic. In this day and age, where we are bombarded with messages of success being synonymous with being the 'best', perhaps it's little wonder their shadow side is often in play. When Achievement is overused or over-prioritised, it can lead to a host of 'shoulds'. These 'shoulds' can be explicit, such as 'I should be working harder. I should have gotten a better grade. I should be prettier,' and thoughts that follow on from that. They can also be implicit or unspoken, hardly acknowledged even by the individual yet deeply impactful on their experience: 'I'm lazy. I'm never going to get where I want to go.'

When noticing that you may be over-prioritising a certain value, approach this situation with curiosity not judgement. Think about how you can dial it back – what could that look like? How will it make you feel? Try to think about the longer term – how can you better action this value for the sake of your broader life? Furthermore, what other values of yours could be picking up some slack in this scenario? How can you better incorporate actions that flow from those values into your experience and actions? Taking a 'values portfolio' approach to the choices you make can enable your core values to each have their time in the sun, without certain values becoming overly dominant to the point of constraining your experience and holistic growth.

How Your Values Play Together

Your core values interact and overlap in various ways that impact your experience. It is typical for several core values to be activated simultaneously in a given situation, or for you to deem several of your values relevant for a particular choice. In that case you will need to balance their needs. Remember that your most important values will never completely align and this is why it's so important to get clear on how you wish to prioritise them in a given instance. While they will have areas of congruence, where they play well together, your core values will also have areas of incongruence, where they conflict or guide you in very different directions.

Your values conflict with one another and overlap in unique ways depending on the context. Their unique areas of difference necessitate that you prioritise them during decision-making, rather than holding them as equally important. The greater the difference in the unique contribution that your values make in determining the actions you'll take, the more important it is to be intentional about how you prioritise them.

Say you have kids, it's the school holidays, and you're taking a day off to spend with them. You're choosing between whether to go to the water park (a one-hour drive away) or the local trampoline centre (more convenient but something they've done many times). Your values of Family, Connection and Adventure are important to this decision. You think that both choices satisfy your values, but the water park does a particularly good job at aligning with Adventure, and after all you have the time. So, you go to the water park.

There's no especial values conflict in this case that is caused by the water park choice. The unique component that your values brought to the two choices was relatively small and uncontroversial. But what about in the context where you're considering whether to take time off at all? The actions 'work' and 'take time off with kids during the holidays' align with very different values. The unique component the values bring to the two choices is relatively large. That is, the actions that flow from these choices are distinct and may elicit a values conflict with some of your values while enabling high alignment with other values. Recognising how your values interact and play as a team can be really useful in forging longer-term, values-aligned growth. They all have areas of overlap, too, which enable them to play well together and coordinate in ways that further support your growth. Looking for these areas of overlap and maximising their potential at times can be an important part of your values journey.

It's important to remember, too, that we don't live in little bubbles, devoid of human interaction and without the complex interplay that is social life. Values-led living is not a solo endeavour. We are social creatures whose lives and identities are interconnected. Values enable us to unite, coordinate, collaborate and succeed together. Our values can help us find common ground when our beliefs alone would divide us. When we're successful in finding values-oriented common ground, we are more drawn together and can better identify with one another.[9]

Some of the world's most challenging and significant issues require values alignment with the longer term in mind, where we strive to look beyond areas of division for the sake of a common goal: humanity surviving and thriving. Collective values alignment does not mean we prioritise the same core values, although ideally, it involves incorporating values from a variety of values domains that have a social welfare and collective growth focus, such as universalism and benevolence.[10] Collective values alignment is enabled through understanding our own and each other's values, such that we can intentionally locate and expand common ground. It enables us to make room for one another's experience rather than assuming everyone does or 'should' hold the same values. In this chapter, we're exploring the benefits of understanding others' values for the sake of our relationships, our own experience, and for the benefit of humankind.

Recognising Others' Values During Conflict

If we start with Deepak Chopra's[11] assumption that 'everyone is doing the best they can with the knowledge and ability they have,' we open ourselves to the disciplined pursuit of recognising another person's core values, even amid conflict or perceived threat. We can consider their past experiences, current needs, and future goals, and better understand their values prioritisation. This process lets us make generous assumptions about someone's motivation and intentions. It reduces our likelihood of activating a spiral of threat-based values caused by a lack of understanding or suspicion about someone else's behaviour.

Values-based perspective-taking in service of generous assumptions is a personal discipline. You can intentionally reflect on a person's core values even if they're currently operating from a threat-based state. Taking a values-oriented perspective toward someone else does not negate you setting boundaries or heeding warning signs of troubling behaviour and putting in place guard rails as appropriate. Such a perspective allows you to extend as much empathy and understanding as possible, both for your own sake in maintaining alignment with your core values and to mitigate another's further descent toward an unhelpful threat-based position.

Threat-based values activation can come from a lack of understanding or intolerance of others' experiences or from interpreting another's behaviour or the values they're prioritising as a threat to us. Yet, as we've heard, values diversity is both inevitable and valuable. Understanding each other's values can mitigate our own threat-based response, which can be especially useful during times of negotiation.[12] In this context, values can help foster trust and rapport, improve communication during the negotiation process, and help you understand underlying values-oriented beliefs, needs and goals. In turn, understanding values enables you to separate these underlying drivers from the negotiation-specific position of the other party (their specific demands or statements).

Values and Negotiation

Whether navigating everyday negotiations about what to have for dinner or where to shop for groceries, through more formal negotiations about the sale of an item, or when settling a dispute, values play a crucial role in shaping our decisions and interactions. By understanding and applying values effectively, you can improve the negotiation process in several ways.

Identify What Matters Most

Before you enter a negotiation, take time to reflect on your values and how they will inform how you show up. Commit to aligning your actions and your decision-making with your values. Reflect on what threat-based values might come into play for you, and remind yourself of the importance of acting in line with your core values.

Knowing your values-based priorities helps you stay focused on what's really important, reducing the risk of you getting sidetracked by less important issues. Furthermore, your values provide an anchor that enable others to perceive you authentically; as someone who has the consistency and such that helps build trust.

Build Trust and Rapport
Establishing common ground by aligning to core values in your language and demeanour can help build a solid foundation for transparent, collaborative negotiation, where you can find a win-win. Identifying and emphasising shared values can foster a collaborative environment and open communication.

Enhance Communication
When you use values-based language that reflects your values and acknowledges the other party's values, this can help frame proposals in a way that resonates. Enhancing communication using values can reduce the likelihood of eliciting a threat-based response, thereby supporting the maintenance of rapport and trust during negotiation.

Manage Conflict
Recognise that moments of disagreement can arise from different values prioritisations rather than personal animosity or misunderstandings. Seeking to understand motivation from a values perspective can help manage conflict by improving understanding and defusing the potential for heightened emotions and interpersonal tensions. As I've

already alluded to, 'Beliefs divide people whereas values bring people together.' Framing conflicts around values rather than beliefs can be useful at unearthing unspoken needs and assumptions, and involves identifying differences in values prioritisation that may explain and make sense of differences of opinion. Doing so can help build a bridge of understanding and lead to a resolution that respects both parties' values.

Maintain Principles

Establishing and maintaining your principles from the start of a negotiation can help set the tone for collaboration and transparency during the process, as well as for your reputation in the longer term. The points at which principles are maintained or broken, other than gradually due to demeanour, is during moments of decision-making. You can approach values-based decision-making with the four Cs of authenticity: consistency, conformity, connection and continuity.[13] When you uphold your core values during negotiation, you are seen as someone who maintains personal integrity even under pressure. Values-aligned choices within negotiation help position you as trustworthy, even in contexts where the other party disagrees with your position. It may also help ensure that your agreements are fair and reasonable for all parties over the longer term, as you are less likely to overvalue 'smaller, sooner' benefits like immediate financial rewards, and undervalue the 'larger, later' value creation and character growth.

Practical Tips for Values-Based Negotiation

While these tips are written with more formal negotiation contexts in mind, they're also directly applicable to other forms of interpersonal negotiation, domestically and in the workplace.

Prepare

Before a formal negotiation, spend time understanding your own values and those of the other party as part of your preparation. Reflect on how these values (yours, as well as the values you're inferring are important to the other party) influence your beliefs, needs and goals as relevant to the negotiation. Given what you know of their character, needs, goals and values, how might you run some hypotheticals around their likely decision-making? How does a values perspective help you best predict the other party's interests versus their positions?

Values-based negotiation is one way of identifying interests (rather than positions), which can lead to more creative and mutually beneficial solutions.[14] Interests in this context represent the reasons *why* someone holds a particular position in a negotiation. They reflect the person's underlying needs, desires, concerns, and motivations. For instance, in a salary negotiation, an interest might be the need for financial security, recognition, and / or career advancement. Conversely, positions in negotiation are the specific demands or statements someone makes as surface-level expressions of their needs. Focusing on interests rather than positions can enable creative and mutually beneficial solutions during negotiation.

Listen Actively

Practising active listening to understand the other party's perspective is a critical component of successful negotiation.[15] When reflectively paraphrasing or summarising what you hear back to the other side, incorporate what you're inferring about their values priorities as part of this. Acknowledge their values and express respect for their priorities where possible. This form of active listening does not mean you implicitly agree with their position; your values-oriented active listening is an expression of empathy-in-action.

Ask Open Questions

Open-ended, values-oriented questions can help you explore the other party's underlying interests – their needs and goals – beyond what is on the table.[16] Open questions enable an answer that is not simply 'yes' or 'no.' They tend to start with 'What', 'When', 'Where', 'How', or 'Why', as opposed to 'Do you' or 'Is it'. Values-oriented open questions help uncover underlying motivations and priorities of the other party in the negotiation. They encourage deeper reflection and dialogue, helping both parties to understand each other's values in service of establishing some common ground. They can also help prime the other party to take a values-based perspective during the negotiation rather than assuming a win-at-all-costs viewpoint, which can erode value for all over the longer term. A couple of examples of values-oriented open questions with priming to begin include:

> 'I'd love to find a bit more time to spend together connecting and hanging out [communicate need], you mean so much to me and I love your company [values-oriented observation]. How do you think we might tweak our schedules to spend a little more time together? [primed proposal]'
>
> 'I agree the redundancies were necessary, albeit so hard on everyone given how much we value the team and our culture [values primer]. How do you think we can be balancing the team's wellbeing and protecting their high performance while market pressures continue? [primed suggestion invitation]'

Reflective Values Debrief

Once the negotiation is complete, reflect on how values influenced the process and the outcome. You can run this process alone, with your team, or with a friend. Values can influence proceedings in small yet meaningful ways. Small orientations to values, when used judiciously, can nudge the trajectory of proceedings in constructive directions. Consider what went well and how to improve next time regarding how you aligned your actions with your values.

Values and Other People: Wrap-Up

When we judge others for not prioritising the values we hold as most important, we fail to make room for their experience and their contribution to the broader whole. We can make incorrect assumptions about their motivations or rationale for a choice. These unhelpful assumptions can reduce the range of common ground we're likely to find where we can have different values, make different choices, yet strive for common goals.

By recognising the different perspectives that values diversity enables, we can reap the rewards that values diversity provides. Again, we're less likely to make poor choices due to assumptions and we can better position ourselves to consider things from a multitude of perspectives. After all, values diversity is not just inevitable as we've discussed; it helps stave off groupthink and promotes innovation and progress. Furthermore, in making room for the experience of others by seeking out the best in them via their values, we can hold space for common humanity rather than seeking out areas of difference and deficiency.[17] And while this talk of common humanity may sound idealistic, at this moment in time it pays to consider how we want to preserve and grow humankind into the future.

Summary About Your Core Values

You can do a lot with your core values. But when it comes down to it, they help explain your motivation and guide your path to what matters to you. Understanding your motivation from a values perspective includes asking questions such as, 'How can my core values serve as a motivating force in this situation, to help inspire me to do what matters?' Or 'Is there a values conflict going on for me around this?' or 'Am I over-prioritising my value of Responsibility just now?' They can help guide your path when you connect your values as goal-directed beacons that keep you on track, not only informing 'what' you want to do with this one precious life, but 'how' you want to go about the goal-directed steps to your version of a brilliant life.

I want to reiterate, however, that this is not a case of pathologising your experience or getting to some 'truth' about your experience using values. Rather, your values help assess the workability of a choice, or of holding onto a thought and feeling like you need to act on it (for example). You can use your core values to start making more generous assumptions both about your own motivations and behaviours, as well as about other people's. So far, we've gone deep on core values. In the next chapter, we'll get further into helping you reflect on the role of threat-based values in your life.

KEY TAKEAWAYS OF THIS CHAPTER:

* Core values help shape your performance, relationships, life trajectory, and satisfaction.

* You can strengthen your core values by actioning or focusing on them more; even so, your core values impact how you evaluate a situation or behaviour, even if you're not thinking about the value itself.

* It's important to personalise your values. Your values are *not* the name and description you read on a values card or a digital app to help you identify your values – these are just tools to get you started. What comes next is personalising your values by ensuring the name resonates with you, and by penning your own description for a value.

* Some of your values may surface very regularly – for instance, values around Family or Achievement – while others may surface less often but are just as important to you.

* Your core values are often prioritised differently in different life domains (such as at home versus at work). Blurred boundaries between life domains require intentional prioritisation.

* Aligning your actions with your core values can promote intrinsic motivation, joy, and longer-term fulfilment.

* Conflicts between your values are normal and inevitable; they signal that you're in an area that matters a lot to you. Getting clear on values prioritisation can help you sit with the discomfort that comes from internal values conflict and still make a decision.

* Making space for the discomfort of a values conflict between you and someone else involves recognising the disagreement as a values conflict, and remembering it is normal and to be expected.

* External values conflicts (with others' values) require empathy and understanding, rather than judgement.
* All values have a shadow side – overusing, misusing, or over-prioritising values can lead to negative consequences.
* Awareness and self-compassion are necessary to balance your values without succumbing to their shadow sides.
* Actively listening, asking open-ended questions, and recognising shared values to build rapport and resolve conflicts is far more constructive than focusing in on areas of values conflict.
* Values are tools for growth and collective alignment, in spite of inevitable disagreement.
* Values diversity promotes innovation and collaboration, and reduces the chance of falling into the trap of 'groupthink'.
* Recognising and respecting different values can help create shared goals, and reduce the likelihood of polarisation.
* Fostering values-aligned relationships enhances individual wellbeing and collective growth.

CHAPTER 4
Know Your Threat-Based Values

When we feel threatened or under a great deal of stress, we've already discussed how we can find ourselves prioritising alternative values that focus on short-term safety and security at the expense of longer-term growth. These are known as threat-based values (TBVs). In today's hyperconnected world with relentless and pervasive access to bad news and idealised versions of a good life, we are more susceptible than ever to feeling under threat. Threats to identity or safety that arise from broader dynamics beyond our control can feel impossible to resolve, and yet sit like a heavy weight for us. This state of being can impact how we interpret, evaluate, and respond to the world.

In these times, then, it is more crucial than ever for us to notice when we're reacting from a place of threat, where we might be prioritising values such as Control or Avoidance. The key is to recognise these moments and consciously reorient our choices to align with our core values instead. Part of managing our threat-based response is identifying when TBVs are activated and deciding whether it's truly necessary to act on them, or if we can redirect our focus toward responses that align with our core values. The reason it's worth prioritising core values more often is they promote long-term growth and fulfilment – whereas acting on TBVs typically does not.

Identifying Threat-Based Values

The first step toward managing threat-based values is to reflect on which are most relevant in your life, and how they show up for you. Below, I've listed a few TBVs I have found emerge in practice. It's not an exhaustive list and you are most welcome to explore your own TBVs. You'll notice that certain values names (such as Health and Stability) are also used as core values. In fact, many of these values can function as core values, but their focus and how they're actioned are different in the context of core values. As TBVs their needs-based focus is very short term and comes at the expense of longer-term growth.

You might also consider these in relation to people close to you, to help make sense of their threat-based responses, too. Sometimes, understanding that someone is acting from a place of threat helps us see they're not just being difficult – they're just acting from a place of threat-related need rather than in line with their best self. Your role, if you choose to take it, is to help them reorient to prioritising actions that fit with their core values that represent them at their best. This list of threat-based values has been compiled over the years, in conjunction with my clients, as a way of making sense of their experience of the values they tend to want to prioritise when under threat.[1]

Which threat-based values are especially relevant to you? Select one to three.

- **Authority:** A focus on respect for hierarchy and adherence to established rules to maintain order and avoid uncertainty.
- **Avoidance:** The tendency to steer clear of potential threats, discomfort, or difficult situations as a way to minimise risk and maintain a sense of safety.
- **Blame Deflection:** Overly shifting responsibility to others to protect oneself from perceived criticism, failure, or judgement.
- **Control:** A need to manage or oversee situations that is often driven by a desire to prevent unexpected or unwanted outcomes and feel secure.
- **Health (threat):** A heightened concern about wellbeing, leading to a preoccupation on behaviours and choices that prevent perceived illness or harm, at the expense of one's broader experience
- **Hypervigilance:** An intense awareness of potential threats or dangers, driven by the belief that constant attention is necessary for safety.
- **In-group Loyalty:** An excessive focus on loyalty to one's own group or community to safeguard its collective wellbeing and to ward off external threats, at the expense of others and one's own group's longer-term prospects.
- **Perfectionism:** The drive to avoid mistakes and ensure flawless results, often out of fear of criticism or perceived inadequacy.

- **Risk avoidance:** Actively minimising exposure to perceived danger or uncertainty, often at the expense of taking opportunities or embracing change.
- **Security:** An overemphasis on safety and protection from threats, prioritising stability over uncertainty to an extent where it negatively impacts on longer-term growth prospects.
- **Self-focus:** A heightened preoccupation with one's own needs, desires, and image, often at the expense of considering others.
- **Self-preservation:** A focus on protecting oneself from harm or loss through overly cautious or defensive behaviours that negatively impact one's longer-term trajectory.
- **Stability / Order:** A desire for predictability and structured routines, often to maintain a sense of control and minimise unpredictability, at the expense of flexibility, learning, and growth.

Practical Exercise: Becoming Aware of Your Threat-Based Values

In the last fortnight, think of a time when you have felt particularly stressed or under threat. You might experience this as a feeling in your body associated with worry, tension, or anxiety. Perhaps you also experience thoughts associated with a stressor that are worries or 'should'-based thoughts such as 'What if this happens?' or 'It shouldn't be like this' or 'They shouldn't have done that'.

Situation description:

- **Describe the situation in detail. You might also like to give it a name.**

Identify associated thoughts:

- **Write down the main thoughts associated with this situation?**
  - What if ...
  - They / I / It should ...
  - If only ...

Notice physical sensations:

- **Were there any sensations (stress, tension) in your body associated with this?**
  - If so, where were these feelings in your body?
  - You might like to take a few breaths with your eyes closed and focus on the part of your body where these feelings were the strongest. Allow any feelings to be there. Make space for them, don't try to push them away. This is an important part of allowing your experience rather than trying to push it away, which can come with self-judgement, shame, and compounding threat-based states.

Recognise any urge to act:

- **Was there something you were compelled to do to handle the situation? This could be anything from avoiding the issue, to confronting someone, to seeking revenge.**

Identify the relevant TBVs:

- **Look at the list of threat-based values and see if any of those words fit the situation for you. Alternatively, describe the value(s) using your own words.**

Take some time to think about the short-term benefits of this threat-based value being activated. That is, how is your incredible mind trying to help in activating this value, prioritising it and trying to get you to take action based on its prioritisation?

How would aligning your behaviour with this TBV undermine your growth in the longer term? That is, how does it hold you back from growing into the version of yourself you seek to be?

What is a short phrase that can help you remember to *in*action this threat-based value?

* * *

Let's move swiftly into one more exercise on how to handle threat-based values simply by allowing them to be there, without acting on them, even at times when you feel you want to, but know you're better off prioritising your core values and what matters most in the long run.

Practical Exercise: Suggestions for Overcoming Threat-Based Values

Begin by taking several deep breaths in through your nose, and out through your mouth. Adjust as you need, and don't forget to pause in between inhaling and exhaling and vice versa. As I've suggested before you may wish to count to four or so as you breathe in, pause, breathe out, pause, and so on.

Once you've done this, allow your body to resume control of your breathing and let's begin with the exercise proper.

Acceptance
- **Take a few minutes to participate in an acceptance exercise.**
    - Guide your attention to your threat-based values, and remind yourself why your incredible thought machine – your mind – might encourage you to act on them out of care. You might like to thank your mind for this: 'Thanks, mind.'
    - Acknowledge and accept the presence of these threat-based values without judgement.
    - Understand these values are part of your natural response to perceived threats.
    - Remind yourself that the presence of these values is normal and natural, and does not mean you have to act on them.

Unhook from Threat-Oriented Thoughts
- **Practise separating yourself from your thoughts.**
    - Repeat the threat-based thought out loud until it starts to sound like a jumble of sounds that has lost its meaning.
    - Imagine the thought as a silly character's voice (in a cartoonish accent for instance).
    - Imagine placing your thought onto your hand, and then use your breath to blow the thought up into the sky, perhaps up onto a cloud.
    - Write the thought down in a book; notice that here you are and there's the thought, there in the book. Now close the book. The thought can wait for later.

Write the thought onto a sticky note and stick it on your window. Walk away, turn around, and glance at it. Notice how you can shift your focus to other things in the room or outside the window. The thought is still there, but it's just one small part of your day. Move it to the bin when you're ready.

Clarify Core Values
- **Values regroup**
  - Take some time to focus on your core values.
    – What are their names? How do you define them?
    – Which of your core values is relevant in the situation where you experienced TBV activation?
    – If you oriented toward these core values during the situation, what action supports this?
    – How does this make you feel about your longer-term growth?
    – Notice any sensations in your body associated with this.

Commit to Values-Based Actions
- **Develop your action plan**
  - Develop a plan to act in accordance with your core values, even when under threat.
  - This may involve setting specific, achievable goals that align with these values.
  - This may also involve developing some short values primers. That is, short phrases or 'mantras' that you can bring to mind and that remind you to view the world through the framework of your core values, even when the going gets tough.

Mindfulness Practice

- **Incorporate a regular mindfulness practice**
  - Mindfulness involves dropping down into the present moment and focusing on aspects of right now.
    - E.g. mindfulness of the senses: Keep guiding your attention back to what you see / hear / taste / touch / smell.
    - E.g. breathing exercises as experienced by your five senses. You can also incorporate intentional breathwork.
  - Don't be concerned about being 'good' at mindfulness. The goal is 'mindfulness practice' not 'mindfulness achievement' after all.
  - The opportunity of intentional mindfulness practice is to guide your attention back to where you intend it to be when it wanders.
  - Every time your mind wanders, treat this moment as a valuable opportunity to guide your attention back to where you intend it to be.

I've lost count of the number of clients who say, 'I've tried mindfulness and I just can't do it.' More often than not, this judgement is born from a belief that you need to be 'good' at mindfulness in order to experience its benefits. You don't. Engage in the practice non-judgementally. Rather than judging yourself as falling short of your objective when your mind wanders, recognise every mind-wandering moment as an opportunity for another 'rep' of the 'attention muscle'. Approaching this process non-judgementally, with curiosity and a focus on the opportunity of mind-wandering, can transform mindfulness practice for those who've tried it before and have concluded it's not for them. Let's get back into mindfulness-related tips.

- If sitting still is an issue for you, try a walking meditation. And as Jon Kabat-Zinn puts it: 'It means simply walking and knowing that you are walking. It does not mean looking at your feet!'[2]
- The goal during a walking mindfulness meditation is the same – practising guiding your attention back to some element of the present moment, in this case the act of walking. I love incorporating a focus on nature into my daily mindful walking. I intentionally guide my focus back to green living things. So, a blade of grass, a thistle growing up among concrete, leaves on trees – try it! Noticing green alive stuff and anchoring to your breath, while you walk. Nothing quite like it for unhooking from your mind, which can get caught up in the past with 'if onlys' or project into the future with 'what ifs'.
- Regular mindfulness practices can increase awareness of your thoughts and feelings so that you don't automatically react to them without being aware there's another way.
- Mindfulness practice, especially in conjunction with slow breathing, can help ground you in a state of 'rest and digest' thanks to activation of the parasympathetic branch of the autonomic nervous system. As discussed, this is gold for reflective and strategic thought, including around how to guide your focus back to your core values, allowing thoughts and feelings associated with the threat-based state to be there without doing anything with them.

Self-Reflection
- **Reflective, non-judgemental journalling**

    Make time to journal about situations where you felt under threat. Rather than justifying 'why' you were under threat (which is a common go-to response), take time to be curious about your *response* and what core values you might bring in to deal with future similar situations.
    - What was the situation?
    - What TBVs were activated?
    - How did you respond?
    - Were you able to overcome an impulse to act on your TBV and if so, how?
    - How could you respond differently next time, in alignment with your core values?
    - What are the lessons for the onward journey, to help you grow further into the version of you that you seek?

Seek Support
- **Therapeutic guidance**

    Consider working with a psychologist trained in Acceptance and Commitment Therapy[3] (ACT) to help you establish a new relationship with your thoughts and feelings. This work can help you more readily align what you pay attention to and how you act with your core values. The central goal of ACT is to increase your psychological flexibility, which involves staying in contact with the present moment and making values-based choices or 'committed actions' (values-in-action) even in the face of difficult thoughts and feelings.[4]

- Alongside seeking therapeutic guidance from a psychologist, you may also want to learn more about ACT. References to material published by the founder of ACT, Dr Stephen Hayes, and Dr Russ Harris, one of the predominant ACT authors and trainer practitioners, can be found in the Notes at the end of this book.

Overcoming Threat for Your Performance

When you're underperforming relative to your ability in your chosen field (e.g. sports, entertainment, business, medicine), it can be because you're so fixated on achieving in the present moment that you find yourself hampered by perceived threat. Blood flow routes to large muscles and areas of the brain needed for fighting or fleeing, rather than performing in ways that require focus and a connection with the present moment. Areas of the brain associated with strategic and reflective thought can function on life support as you focus on scanning for threats and danger, including 'what if' thoughts (e.g. 'What if I miss the shot?', 'What if I forget my lines?'). Negative thoughts characterised by 'what ifs' around performance shortfalls can crowd in on your attention. A sense of ease, flow, weightlessness and timelessness eludes you. It's little wonder you're underperforming.

As counterintuitive as what I'm about to say might sound, one of the best things you can do in moments of performance is to home in on what matters most to you in the long run and stop concerning yourself with whether you rise or fall today. Zoom out and intentionally look at the bigger picture.

KNOW YOUR THREAT-BASED VALUES

Have you seen that incredible image of Earth – *Earthrise* – taken by astronaut William Anders while undertaking a lunar orbit in 1968 during the Apollo 8 mission? Peering down on our blue planet from outer space puts into perspective everyday struggles and strife in the grander context of our shared planet. I invite you to go looking for your own *Earthrise*, with the help of your values and your 'why'. Doing so can help you more effectively contextualise daily struggles and transcend a threat-based response to momentary concerns – even the ones that feel big – for the sake of optimising performance.

Your values allow you to zoom out and look at things in terms of what matters to you most over time, including within your domains of performance. The performance paradox is that caring less about your performance today, while working extremely hard of course, can enable you to achieve higher results over time. That is, it pays to focus on *why you're there performing today* and care about that, rather than overly concerning yourself with the outcomes of today's performance.

Getting clear on your values and your 'why' enables you to remain anchored to what matters most. And play can really help with this, too. Get curious about your performance and find moments of play in the nitty gritty of how it's unfolding. Allow the play to eclipse any judgement. From this position your mind and body can remain fully present, and able to optimally perform, whatever that means to you on this day. Optimal performance today might not be your peak performance, and that is okay. Do all you can to perform in alignment with your values and what matters in the longer term, rather than trying to win the day at the expense of the longer term.

Let's dive into another practical exercise, which is focused on overcoming feelings of threat during moments of performance to improve long-term outcomes. The paradox of performance is that optimising over time improves when you can anchor to what matters most to you and reduces your focus on your immediate performance. It may feel challenging, even risky, to loosen control in the moment, yet evidence suggests that doing so can actually lead to better performance in the long run.[5] In this exercise, we'll be focusing on helping you connect with your values in the moment, in order to maximise your performance in the longer term.

Practical Exercise: Contextualise Your Values to Overcome Threat

Begin by taking some deep, slow breaths in through your nose if you can, and out through your mouth. Notice the feeling of the air moving in and out of your lungs. Guide your attention back into the present as much as you can; to small, granular details like your breath. From here, there are a range of activities you can engage with, depending on where you are and how much time you have.

- **What are your most important values?**
- **What is your values-aligned 'why'?**
    - Remind yourself of your 'why' when it comes to your area of performance. How does this relate back to your values and to the version of yourself you seek to cultivate that is more than the superficial short-term stuff?
- **Shift your focus from outcome to process: Be present.**
    - Guide your focus again and again to the process of your performance. Trust in that, rather than getting pulled into the future with thoughts about the importance of the final result. This focus on process enables you to stay in the present and reduces pressure that counterproductively diverts blood flow.

KNOW YOUR THREAT-BASED VALUES

- Set process-oriented goals in the present moment, based around what you can control rather than shaming yourself with 'You should be able to ...' or 'You should have ...'

My grandpa, Don Bradman, was a cricketer and businessman who lived and breathed his values. He even professed them publicly on numerous occasions. His interest and focus on values throughout his adult life helped him achieve what he did in moments of high pressure on the cricket pitch. He passed his interest and appreciation for what values can do on to his children and grandchildren and for that I'm eternally grateful. He once wrote a line on a piece of card, which remains stuck above the door to a changeroom at the Sydney Cricket Ground: 'If it's hard I'll do it now, if it's impossible I'll do it presently.'

Grandpa was one of the biggest believers in the transformative power of values I've ever met. He also believed that being present was vital, and that living your values in the present moment was key — that it's too easy to defer values alignment, when the only moment we ever have to act on our values is right now.

There is perhaps no state that you're more fully present than play. Bringing play into your performance helps you to access the present moment and stop fixating on the outcome.

Practise Mindfulness

- **Being mindful involves the intentional practice of dropping down into the present moment, so that you can 'be here now'.**
  - Use controlled breathing exercises to regulate your autonomic nervous system (the extent to which you're

activating your sympathetic – fight or flight – versus parasympathetic – rest and digest – branch of your autonomic nervous system). Being in a 'rest and digest' state can enhance your attention focus.[6]
- Use progressive muscle relaxation to help you systematically relax your body when you need to.
- Practise visualisation techniques. For instance, practise transporting yourself in your mind's eye to a specific place that means a lot to you, perhaps somewhere from your childhood where you felt safe. For me, it's sitting on the bank of a dam on the farm where I grew up, looking at a specific pebble there. It anchors me and reminds me of who I am and what matters most to me. Visualise that place, as though there was a felt memory of it that still endures inside you. Allow that feeling to grow, breathing air into and around it. Allow that place to be a source of strength for you, which you can bring to mind in moments when you need to reconnect with a deeper part of you.

Develop a Pre-Performance Routine

- **Create rituals**
  - Establish a gentle and flexible routine that you can use to calm and focus you before you perform.
  - Bring to mind the mantras you've developed for your values, or your purpose mantra; phrases that are very short and super memorable, which you've practised so that they emotionally connect with a 'felt sense' of what's important to you. This way, they can motivate and

ground you, providing you with not just an anchor but wings of courage to fly.

Recognise Growth Opportunities When They Come

- **Accept 'mistakes'**
    - Rather than reflecting on misses or errors as 'failures', recognise them as growth opportunities in the context of your values.
    - Learn from setbacks and integrate them as opportunities to learn and improve, to help you overcome similar setbacks in the future.
- **Practise intentional self-compassion**
    - Remember that self-compassion is a route to accepting imperfection. It helps us put down the judgemental 'imperfection microscope' where we focus in on and magnify shortcomings. Rather, we zoom out and see imperfections as a natural part of a whole.
    - Take a moment to place your hand on your chest. Breathe in and out one intentional breath. This is a committed action that reminds you that your values practice includes making space for errors, 'mistakes' and imperfection in service of growth and being able to focus on what matters.

Engage in Reflective Practice

- **Reflect on your values**
    - Regularly take time to reflect on your values and how they are relevant to your performance practice.
    - Cultivate your 'why' so that you can bring it – and bring your values – front of mind during performance

when you need, in order to settle and calm yourself, and unlock all you have to offer in that moment.
- Reflect on recent performance opportunities and how you went. Intentionally celebrate your values-led efforts and improvements.

* * *

Values are relevant to your present moment, your future self, and to make sense of how you feel about prior choices. The motivational impetus that values provide will forever influence your experience. You are a dynamic, values-enabled person with much more to offer when you have insight into your values and their impact on you and your life. This includes how they can guide the way you show up around others and respond to their actions.

Threat-Based Values and the Drama Triangle

There are many ways you can think about your TBVs in order to simplify them and get to a point where you can have insight when they're activated for you. One framework I like, which I have my husband, Didier Elzinga, to thank for introducing me to, is the 'Drama Triangle'. The Drama Triangle is a social model of human interaction developed by psychologist Stephen Karpman in the late '60s.[7] In this context, 'drama' can be understood as playing a role on a stage — as opposed to taking the more recent understanding of 'drama' as necessarily meaning something overly dramatic in real life.

Roles Within the Drama Triangle

The Drama Triangle can be a helpful framework for thinking through how you or another may take on certain dysfunctional roles during threat-based interactions. There are three roles that you can assume in the Drama Triangle – the Victim, the Persecutor, and the Rescuer. Across different threat-related situations you may cycle through all of these roles. In a single situation it's possible to play two roles at once, such as during an argument where you take on the roles of both Victim and Persecutor. I find the Drama Triangle a helpful framework in which to consider how your TBVs are showing up in various situations.[8]

The Victim. This is when you show up as the helpless victim to a situation or to life itself. The Victim holds that a situation has happened *to* them and they have very little influence or control over what has transpired. It's a role characterised by feeling oppressed, helpless and hopeless. As the Victim you may believe you have no power over your circumstances. You may seek sympathy and support, portraying yourself as wronged or suffering more than others. Where this is reinforced, by yourself or others, it may initially be validating and constructive, but over time it may hinder growth beyond the role of Victim, toward owning your own voice and power in the world.

When you can intentionally reflect on and begin to reconnect with your core values, this can represent the start of taking small, manageable actions that will reconnect you with a version of yourself that is more than and separate to your experience as a victim. Reconnecting with your core values is a powerful way of starting to reclaim your authentic voice.

The Rescuer seeks to save the day, potentially because they feel guilty if they do not step in, or perhaps because they have a deep-seated need to be seen to be 'doing the right thing', or because they have internalised a belief, rightly or wrongly, that 'If I don't do something, no one will'. As the Rescuer, you may forgo many of your own needs for another person, or you may inadvertently deepen their sense of victimhood and helplessness, rather than supporting them in more constructive ways. The Rescuer feeds the person fish rather than helping them learn how to catch them for themselves.

By reorienting to your core values, this can pave the way for you to shift from this role of Rescuer to one of values-led Guide. In order to do so, reconnect with what matters most to you and ensure your own needs-based oxygen mask is fitted, before looking at how to support another in need in ways that support their longer-term growth rather than just focusing on their short-term survival.

The Persecutor is the role of the accuser or criticiser. When playing this role, you're likely to adopt a position of authority or superiority. As the Persecutor you may blame, criticise, or try to dominate others. You may appear controlling, aggressive, hypercritical, or dismissive, exerting your views or decisions on others. Over time this may erode relationships and exacerbate any feelings in you of isolation or even abandonment.

Left unchecked, this can create a vicious cycle where you seek greater control while feeling increasingly unheard or alone. Reconnecting and activating core values and shifting away from the role of Persecutor amid TBVs is a way to break the cycle and reconnect with your better self.

Threat-based values can show up differently depending on the role being played. Let's examine two threat-based values, Control, and then Avoidance, and how they show up differently across the three roles of the Drama Triangle – remembering that several roles can be assumed by someone at once when they're under threat.

TBV of Control and the Drama Triangle

As Victim

Manifestation: The person may feel powerless and overwhelmed, as though they have lost control over their circumstances. External forces might be seen as entirely responsible for their challenges. They may say things like, 'I can't control anything that happens to me', or 'Everything is outside of my control'. This sense of helplessness can lead to passivity, reinforcing the feeling of being dominated by outside events.

Impact: As the Victim, the person may believe they lack agency, making it harder to take steps toward change in big ways. It can be that the Victim tries to control other elements of their experience, such as the orderliness of their house or what they eat.

As Rescuer

Manifestation: The person may feel compelled to take control of others' situations, stepping in and 'fixing' things because they believe they know best. This includes micromanaging rather than enabling someone to help themselves. They might say, 'Let me handle this for you', or 'Well the way I'd suggest we do it is …' The Rescuer essentially ends up controlling the situation, preventing others from learning to handle it themselves.

Impact: The Rescuer's need for control can relegate others to passive onlookers who don't develop key skills themselves, or even Victims who perceive a lack of agency, and experience an erosion in engagement, self-confidence, and competence that can come with that.

As Persecutor

Manifestation: In the Persecutor role, the person with the TBV Control might become rigid or domineering, criticising others for

not meeting standards or doing things the wrong way. They may have an attitude of 'Others are incompetent', or 'If I don't control this, everything will fall apart'. This may result in a high level of criticism and micromanagement of others, and a lack of flexibility.
Impact: This approach can push others away or create resentment, as the Persecutor's control-oriented behaviours feel stifling, oppressive, or just plain inappropriate to those around them.

TBV of Avoidance and the Drama Triangle
As Victim
Manifestation: In the Victim role, someone with an Avoidance TBV may avoid taking responsibility or making decisions due to fear of failure or confrontation. They might think, 'It's better if I don't get involved, I don't want to mess things up', or 'Everyone else is better if I stay out of it'. Avoidance can reinforce their sense of helplessness, as they feel unable to face or influence their situation.
Impact: Avoidance in the Victim role can lead to missed opportunities as the person sidesteps challenges rather than moving toward and through them in order to embrace opportunities for growth.

As Rescuer
Manifestation: In the Rescuer role, Avoidance can appear as a reluctance to confront the deeper issues of the person they're trying to help. Problems might be glossed over and difficult conversations are avoided. The Rescuer might instead home in on praiseworthy details, even if they're in the minority, for the sake of bolstering the other person's experience and avoiding a difficult interaction. This avoidance can prevent both the Rescuer and the other person from tackling deeper problems that require work for the sake of the longer term.

Impact: This form of avoidance can keep the Rescuer from providing truly constructive support, as they shield the other person from uncomfortable truths rather than fostering growth. Furthermore, it can negatively impact their experience and workload over time – especially if in the end, a very challenging conversation needs to be had with the other person, which to them feels like it is out of the blue, because the Rescuer hasn't been providing them an opportunity to deeply remedy their own shortcomings sooner.

As Persecutor
Manifestation: The person with an Avoidance TBV, in the role of the Persecutor, may withdraw or refuse to engage when things become challenging. They may act dismissively, saying things like 'I'm done with this', 'This isn't worth my time' or by blowing situations up while simultaneously avoiding direct communication. Instead of addressing the issue, they avoid confrontation or shut down conversations, which can come across as cold and uncaring.
Impact: The Persecutor within an Avoidance TBV can create a cycle of unresolved conflict, as issues are never fully addressed, leading to frustration and tension both for the person and others involved.

When thinking about how to shift back to alignment with your core values at times when your TBVs are activated, it can be helpful to understand not just which threat-based value is coming to the fore, but how to frame the role you're playing within that value.

It can also be helpful to reflect on the Drama Triangle for yourself, in the context of your own TBVs experience, remembering there are no rights or wrongs.[9] This work is about gathering insight that enables you to make sense of and *in*action a threat response when it is not essential. It is not about providing a framework that further pathologises your experience of what are, in essence, entirely normal and natural processes and experiences.

In the next chapter, we're moving into a specific realm where threat-based values can come to the fore, but more than anything where your core values can help ground you and remind you what matters most, for the sake of your performance when you feel like an impostor.

KEY TAKEAWAYS OF THIS CHAPTER:

* When we're feeling threatened, we tend to prioritise survival-related values, which I call threat-based values (TBVs).

* TBVs prioritise survival now over growth later. That is, there's a focus on protecting short-term safety and security, over and at the expense of long-term growth.

* TBV activation is 'contagious' – when someone else acts from a threat-based stance (or you perceive it to be so), you're more likely to adopt a threat-based stance also. Reducing an unnecessary threat-based response in someone else involves helping them reorient to what matters most to them from a growth perspective.

* Identifying your most commonly activated TBVs can help you recognise when they're in play or are likely to be so.

* *In*action TBVs more often. Notice when they're being prioritised and reflect on whether it is really necessary to act on them. If it is not necessary to do so then intentionally choose to *in*action them, and redirect your attention toward actions that fit with your core values.

* Acceptance and mindfulness can help you notice TBV-related thoughts without judgement. Allow yourself to separate from them and observe them, thank your mind and make room for them, and *in*action them more often.

* Practical activities for overcoming TBVs include intentional actions that align with your *core* values – these are 'toward' moves (toward what matters most, and toward the short-term discomfort this can involve). Other reflective activities can also help, such as journalling or mindfulness, as well as seeking therapeutic guidance.

CHAPTER 5
The Power of Meaning in an Uncertain World

It can feel hard to focus on personal growth and self-actualisation until more basic needs are met, but it's possible. And unlike other animals, we humans don't just look around our current environment to assess our safety. A family dog is not going to feel unsafe after seeing a social media feed, but we might. Furthermore, the inequity in the world necessitates that growth occur, as best it can, under pressure. The world has added layers of connectivity since Abraham Maslow created his Hierarchy of Needs, but it remains a relevant and simple framework in which to consider how you feel your needs are met, and how this might be impacting your ability to live in line with your core values more of the time.

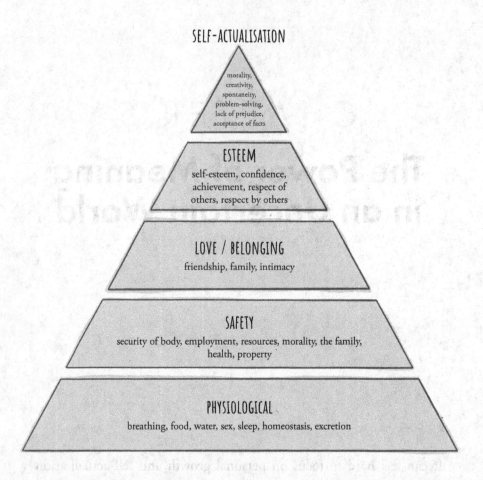

Maslow presented two broad types of needs that we humans are motivated to satisfy.[1] We have 'basic needs' for survival as well as safety and security, connection, and achieving a net-positive sense of self. Basic needs are motivated by 'deficiency' (e.g. 'I need more safety, I need more connection'). And we have 'growth needs' that are motivated by an innate desire for growth and self-actualisation, where we can uniquely create and contribute to the world. Our perception of whether our basic needs are met varies a lot between people, and if we wait until they're met before we start making time for growth needs, we may never get there.

The Role of Needs in Values

Self-actualisation is intrinsic growth of what is already in the organism, or more accurately of what is the organism itself. Just as our tree needs food, sun, water from the environment, so does the person need safety, love, and respect from the social environment ... this is just where real development (i.e. of individuality) begins ... [where] each human being proceeds to develop its own style, uniquely, using these universal necessities to its own private purpose.[2]

When our basic needs are not met we can feel motivated to overly focus on achieving them. Yet Austrian neurologist, psychiatrist, and Holocaust survivor Viktor Frankl's experience showed that even in the most desperate of circumstances, humans are capable of reaching for values associated with what Maslow would call self-actualisation. Despite unimaginable suffering and starvation, some prisoners in Auschwitz found ways to connect with what mattered to them beyond survival, for instance by offering kindness to others, finding beauty in nature, or holding on to their sense of purpose in spite of the hopelessness of the situation. Frankl's observations of how people can strive for a sense of meaning and purpose, and hold on to hope even when basic needs around food and safety aren't being met, helped form the basis of his famous logotherapy.[3] Frankl held that rather than humans' primary driver being pleasure (as Freud suggested)[4] or power and superiority (as Alfred Adler proposed),[5] our primary driver is the pursuit of meaning.

Frankl reflected that not all prisoners in Auschwitz managed to do this. However, he found that those who managed to do so were more likely to survive despite their equivalent suffering. The apparent paradox was that intentionally holding on to a sense of what mattered, over and above sheer survival, appeared to improve one's odds of surviving.

Broadening this principle to acts of performance – whether in sport, the arts, business, and so on – I have observed the same pattern. When you hold lightly the act of performing, and intentionally orient to your values and purpose, it supports your optimal performance over time. It is essential to not rely on trying this once or twice as evidence of whether it works, by the way! Anchoring to your core values in such moments requires a leap of faith. It can feel like you're relinquishing control over variables that contribute to performing well. It takes great intentionality to prioritise core values over immediate needs for survival (be this reputationally, identity wise, role wise, or beyond) or over actions that satiate short-term desires or cravings. But this trade-off is worth it because you are switching out 'smaller, sooner' rewards today for 'larger, later' rewards associated with longer-term growth that take you where you want to go.[6]

Interestingly, modern or 'third-wave' cognitive behavioural therapies, such as Acceptance and Commitment Therapy, as well as Martin Seligman's PERMA+ model for flourishing, have meaning-making embedded, both as fundamental components of therapy, and longer-term human fulfilment and happiness. Values offer essential insight into what matters to us and help make sense of our motivations. They pave the way for people to improve their relationship with their thoughts, feelings, and actions.

Your Relationship with Your Thoughts

Values and Acceptance and Commitment Therapy (ACT)

In therapies such as Acceptance and Commitment Therapy (ACT), the focus has shifted away from trying to establish the 'truth' of thoughts toward assessing how 'workable' they are. That is, rather than asking a person to complete a thought record where they weigh up evidence for and against a thought being true, the question has become: 'Whether or not this thought is true, how workable is it?'[7] That is, to what extent can you productively deal with this thought right now, and how much does it contribute to where you want to go in life, where you want to spend your time, or cultivating your relationships in ways that are positive for you?

Workability, then, involves making values-based choices. If I'm thinking, 'I really bombed that test, I mean, it went terribly. At this rate I could very well flunk out of the year,' and I receive a grade of 32 percent when the test comes back, practically my thoughts and fears have truth to them. But are they workable? From my experience with clients, I would say that in the majority of such moments, there is a tendency to focus so hard on these thoughts and associated 'what ifs' that they are not workable, because they crowd your attentional capacity, making it very difficult to focus and study.

If a thought is not workable, whether or not it's true, then in ACT, a client uses strategies to allow that thought just to be there, in their mind but not occupying all of their attention, until it dissipates. That is, the person asks, 'Is this thought workable?' or the slightly longer version of the same thing, 'How helpful is it for me to hook into this thought – to hang on to it, to reason with it, to follow it along and allow it to take me on a cascade of other, related thoughts?' If the answer is 'In this moment, it's not helpful', simply let it be there. Recognise it for what it is – a thought that is generated by your incredible mind, which generates thousands of thoughts for you every day.[8] Thoughts do not demand your attention, nor your action, even when they feel like they do.

You don't *ask* for every thought your mind brings you. And you certainly don't *need* every thought that is generated. Remember that you're applying awesome, super-sophisticated but ancient brainy-part technology within a modern context. And it turns out that much of the time your mind is trying to do certain things with 'what if' thoughts generated by the same tech that was anticipating tigers in bushes: it is trying to keep you safe, protect you, prepare you. For that, you can be most grateful! 'Thanks, mind, for working so hard to keep me safe!' In the modern world where we engage in so much thinking that has us leaping through time and space with our thoughts, using your values to anchor you to what matters most enables you to gain deeper insights into what thoughts and inclinations are workable, and which simply require acknowledgement.

ACT's ultimate goal is psychological flexibility.[9] Part of 'the work' in ACT is learning how to embrace a pragmatic willingness to change up our relationship to our thoughts and feelings. In the context where we need to help calibrate our mind for the modern environment, ACT is most useful. Part of its utility is that we no longer have to twist ourselves in knots over whether or not something is 'real' or true, because that is not the question we need to answer. As I have said, workability becomes the benchmark. And workability intersects with values alignment – if something is taking you *toward* the version of yourself that you wish to grow, then chances are it's workable. If it's not (i.e. it's an 'away move'), then it's probably not workable.

You might say, 'But that doesn't stop me thinking "what if" and feeling anxious and uneasy about things, or thinking "if only" and feeling sad or disappointed in myself.' Yes, that is true – I am human and feel that (a lot), too. Discomfort is not an unnatural phenomenon and I believe that our recent inclination to avoid discomfort at almost any cost is responsible for the current avoidance epidemic. But rather than avoid, or control, we can make space for our experience and get intentional about reorienting to our values, and actions that flow from those.

Now that we understand that prioritised values are informed by our current needs and can help guide how we consider the workability of our thoughts, we'll get into one application of values where I see them playing an especially important role: at times of feeling anxious, either in general, or when it comes to an act of performance (be this on some sort of a stage or just about leaving the house).

Values, Emotion, and Navigating Fear

Values that seem to come so naturally in some contexts may, at other times, feel very difficult to prioritise. As we discussed back in Chapter One, this experience can lead people to question the 'authenticity' of their own (or someone else's) core values. But if you've done the work – exploring your values through what brings you joy, who you admire, and what ignites your emotions – and you have conviction around your values, then they are not 'false'. Your values are yours;

they resonate with you, if you've chosen them, if you have noticed them being activated and bringing you fulfilment in the past.

However, if you've ever experienced that overwhelming sense of impending doom, where 'what ifs' crowd in from every side, you'll understand how hard it can be to resist responding out of fear. The alternative is to accept fear's presence, to let those feelings be there without acting on them, even when they feel tsunami-esque in size. Remember, you are always bigger than your feelings and thoughts. Instead of avoiding or reacting out of fear, I invite you to reorient toward what your values would guide you to do in that moment. Is it easy to resist acting on fear? No, but it gets easier with practice, and it's worth it!

Case Study: Navigating Fear and Reconnecting with Values

David had seen me for anxiety issues, and after a break of some months came to see me several weeks before he was due to emcee his company's Christmas party. While initially he'd been excited about the opportunity, his anxiety had begun to build as the event got closer, leading him to question saying 'yes'. Indeed, the way he put it to me was, 'In a moment of insanity, I said yes.' He'd started sleeping poorly and was experiencing a pervasive sense of impending doom, even at times when he was doing things like taking a shower.

David appeared to be grappling with two sides to this opportunity. On the one hand, he saw this as an opportunity to put into action some of the values-led work we'd been doing about making 'toward' moves at work, toward the sort of opportunities that would take him career-wise where he wanted to head. On the other hand, however, the opportunity of emceeing the Christmas party appeared right at the edge of the 'anxiety equation' for David, where there was some doubt in his mind about whether he could cope with the challenge before him.

The anxiety equation is used in cognitive behavioural therapy to express the relationship between the ability to cope and the perceived size of the challenge. At times when you think your ability or 'resources to cope' are greater than the 'size of the challenge,' then bodily responses like your heart pumping faster are more likely interpreted as excitement or alertness. However, when the 'size of the challenge' is perceived as greater than your ability or 'resources to cope,' then the same physiological characteristics are likely interpreted as anxiety.

$$\text{ANXIETY} = \frac{\text{RESOURCES TO COPE}}{\text{SIZE OF THE CHALLENGE}}$$

David and I discussed this, including the work we'd been putting into managing anxiety symptoms and dealing with the uncertainty that can come from public speaking opportunities. I reminded him of the hard work he'd been putting in around this, and the likelihood that his boss Sylvia's invitation for him to emcee was a testament to her belief in his ability to do the job. As the Christmas party had got closer, the initial focus on the opportunity as a major 'toward' move had shifted toward a threat-based mode where David was reaching for all the potential negative implications of the experience. This had manifested already in self-monitoring during presentations to colleagues. He found himself assessing his performance and distracted by thoughts such as 'Gosh, imagine if I did that while emceeing the Christmas party.'

The cognitive load used to hook into all these distracting thoughts was impacting his performance during meetings. He had also started 'mind reading' what his colleagues must think of him, and forecasting what they might say about him after the Christmas party. For instance, he imagined his colleagues saying about him: 'Who does he think he is emceeing the Christmas party?' or 'How about David emceeing? Yeesh that was painful.' Each day, the fear seemed to grow in his mind. He spent increasing time conjuring scenarios of embarrassment and failure. He was living with these uncomfortable feelings and associated threat-based thoughts about other people, which had been crowding in on his experience and occupying his mind. A vicious cycle of prioritising threat-based values (Control, Avoidance), fortune telling ('what if …') and fusing with thoughts (hooking into them and believing it necessary to engage with them actively) had left him in a state of heightened anxiety and feeling exhausted, distracted and, frankly, miserable.

We stepped back, observed, and (eventually) marvelled. 'Wow!' I said. 'What an incredible protective system you have. It's something to behold and be grateful for!'

David seemed stunned, shocked that I would say such a thing. 'But Greta, don't you *know* how uncomfortable and paralysing this is for me?' he replied. 'Not to mention exhausting. There's clearly something very wrong with me. Why did I ever think I could get up and emcee at the Christmas party? I must have been out of my mind. And now look at me; my work more generally is suffering; I'm questioning everything I do; I *never* should have said yes to this.'

'It must be exhausting and distressing for you right now,' I reflected, validating his likely emotional state. 'Can I ask, what mattered enough for you to say yes to this opportunity in the first place?'

'Well,' David responded with a twinkle in his eye, 'I guess it had something to do with "living in line with my values" and stepping up.'

This moment was a turning point for David. Often, when considering the anxiety equation, there is a tendency to think about increasing resources to cope, or reducing the perceived threat. But there is another way. Rather than changing anything about either resources or threat perception, you can hone in on what matters most and allow your connection with that to enable you to allow the discomfort and do the values-aligned hard thing anyway. Where you can establish a connection to values-based goal direction (i.e. purpose), discomfort can feel more manageable. And if you see that as increasing resources to cope, well so be it. The main thing is values can help anchor you to what matters in your life.

In our work together, we revisited David's core values: Connection, Leadership, Care for Others, Work Ethic, and Family. David reflected that his initial 'yes' had flowed from his desire to grow as a leader. He had envisioned the moment of emceeing – he'd seen himself stepping into that role, in front of his team, and embodying the person he wanted to become and making the contribution he wanted to make. It was energising and had given him what he needed to say, 'Yes!' However, as the event drew nearer, his anxiety had shifted his focus to short-term safety and security – away from his long-term goals and values.

Together, we gently explored the roles of avoidance and control – he had thought about stepping aside and letting someone else emcee, or scripting the whole thing tightly so that he couldn't 'eff it up for everyone'. He had been sitting with an overwhelming desire to pull out. 'But it doesn't feel right to back out,' he admitted. 'Deep down, I want to do it and honour the commitment. Bowing out just feels like a cop-out, and I'd feel like I was letting myself down values-wise.'

As we continued our discussion, David further reconnected with his 'why'. He reflected that he had turned his mind from a 'why' that grounded emceeing as something he wanted to do for *him*, to a 'why' that framed emceeing as an obligation that others had foisted upon him and which he resented. He also reflected that he resonated with 'the Victim' and 'the Persecutor' in the Drama Triangle; he felt out of control of the situation and that it was being imposed on him (Victim). In his mind David had started to criticise his boss for doing so (Persecutor), and he'd found himself going looking for further evidence that his boss was just trying to get him to do it in order to solve a problem of who will emcee – generous assumptions toward his boss had well and truly evaporated during such thought processes. Now, though, David homed in on one phrase, which ended up becoming somewhat of a mantra for the event: 'I guess this is about levelling up my leadership.'

'Levelling up leadership' became something David spent time getting curious around. Thinking about how that connected back to and enabled his core values. Part of this reflection was that 'It doesn't have to go perfectly. Whatever happens, I'll learn and grow from it.'

David reflected that this connection to 'why' increased his perceived resources to cope with the challenge ahead. He realised that as the event had got closer and he had anchored increasingly to threat-based values, he had equated success with 'doing a perfect job' (Perfectionism), and the thought of being unable to control all the variables around the event (Control) had been extremely distressing for him. But now, he acknowledged that his performance didn't have to be flawless – not even close. It just had to align with his values, to what mattered most to him, and he needed to trust that given his skills and experience, this was enough.

A few days after the Christmas party, I got an email from David – the subject line was 'Level up, achieved'. During the event, David used breathing techniques, his mantra for the occasion, and moving 'toward' imperfection as well as making room for play, to keep shifting him away from occupying a threat-based state and toward his core values-in-action. He said there were a few curly moments, but that on the whole, he'd been happy with how the evening had gone. Several of his colleagues had reached out afterwards to express their congratulations and thanks to him, which he hadn't expected, and he noticed a subtle positive shift in the way some of them treated him in meetings. 'It's as though they feel they know me better now.' David reflected that values had done more than just provide the motivation he'd needed to not run away from the opportunity – they'd provided the basis for *how* he conducted himself.

Reflection

Having second thoughts about doing something that pushes out into your zone of discomfort – into your zone of growth – is normal and natural. The litmus test on whether bowing out is a good idea involves connecting to your values, and considering the implications and considerations of the choices available to you. Being buffeted by fear in how you live, however, can hold you back from the growth, contribution, and fulfilment you're capable of.

So far in this chapter, we've learned that when you're in a state of fear, it's important to be intentional about how you respond. Sometimes, there will be a disjoint between how you want to act in the moment and what might best serve you for the longer term. Sometimes, even actions we dream of can seem like 'not such a good idea' when fear takes hold. When you perceive a threat, it is natural to want to avoid or control the situation to eliminate or reduce the danger. Further, when in that state of fear, you're inclined to scan your environment for more potential risks. As the saying goes, 'Seek and ye shall find.' There are always threats to behold. If you look for them, you will find them. Once found, we tend to amplify those threats, which reinforces and escalates our sense of danger.

To grow into the version of yourself you desire, it pays to act intentionally when faced with fear. This begins with noticing your fear response, and observing any prioritisation of threat-based values occurring. Make space for the desire to act on them, while doubling down on your commitment to act in line with your core values. Aligning your actions with your core values tends to yield a better return than succumbing to fear and acting on it instead.

We humans are hardwired to judge ourselves, others and our environment. Much of our experience, especially in social contexts, involves constantly scanning for threats. This process is normal and natural, but the degree to which threats affect us depends on how necessary we feel it is to monitor and respond to them. A 'threat-free' environment exists when we don't perceive threats. Perhaps in some contexts with loved ones, when we're asleep, or under the influence of some substances, our perception of threat will be especially low. But it's unrealistic to wait for the absence of threat before pursuing values-aligned growth. We must find ways of turning our mind toward growth even at times when we are working to survive.

No matter where you are or what your circumstances, your time to grow is now. Rather than spending a lifetime waiting for the perfect growth conditions, we can change our relationship with our thoughts about threats. That is, we're not looking to change the thoughts, or push them away, but rather – we make room for those thoughts. We allow them to be there and we use mindfulness in conjunction with our values to help guide our attention and action some place else. Furthermore, we can be grateful to our mind for bringing us those thoughts – the way we might genuinely thank a friend when they give us a present we don't much fancy; it's the thought that counts, as the saying goes. However misguided, your mind is offering up threat-based thoughts in an attempt to help you survive – because it cares. Making a generous assumption about the intent of your mind involves anchoring to intentional gratitude toward your mind in such moments. To recap, then, you can notice threat-based thoughts and feelings, allow them to be there, thank your mind, and 'unhook' or consciously disengage from them by guiding your attention back to other elements of the present moment. Use your values and your 'why' to motivate this shift in focus. Remember why facing this anxiety-provoking challenge is worth it, with your values as an anchor.

Anchoring to values-led actions that reflect our best (albeit imperfect) selves, rather than necessarily relying on how we feel, can help keep us on track over time. Not because our emotion system isn't to be trusted – our emotion system is incredible and a worthy goal is becoming more intuitive with values-led living. In the short term, however, if we've lost touch with our intuitive sense of what matters most to us, using 'feelings' as our guide can lead us to anchor to threat-based values and associated safety behaviours involving avoidance and control. With practice and over time, we can become more in tune with our values such that we may increasingly rely on our emotions or 'intuition' to inform our choices. But first, we need to understand and overcome any undue influence of being pulled and pushed around by fear.

If we succumb to our emotion system without checking in with our values, it can be that our emotions seem to urge us to respond as though our very survival is at risk. This can lead us to look for proof that we are right to feel the way we do, by scanning for threats. In such moments, longer-term goals may seem irrelevant. We can even experience our emotions as representing a 'felt sense' of unquestionable truth that we need to abide by. To reiterate, I am not suggesting our emotions are to be ignored – not at all. But I am suggesting that a check-in with our values at such times can help us gauge to what extent our emotion system has become overly sensitive to threat, clouding our ability to focus on our long-term growth potential and the choices needed to take us where we want to go.

In order to become intuitively connected with our emotion system in a way that can better serve us, we need to program it so that it is calibrated to what is important to us. This takes time and work with values.

In the rest of this chapter, we'll explore the role of emotions and their links with values.

Some Reflections on Emotions

Through much of the 20th and into the 21st century, psychologists largely viewed emotions as basic physiological responses to events, which reflected some inherent 'truth' about the event's impact on the individual, or their motivations associated with the event. Emotions were also seen by psychologists and economists alike as connected to our 'irrational' side, potentially undermining our capacity for rational thought and decision-making. More recent theories emphasise the critical role emotions play in motivation, learning, and decision-making especially the ability to improve decision-making over time.[10] They enhance our understanding and provide motivational impetus for our actions. Later, we'll dive deeper into this in the context of values-based decision-making. For now, we're focusing on how we perceive and experience emotion, and how our perceptions of them impact how we respond.

American psychologist Paul Ekman proposed that people universally perceive six 'basic emotions', irrespective of culture or background, which can be distinguished based on when they occur, their onset, duration, and the facial expressions accompanying them.[11] These six basic emotions were proposed as fear, anger, joy, sadness, disgust and surprise. They were (and by some still are) considered universally perceptible through facial expression, posture, prosody (speech patterns) and eye movement. They were taken to reveal a deeper 'truth' about our motivations and intentions. An implication in Ekman's research is that there should be a distinctive pattern of neural activation for different emotions – that is, he anticipated that on brain scans (which weren't available at the time), each emotion would be recognised for its own universally applicable 'emotion fingerprint'. Modern-day neuroimaging research, however, has not neatly supported his predictions.

Thanks to advances in neuroimaging, neuroscientists have joined the party in investigating brain-based origins of emotions. One competing explanation of our emotion system that has emerged is that of neuroscientist Lisa Feldman Barrett and her team, who painstakingly retested Ekman's research, as well as performing their own neuroimaging research.[12] Barrett's research comes with the benefits not just of modern neuroimaging, but the abundance of research it has allowed that has elevated our appreciation of how malleable and neuroplastic the human brain is when it comes to learning and development.[13]

The research of Barrett and her team suggests that emotions such as 'angry' and 'excited' are constructed from many instances of learning, just as our mind constructs other 'complex concepts' from 'dog' through 'existence' and 'igloo'. Our mind trains on these complex concepts from the earliest moments of our childhood, over millions of instances up to the present moment, and an instance contributes to an existing complex concept when it has certain features in common with the concept. Say, our idea of 'disgust': In the dog park we see someone step in something rather unfortunate, we see their facial expression, and this is understood as 'disgust' thanks to our prior learning about the concept. Further, the experience reinforces our understanding of disgust; what it looks like and the circumstances in which it may arise.

The dog park example is a simplification of how we make a prediction about a complex concept – including an emotion – belonging to a certain concept and, once tested, our prediction is tagged as 'true' or 'false' and our understanding of the concept is updated. Barrett holds that we learn emotions when others help us make sense of our own and others' emotion-oriented behaviours. So, again using the example of disgust, we understand what that looks like and feels like thanks to others, such as caregivers, talking with us about this at some point when it has arisen.

Rather than being innate, biologically hardwired responses then, Barrett and her team believe that emotions are learned, constructed categories, which are based on our experiences as well as our culture and language. We learn to categorise and label emotional experiences through repeated exposures and via the interpretation of emotion states by those around us. A further example would be when, during childhood, we're in the playground with our caregiver. Another child in the playground is crying and making certain facial expressions, and our caregiver says to us, 'Oh, Luca is sad.' We don't just learn from what our caregiver says but the way they say it, and this information, including what we see from the other child and the context, further contributes toward and reinforces our understanding of 'sad'.

From this perspective, our brains are prediction machines, constantly drawing inferences about what is happening around us based on past experience. These predictions shape our understanding of our world. Human values offer the ultimate bridge that links thoughts and behaviours with emotions. By understanding a person's values, we can better make sense of their thoughts and behaviours and predict how they might feel about certain situations, and what they might need in response to them.

The origins of nuanced emotion beyond 'positive' and 'negative' remain a hot topic in research. From the perspective of constructed emotion, it seems we are continuously weaving our own emotional tapestry, adding to it over time. Rather than being entirely at the mercy of predestined biology, we construct emotions over time, which are framed by our cultural and interpersonal context. Emotion plays a critical role in memory, motivation, and meaning-making.[14] Our brains are highly plastic and designed for learning, and they rely on the same malleable operating system that has been in place for millennia. And our operating system is highly skilled at acquiring culturally encoded learnings about meaning-making – including emotion. In this sense, we're born with a blueprint for learning and constructing concepts and categories, rather than a pre-programmed understanding of pre-existing complex concepts like emotions.

As for an emotion 'centre'; emotion activation involves a distributed network of brain regions.[15] Neuroimaging has shown how emotions are distributed across multiple brain regions rather than being confined to a discrete area.[16] The jury is still out around how much heritable differences, versus the culturally constructed view of emotion, play a part in our experience of emotions.[17]

What can be said is that researchers have found that far from being universal and innate, perceptions of specific emotions beyond 'positive' and 'negative' appeared to be culturally embedded and rely on a conceptual context shaped by language and experience, rather than reflecting purely biological emotion states.[18]

The theory of constructed emotion holds that emotions are socially and culturally shaped over time. How does this relate to human values? Emerging research suggests that complex concepts, like human values, are primarily learned rather than innate, challenging traditional views that values are hardwired from birth. We also know that when values are activated, they elicit an emotional response, demonstrating their influence on our psychological and neurological states. These insights suggest that values may serve as crucial connectors that bridge the gap between our 'cognitions' – our thoughts about, and interpretations of, the world – and our behaviours.

This bridging role of values is key to understanding human behaviour in a more nuanced way. Values don't just influence our decisions (or how we feel about them); they shape our emotional responses to the world, which in turn significantly impact our actions. For example, someone who places great importance on 'fairness' might have this value activated positively (leading in satisfaction) or negatively (leading in indignation), motivating them to take actions like supporting equitable policies or protesting an injustice.

The emotional component of values also highlights their role in both learning and reinforcement processes. Over time, emotion activation tied to specific values may either strengthen or alter the level of importance we attribute to them. This dynamic interplay between our emotions and values further supports the idea that values are not fixed; they evolve as we encounter new experiences and information. These new experiences and insights can influence and reshape our beliefs, needs, and goals, which in turn reinforce or disrupt our values prioritisation. This cycle feeds back into how we evaluate and respond to the world, perpetuating the evolution of values throughout one's life.

Another area where this cyclical process of values activation, prioritisation, action, and reinforcement occurs is during times of chronic perceived stress. In such times, we endure an ongoing state of survival mode, and our threat-based values may surface more readily. This brings us to the concept of 'safety behaviours', which are often talked about when working with clients experiencing anxiety, and which can be relevant when wondering why someone repeatedly acts on their TBVs.

Deploying Your Core Values When Navigating Fear

Imagine yourself as a senior associate at a prestigious law firm, where even getting in the front door was a fiercely competitive process. The pay is great, the prestige is a major career booster, and intellectual challenges are big and meaningful. Whether you measure success by power, prestige, contribution, or stimulation, it seems like an enviable job. Along with this comes a history of a whole lot of hard work that made it even possible to apply in the first place. The years of education, of learning and keeping in line with other people's wishes and expectations. By the time you've reached this senior associate level, you likely perceive the position as high-value. However, that does not necessarily translate into happiness, satisfaction, or values alignment.

For some in such rarified positions, the achievement of career goals can serve to increase the volume switch on that inner voice saying, 'Is this all there is?' Others may experience an increasing sense of feeling like an impostor. They begin to doubt their aptitude in the role, relative to their peers, and they compensate by overpreparing or procrastinating. They work hard at not being found out. At the same time, they may have 'I'm so lucky to have this opportunity I can't lose it' playing on a loop in their mind. Some lean into the competitive nature of their work as a way to mask their insecurities, viewing others as competitors in a race they're not even sure they want to run.

If you find yourself feeling trapped by metaphorical 'golden handcuffs' – whether it's because of good pay, sunk cost (all that time and money) or your sense of identity being tied to your role – you may experience a constant, low-grade state of threat activation. Similarly, if you enjoy your work but feel like an impostor, you are likely in a state of ongoing perceived stress. In both cases you're more likely to scan for threats and approach others from a defensive position. The way out of this threat state begins with recognising your emotions and then doing intentional work to clarify your 'why'. Given your values, why are you here? Why are you doing what you're doing? Chances are, there are some very good reasons for staying where you are, and more often than not I see people recognise the changes they want to make are less extreme than they initially dreamed of.

Once you have identified your 'why' and clarified whether on balance you wish to stay where you are, you can begin by making micro-changes – small, experimental shifts that align more closely with your values without disrupting your entire life. These small changes can sometimes lead to meaningful shifts in perspective, reducing the need for larger life changes. Sometimes, the impulse to make a big change stems not from a genuine, values-driven need but from the discomfort of sitting with uncertainty. In such cases, the desire for drastic change may present itself as being core values-led when, in reality, it's a threat-based response – a way to control and resolve uncertainty.

It's important to remember that your emotions do not reflect a hard and fast truth or reality that you must listen to and act upon. Instead, they are constructed responses, shaped by past experiences and your interpretations of them. Your current emotional state in part reflects a perception of what is happening now, informed by probabilities based on previous learning, rather than reflecting some literal reality of the present moment.

Your incredible mind is particularly attuned to identifying potential dangers – after all, its job above all others is keeping you alive. It makes a judgement about whether a situation poses a danger to you by weighing up the probability of danger, based on what you've previously learned (both directly through your own experience and indirectly through what others have taught you). If you've responded to a similar situation in the past as though it were dangerous, you're more likely to do the same again. Further, where you've internalised actions as having kept you safe before, you'll likely be drawn to doing them again, too, irrespective of whether they actually helped or not. Safety behaviours include any action we take when we perceive a threat, which we do because we've internalised a sense that it keeps us safe, but which is not necessary and comes with a longer-term cost. Safety behaviours reinforce both a belief that you need to engage in them to keep you safe, and a belief that you were unsafe to begin with. Threat-based responses stemming from the belief that prioritising survival over growth is necessary (when in fact our survival is not really at risk) can be thought of as safety behaviours.

One area of safety behaviours involves avoidance. When we avoid difficult conversations, we internalise the act of doing so as having kept us safe, which serves to reinforce both the sense of the conversation as having posed a threat, and the belief that avoiding the conversation kept us safe. We're more likely to perceive a threat and feel compelled to repeat the response the next time it occurs. I used to experience anxiety about answering the phone. My survival clearly was not at risk from answering the phone, yet it really felt that way. Each time I chose to not answer the phone, I reinforced to my interoceptive system – my sensory system that enables my brain to perceive and interpret signals from my body[19] – that not answering kept me safe. The next time the phone rang, my body reminded me that answering was a dangerous move by sending me signals I interpreted as anxious feelings, which came with thoughts around 'Don't answer the phone!'

Each time I went to answer my phone, having not answered it the last time, the anxiousness around doing so was stronger because my mind and body together treated avoidance as necessary to keep me safe. It took reflecting on what mattered most to me, and making small, intentional choices to approach my phone more flexibly, for me to start breaking down the safety cycle. Safety behaviours can show up in situations where some level of risk is involved – like taking phone calls, flying, or public speaking – but where the action is meaningful to you. For instance, you may choose to board a flight to be part of a family holiday, or speak publicly to grow your career, even when it triggers an anxiety response. Indeed, it's important to remember the response is neither good nor bad; it's just the body's way of getting your attention. It's then up to you to make a call whether to cope with and allow the experience, or move away from it.

It takes moving *toward* the anxiety (in my case by answering the phone) to gradually break the connection and teach your body that it's okay to do so. It's far from easy! Nowadays, I still set boundaries around my phone use to ensure I have the focus time I need for work or being present with my kids. But I am far more deliberate about when I will answer, no matter the situation, in order to not reinforce unhelpful safety behaviours that take me away from the version of myself I seek to be.

Chances are, you engage in safety behaviours without even realising it. An area where these behaviours can show up is around the impostor experience. Just as my values helped me overcome phone anxiety, they can also guide you in unpicking and moving beyond impostor feelings.

KEY TAKEAWAYS OF THIS CHAPTER:

* Don't wait until your survival needs are met before seeking growth. Attending to your growth, meaning-making, and contribution not only supports your longer-term journey; it can help you foster resilience.

* Viktor Frankl's insights suggest that intentionally actioning core values in manageable ways during challenging times can enhance your chances of survival. So – anchor to your core values even when under threat, although your first inclination might be to anchor to TBVs instead.

* Third-wave cognitive behavioural therapies like ACT focus on how 'workable' a thought is, rather than how 'true' it is.

* Mindfulness and your values can help ground you in the now.

* Safety behaviours reinforce threat responses. They are actions you take to avoid perceived danger, which can inadvertently reinforce your belief that the threat is real and substantial.

* Safety behaviours can serve an adaptive purpose at first, while over time they become counterproductive. Removing them needs handling with care, perhaps under therapeutic guidance.

* *Toward* moves often take you toward your values-aligned self and toward anxiety-provoking situations. *Away* moves take you away from your values-aligned self and away from anxious feelings.

* Values are key to navigating fear and anxiety in ways where you continue to honour your best self.

* Emotions can be thought of as complex concepts. Our understanding of emotions, such as 'disgust' or 'love' are built up over time and through experience. Our values trigger emotions and can help explain how we feel at times.

CHAPTER 6
'Shoulds', Being Enough, and the Impostor Experience

Release the weight of 'shoulds' and embrace your journey; you are not an impostor, rather, a work in progress.

Expectations or 'shoulds' point us to states of being that aren't real, but which we feel strongly ought to be. 'Shoulds' involve a gap between the reality that is (or that we perceive as reality) and the reality that we believe 'should' be so. This gap can come from various factors ranging from tragedy to judgement, social pressure, self-criticism and beyond.

We humans are inherently contrarian. If I say to you, 'You are enough,' at some point in your life there's a good chance I would get back, 'You don't understand; I'm not enough in x, y, z ways ...' Implicit in that statement is a 'should' – 'I should be doing x, y, and z in order to be enough.' Humans tend to counter statements others make, especially when those statements are about us.[1] This is especially so when it comes to receiving praise when we feel unworthy.[2] Our incredible mind (it genuinely is incredible!) is programmed to protect us, keep us safe, and ultimately alive. As we've discussed a big part of its work is keeping one step ahead of danger and, indeed, helping us identify and overcome 'not-enoughness' that might leave us at risk of not having the resources to cope with what comes our way.

In this chapter, we explore just a few categories of 'should'. One particularly potent varietal of 'not-enoughness' (and associated 'shoulds') is the impostor phenomenon, also known as the impostor experience (or colloquially as 'impostor syndrome'). It might be experienced along the lines of, 'In order for me to be enough in my role at work or in class, I should be more, and as I'm not, I fear I am not enough and am, in fact, an impostor.'

The Impostor Experience

The impostor experience involves a particular variety of 'should' where we perceive ourselves as less than what is needed to be the 'real deal'. The person we see in the mirror doesn't align with the (idealised) version of self that would be qualified to do a certain task. The bigger the gap between where we perceive our skills and aptitude to be and where we believe they should be for us to be the 'real deal,' the greater our sense of being an impostor or 'phony'. Being an impostor is one example of being 'not enough' because of 'shoulds'.

What is the Impostor Phenomenon?

To help understand why and how values can support overcoming the impostor within, let me provide a brief overview of the impostor phenomenon.[3]

Psychologists Suzanne Imes and Pauline Rose Clance first described the 'impostor phenomenon' in 1978 as 'an internal experience of intellectual phoniness', which they observed among 150 highly successful women, all of whom had earned PhDs and were respected in their fields.[4] As Imes and Clance put it, these women, despite considerable success and the respect of others, 'consider themselves to be impostors'.[5] Far from an innate trait, the impostor phenomenon is an experience of the world, which comes with pros and cons as you'll hear. This is why I tend to call it the impostor experience.

The impostor experience is characterised by five key characteristics, which can crop up at different points on the impostor cycle.[6] Say you have a task to do, and the impostor experience creeps in. The most common behavioural responses are one or more of the following: over-preparation, procrastination and / or perfectionism. Once a task is achieved, denial of ability and / or deflection of blame can be present.

Picture this. You have a work or study task to do. It involves new skills and material. You notice anxiety, self-doubt and worry creep in and impact your thoughts about the ability to complete the task. Over-preparation, procrastination, or perfectionism follows – where you either spend far more time than necessary to complete the task to a reasonable standard, wait until the last moment possible before doing it, or over-invest in the required standard to the detriment of other tasks or life domains.

Once the task is completed, it brings momentary relief and perhaps even jubilation – 'I did it!' However, this jubilation is short-lived. When task completion follows perceived or actual over-preparation, there can be a sense of dismay at the amount of time it took to complete the task: 'I take so much longer than others do for that sort of task. I should be able to do it much faster.' (A sidenote here; I can tell you, hard things are hard and take time. When 70 percent of the population are dealing with the impostor experience, it's little wonder often we don't see the half of the work involved.)

When procrastination preceded completion of the task, the accomplishment might be eclipsed by beliefs about how a task should be carried out: 'I can't work until the last moment; it's not a way folks should work on this stuff. It's a miracle I got away with it – one day I'll be found out for doing it in such a haphazard way.'[7] And with perfectionism, we can find ourselves picking the eyes out of our work and focusing in on the tiniest detail that wasn't right. We can even lose respect for someone else who deems our work good enough: 'Huh! Tina thought it was good enough? I didn't pick her as an impostor but there you go. There's no way she'd think that was good enough if she knew what she was on about. Those mistakes shouldn't have been there.'

So, what keeps the impostor experience going, even long after we might have settled into a role or course? The impostor cycle is the mechanism that perpetuates the impostor phenomenon. You can think of the fundamental characteristics that keep the impostor experience going as safety behaviours, which the 'impostor' engages in to avoid being 'unmasked'. Alongside over-preparation and procrastination, which I've already discussed, allow me to elaborate on some other characteristics of the impostor phenomenon.

Perfectionism was first described with reference to impostors by Clance as 'The need to be special or to be the best', where unattainable standards and goals are self-imposed.[8] Impostors compared with non-impostors tend to overestimate the number of mistakes they've made, report greater dissatisfaction with their performance, view their performance more harshly than non-impostors, and attribute success to external factors.[9,10] Interestingly, as we'll learn later, certain elements of this attitude are associated with high performance at work – as long as it is managed and doesn't either lead to task avoidance (i.e. perfectionism and procrastination working together), or slow down task completion (i.e. perfectionism and over-preparation working together).

Clance found that perfectionism and a desire or need to be 'the best' were connected to *Super-Heroism* – a tendency to over-prepare and seek to save the day, perhaps through solo acts of heroism rather than playing as a team. A drive toward flawlessness in one's life, with high and near impossible standards, leads the superhero impostor to feel often overwhelmed, disappointed, and even more past this into the realm of core beliefs – 'I'm not just an impostor, I'm a failure.' What I have seen in my practice is that perfectionism as part of the impostor experience can emerge as the shadow side of Achievement, especially when that is paired with conforming to unrelenting standards.

A Fear of Failure has been suggested as an underlying motive of most impostors.[11] It can lead to overwork or procrastination, which can negatively impact mood, anxiety and performance. Again, I have found it useful to look at core values and how they might be impacting one's experience of 'enough' – are there certain values around Achievement or Work Ethic (or even Intelligence or Competence) that are being overused? Furthermore, I would consider a fear of failure one side of a coin. The other side involves success.

Fear and Guilt About Success. In my clinical work, I often see a fear of failure and a fear of success either being mistaken for the other, or co-occurring. When you experience success in an area associated with feeling like an impostor for you, especially when the success involves the safety behaviours mentioned above, it can come with a feeling of worry or threat about being 'found out' rather than simply relief at having succeeded. There's concern that the demands of the task were 'barely manageable' and next time you will be exposed.

Denial of Competence and Discounting Praise is also part of the impostor experience, and this can extend beyond simply waving away compliments for fear of being seen to accept and therefore implicitly agree with them. Denial of competence and discounting of praise can also include filtering for evidence that 'proves' their impostor status; that they do not deserve praise or credit for an achievement. The wording is picked apart, and the weakest link of praise, which may implicate a 'but' or a disclaimer, is magnified as evidence of having fallen short. Far from a display of false modesty, this can be a way for an impostor to feel like they're keeping themselves 'in check' and safe from being unmasked.

While well documented for its features and impact, the impostor phenomenon is not a diagnosable condition in the *Diagnostic and Statistical Manual* (DSM-5). It is not pathological but rather is a culturally embedded phenomenon that around 70 percent of adults are thought to experience at some point.[12] A growing evidence base points to its detrimental influence on people across professions, gender, age, race and culture.[13] However, this detrimental influence might be bound up with the meaning people ascribe to its experience rather than there being anything inherently wrong or abnormal about the experience itself. It may be another case of our thoughts about thoughts, in this case our thoughts about impostor thoughts, having a detrimental impact on our experience and growth.

The downside of the impostor phenomenon is not just the immediate feelings of distress or overwhelm but the gradual deviation between the choices you make and the values-based life you seek to grow for yourself. It can keep you in a cycle of threat, where you are prioritising actions that align with threat-based values around control (such as Over-preparation and Perfectionism) and avoidance (Procrastination). The need to do so can seem very real, and the reason I refer to them here in terms of being 'values' rather than merely 'responses' is because this is not just some knee-jerk response; there are thoughts involved, too, which are grounded in beliefs, needs, and goals.

The impostor experience can create a ceiling in the work context that becomes difficult or painful to rise above over time. In the short term, a noticeable downside can include feelings of suffering and preoccupation with proving yourself or hiding your perceived phoniness. This state leaves little room for showing up and being present. The 'attention trap' created by feeling like an impostor – where your attention keeps being directed toward distracting thoughts around what you should be doing, or how you're not enough, rather than being directed toward the work at hand – can lead to dissatisfaction and disconnection with the present moment and with other areas of life, too. Associated thoughts can include:

- **'My work is never good enough.' You may find yourself striving for perfection in your work, which necessitates more time and energy than is reasonably spent on a given task.**

- **'I should have started that work already.'** You may find yourself overly procrastinating on tasks, creating a bottleneck before the task is due. You may find it increasingly difficult to reach out to others for the information you need, as it reveals you haven't started yet, thereby further delaying your start.

Either scenario can impact where you spend your energy, time and attention. It can create upheaval or lead to deprioritising meaningful relationships or other areas of life.

Values can help by providing a structured way of bringing in a more holistic consideration of life domains and areas of importance. This remedy is no different really from deploying values in other areas of performance. Aligning more small moves with your most important values can help you 'do' what is important, even when you 'feel' you need to devote all your time, attention and energy to an area where you're an impostor. More on the 'what to do' soon enough. But first, let's return to characteristics of the impostor experience and how it's not all bad.

Forty-one years after Imes and Clance first described the impostor phenomenon, the first systematic review was published[14] – forty-one years! It found that 'impostor symptoms are prevalent among men and women and members of multiple ethnic groups, and are significantly associated with worsened experiences both in academic and professional settings'. That is, the impostor experience itself, due to its impact on our attentional capacity, as well as its influence on us to focus on mitigating danger rather than leaning into growth, can negatively impact our wellbeing and performance.

Interestingly, MIT Assistant Professor of Work and Organization Studies, Dr Basima Tewfik, has found that the impostor phenomenon at work, or 'workplace impostor thoughts', can benefit employees' work performance.[15] It is associated with higher 'other-focused orientation' – an ability to consider and care for the needs and perspectives of others – as well as interpersonal effectiveness. However, while the participants themselves reported having a high consideration of others, they did not report they were more effective interpersonally. Rather, it was other people who worked with them who were likely to rate them as terrific interpersonally.

Tewfik's research found that individuals with impostor-related thoughts made a particularly positive contribution to the business and team. This contribution largely flowed from how they interacted with others, and were willing to take a values-based, team-oriented mindset, which benefitted team and organisational culture and performance.[16] It may be that the benefits of impostorness for an organisation flow from prioritising actions associated with values involving Humility and Conformity (which have a social, survival focus) in conjunction with values that involve Achievement and Self-direction. Promoting this combination of values at work may unlock some of the benefits of impostorness without coming with the impact to an individual's career and self-esteem.

The most marked difference between the group who recalled workplace impostor thoughts and the control group was self-reported self-esteem. Tewfik found that on average, those who engaged in workplace impostor thoughts had self-esteem that was 23 percent lower than those in the control group. Of particular impact for individuals and businesses, Tewfik's research also showed that self-esteem explained 42 percent of the differences in anxiety levels and 29 percent of the differences in feelings of belonging. People with workplace impostor thoughts tend to feel more anxious and less like they fit in, which has implications for performance and retention. The results indicate that workplace impostor thoughts can detrimentally impact the individual and the business over time, while certain areas of the impostor phenomenon (other-focus, humility) may benefit the business. I have suggested that through honing in on certain values domains at work, the benefits associated with impostor phenomenon may be harvested without the negative implications.

Later on in this chapter, I will discuss self-compassion as an important panacea to mitigate the negative effects of impostorness and poor self-esteem on performance and decision-making. Working to overcome issues with low self-esteem is best achieved not by seeking to bolster it, but by letting it go. That is, by letting go of the 'shoulds' that give way to the comparisons and perception of one's self-esteem as a relative construct, compared with other people or an idealised version of oneself. Why? Because self-esteem can significantly impact productivity, employee motivation, satisfaction, commitment, and turnover intentions, among others.[17,18] Low self-esteem puts people at risk of experiencing burnout and increased stress levels, which also heightens the risk of burnout.[19] So, while Tewfik might have found that the impostor phenomenon is handy when it comes to teamwork, there's the curly matter of overcoming its impact on self-esteem.

So, where do values fit into all this? I've already alluded to the 'shoulds' – those internalised expectations that whisper, 'I should be / have / do …' and how they fuel the impostor experience. As someone identifying with the impostor phenomenon, you carry deeply ingrained beliefs about how someone in your position *should* act. These beliefs not only shape your actions but, more importantly, how you feel. The fear of being exposed as an impostor drives the use of safety behaviours – actions that give the perception of keeping you 'safe' but, in reality, only perpetuate an anxiety response. These behaviours reinforce the sense of threat next time, maintaining the cycle of self-doubt and the fear of being found out. In turn, your focus remains on safety behaviours and other threat-based actions, rather than on values-led actions. This focus on self-protection for the shorter term can take you off course.

A disconnect can develop between what seems most important to you at the time and the actions that would contribute to your longer-term growth. Even when you recognise that the behaviours you're engaging in are unsustainable or unhelpful longer term, they may nevertheless feel like the only 'viable, immediate solution'.

Impostor-related safety behaviours – like over-preparation, procrastination, or perfectionism – can seem small or relatively harmless, but their impact compounds over time. For example, repeatedly working late rather than making it home for dinner can gradually strain relationship dynamics, taking it in a direction you don't aspire toward. Spending extra hours on project after project takes time away from other important pursuits, like another assignment, sleep, or time spent nurturing relationships. Putting off a task until the eleventh hour can create a reliance on pressure to complete something that otherwise feels unachievable, and over time accumulates into more and more time spent in the chaos of 'firefighting' missions where everything else is dropped so that the latest last-minute task can be undertaken.

These impostor-related safety behaviours even extend to our thoughts. For instance, we may feel that it's essential to keep certain thoughts (e.g. worries) associated with a task front of mind so that we remain vigilant and prepared. However, this constant preoccupation with work-related tasks prevents us from being as present in other areas of our life, be it spending time with loved ones or taking a shower. Staying mentally tethered to work, even outside of work hours, deprives us of the necessary breaks and time out to disconnect from the 'doing' and just 'be'. It increases our likelihood of developing burnout, adds to our sense of needing to always be 'on', and can compound our impostor experience.

Impostor-driven responses can also influence big life decisions. For instance, making career decisions based on thoughts around 'Who do I think I am?' or 'I couldn't possibly do that,' even when the interest and aptitude are there, likely flows from an impostor-related 'should' of not-enoughness. I've had numerous clients, especially women, say, 'I can't possibly go for that promotion / pay rise / position.' They worry that taking up such an opportunity would signal that they're claiming a confidence and competence they don't feel they have, leading to public unmasking and shame. That is, for someone who feels like a phony, taking up a growth opportunity risks not one but two things: (i) their being unmasked as an impostor; and (ii) being recognised as dishonest or delusional for thinking they are better than they are. Understandably, it's more than they can risk and they orient toward control or avoidance by turning down the opportunity.

Normalise Don't Pathologise the Impostor Experience

When I describe the impostor cycle and the impostor experience, many people resonate with it immediately: 'Yes! That's me!' Some may even arrive at my door saying, 'You know that thing, impostor syndrome? Yeah, that's me.' Despite this insight, however, they still work hard to avoid being unmasked. They carry shame about their experience – a contradiction between knowing they shouldn't feel like an impostor and yet still feeling that way. This shame often reflects the presence of 'shoulds', such as: 'I shouldn't feel this way' or 'I shouldn't experience the world like this.' The experience of impostor-related 'shoulds' can isolate someone further, even when intellectually they know many others feel like impostors, too. They believe, 'Yes, others may feel like impostors, but I'm somehow different. The reality is I have to work a lot harder than everyone else, to do the same thing.' The irony is that this sense of difference is one of the uniting features between my clients who experience impostorness.

Our tendency, thanks in no small part to 20th-century psychology with its propensity to falsely dichotomise the human experience into 'normal' and 'pathological', is to view our own impostor experience as evidence that somehow, we are broken or not normal. We may feel shame that we cannot overcome this 'deficiency', rather than recognising this part of our experience as relatively run-of-the-mill and typical. We're inclined to do several things when we view our impostor experience as pathological. First, we keep it to ourselves. Second, we hook into lots of 'should'-based thoughts, often in an attempt to rid ourselves of the pathological way of being – for instance, 'Oh, just get over it' (the implication being we 'should' be able to), or 'You shouldn't procrastinate, it's not helping' (and yet we continue to do just that). Third, we experience shame.

Our self-monitoring and associated judgements compound our engagement with the impostor cycle. In turn, our engagement with the impostor cycle and identification as an impostor exacerbates our sense of shame, along with our sense of being different and isolated in our experience. It's exhausting and can leave you feeling stuck, alone, and unable to grow into the version of the self you aspire to. As

Brené Brown says, 'Shame needs three things to grow exponentially in our lives: secrecy, silence, and judgement.'[20] And all three things can emanate from within rather than having to come from others.

Using Values to Help Overcome Secrecy, Silence and Judgement

In the context of the impostor experience as in other areas of life, harnessing your values can help you overcome secrecy, silence and judgement. They can lay the foundations for a different way of countering your impostor experience, where you don't have to do away with it – you can recognise it as part of your experience and understand it reflects that you care. Because there are vital things you especially care about, be it how you connect with people who are meaningful to you, your career trajectory, your sense of loyalty, your family. These things are bound up with your most important values.

A sidenote: your threat-based values can provide clues about safety behaviours you are likely to engage in following on from impostor thoughts. I find, perhaps unsurprisingly, that people inclined toward control tend to over-prepare, while those inclined toward avoidance tend to procrastinate. Perfectionism as an impostor-based response appears to be associated with both control and avoidance.

By identifying your core values and reflecting on how they relate to your impostor experience, you can start to understand in more detail why you care so much. You can also begin to intentionally align more of your actions with your core values rather than with impostor-related 'shoulds'. I have noticed that impostor-related responses can be particularly intense when values conflicts are in play, such as during transition moments when multiple life domains are relevant. For instance, at the end of the day, when there is a transition from work to home, values conflicts may arise. At the same time, there may be a desire to stay and finish a piece of work, which compounds a sense of wanting to stay at work even when plans with loved ones have been made, and the sky will not fall if you leave work. Let's explore this in further detail, using the earlier example of the values conflict between Family and Achievement.

It's the end of the day, and Fred (who values Family and Achievement) is considering working late – it's optional, but there's plenty to do. Fred may experience a values conflict: prioritising Family might have him head home now in time for dinner, whereas prioritising Achievement might involve working late. As I've discussed, there is no right or wrong to this values conflict; it's a choice to assess, given the specifics of the situation. Fred is no stranger to the impostor experience, and recognises his tendencies to over-prepare and prioritise work in order to not be 'found out'. For Fred, then, prioritising Family and heading home can come with a sense of threat or unease because of the pull to just keep working.

This sense of threat comes from the emotional weight that an impostor-based response adds to values activation. An impostor-based response provides an emotional and motivational boost to the work-oriented value of Achievement. As a result, working late is likely chosen more naturally than heading home. Alternatively, Fred heads home, but hurriedly eats dinner and swiftly opens up his work again. The feeling of danger associated with shifting into Family-oriented actions flows from fears that in not prioritising Achievement and work, Fred risks (i) being unmasked as an impostor because the work is not good enough; or (ii) losing the safety net of 'I might be an impostor, but I'm a hard worker and I make up for it.'

Understanding your core values helps you begin to unpack why you feel and think the way you do in these moments, without resorting to shaming or blaming yourself. Shame and blame can act like mental cattle prods – pushing us into action – or like mental straitjackets, shutting us down. However, shame and blame tend to erode our sense of self, leading us to retreat into threat-based thinking. We can resort to shame or blame when we're dealing with things that really matter to us. That is, we try to force ourselves into action using shame and blame *because we care*. Values activation can serve as an indicator of importance; a litmus test for how much you care. Rather than hooking into thoughts associated with shame or blame, you can notice it as a sign of caring: 'Wow, I must really care about this! Look how hard my mind is working to try to shame me into action around it – thanks, mind!' Recognising the connection between impostor thoughts and your core values can help you reframe your impostor feelings as a sign of caring rather than personal deficiency.

Acknowledging and reflecting on your core values and their role in your impostor experience enables you to more compassionately understand your motivations and reactions. Psychologist and shame researcher Brené Brown has written about the importance of understanding and embracing our values to navigate difficult emotions and avoid the trap of self-criticism. By taking an approach of self-insight around values, in conjunction with self-compassion around how those values impact how we show up in the world, we can significantly reduce the negative impact shame can have on us, and enhance our personal wellbeing.[21]

Practical Exercise: Some Questions and Self-Compassion

When you experience the impostor phenomenon, here are some questions you might like to ask yourself, to start unpicking where these impostor-related thoughts and feelings are coming from.

- **In this moment, what do I care about?**

- How does this relate to my values and what matters most to me?
- Given what I care about, how does it make sense that I feel like an impostor?
- How would I comfort a friend, if they were in this situation?

1. **Acknowledge the experience. Say to yourself:**
   'I understand that you feel like a fraud just now. It's a symptom of how much you care about this, and how much you want to honour it by doing it right.'

2. **Reflect on its universality:**
   'When someone really cares about what they're doing, it's normal for them to worry they're not doing it well enough, or to feel like they should be doing better to do it right. We can forget that none of us have a guidebook for life and are all muddling along as best we can. We can all feel like impostors at times.'

3. **Offer yourself comfort and compassion:**
   Start by taking three slow, intentional breaths in through your nose and out through your mouth. Place your hand on your chest if you feel comfortable doing so.
   'I recognise this as a moment of suffering in my thinking that I'm going to fall short with doing the task in front of me. I extend warmth and loving kindness, as though I were extending this to a friend I care deeply for. I make room for this experience, and I seek not to judge myself for this suffering, but to recognise this experience as normal, natural and as a sign that I care deeply.

> *'I care deeply. I care deeply. It's okay to care deeply. I allow my experience.'*

* * *

With this insight, you can extend understanding and compassion to yourself. Alongside understanding your core values, it's helpful to recognise 'should'-oriented values. That is, values you may feel you 'should' prioritise, but in fact don't hold as most important (in the context of your one precious life). Actions that flow from 'should'-based values may not align with what truly matters to you if you examine them closely. For example, in the context of the impostor experience, a 'should' around 'things should be perfect to be good enough' may sit as an assumption that is hooked into and contributes to that sense of not being enough as you are. Recognising these 'shoulds' and reorienting to what really matters to you at work can help you ground yourself and reconnect with something meaningful.

All-or-nothing thinking, grounded in the idea that something less than perfect, for instance, will cast doubt about your legitimacy and lead to your 'unmasking' often goes unquestioned until you start reflecting on your values. With added insight into your values and assumptions, you can reframe impostor-related actions and thoughts as indicators of what matters to you, rather than fixating on what these thoughts might say about you. Without this values work, those who experience impostorness often judge success in ways that reinforce their identity as an impostor. These judgements of not measuring up impact their beliefs about their abilities during key times of performance. Instead of hooking into these thoughts, you can allow them to be there, recognise them as normal, natural indicators of how much you care, and draw on your values for guidance and motivation to recommit to what matters most to you.

Impostor-Related Thoughts Are Normal and Natural

With values work on board, the impostor experience takes on a different hue. Impostor-related beliefs can be seen for what they are: as natural phenomena – a symptom of caring rather than reflecting personal shortcomings. One can make room for the impostor experience rather than feeling that impostor-related thoughts and feelings need attention. Allowing the impostor experience to be there without doing anything with it enables the individual to reorient their actions around their values. From here, it ceases to matter whether success comes from external factors like luck or timing or internal factors like innate ability. The litmus test for what matters and constitutes success becomes values alignment: Are you acting in line with what truly matters to you? How can you adjust your alignment to better balance your priorities?

Aligning your actions with your core values can foster a sense of competence and autonomy, which are fundamental components in overcoming the impostor experience. This is not so you will start thinking, 'I am the best' – far from it. Overcoming the impostor experience can involve making peace with related thoughts and feelings rather than ridding yourself of them. Instead, your measure of success can shift from being the 'best' to being 'aligned'. And when climbing a mountain, as much as it pays to have great (if not the 'best') gear, it's far more important to be aligned with the path and heading in the direction of the summit you're aiming for. But what happens when you're unsure if you're heading for the right summit – if in fact your values are your own, or if you're being pushed around by values you believe you 'should' hold?

Indicators of Core Values Misalignment

When your values and actions are in sync, you feel content; when they're not, you feel off. I suggest that the degree to which you're living in accordance with your values is proportionate to the volume of your inner voice that's saying, 'There has to be more to life than this.' This voice can get so loud that you may look for ways to distract from the perceived disconnect between who and where you are and would like to be.

Practical Exercise: Identifying Values Misalignment
Here's a list of behaviours I've witnessed clients use to distract themselves from this disconnect. See if any resonate with you.

- **Filling your days with 'busy' work or errands, to bolster your sense of being enough and avoid feeling lost or disconnected from what matters most to you.**
- **Over-indulging in media consumption:**
  - Binge-watching TV shows or movies at times when you probably should be working.
  - Scrolling social media: constantly checking and updating social media to stimulate, distract and validate a superficial sense of self to avoid confronting deeper issues of disconnection.
- **Engaging in 'retail therapy':**
  - Shopping for items you don't need as a way of temporarily boosting your mood and avoiding feelings of inadequacy or emptiness.

- **Seeking constant validation:**
  - Overly relying on external approval via praise and validation from others to compensate for a lack of internal fulfilment.
  - People-pleasing behaviour at the expense of your own needs and values.
- **Immersing yourself in work:**
  - Dedicating an excessive amount of time and energy to work tasks to avoid looking more closely at whether you're finding ways of aligning your work with your 'why', or to avoid issues of values misalignment in your personal life, or a sense of purposelessness.
  - Overcommitting: A tendency to take on too many projects or responsibilities to stay constantly busy and distracted, or because you're looking for the 'next best thing' to provide a sense of validation in the absence of values alignment.
- **Other numbing behaviours:**
  - Engaging in unhealthy practices with food, substances, gambling, sex, to stimulate quick dopamine hits that numb the pain and suffering from feeling lost or disconnected.
- **Focusing on the superficial:**
  - Steering clear of deep connections to avoid vulnerability and running the risk of confronting personal misalignment.
  - Engaging in excessive socialising, not to satiate a social appetite but to avoid being alone with your thoughts and feelings.

- Focusing overly on physical appearance as a way of seeking and maintaining approval and avoiding deeper self-worth issues.
- Pursuing perfection: using the pursuit of perfection around one's appearance, behaviour, or lifestyle to mask feelings of inadequacy.

* * *

Identifying your values is an iterative process that takes time. It is best divided into time spent in self-reflection, and time spent discussing them with others – either with a coach, psychologist, or friend who is perhaps interested in doing values work alongside you.

The long-term personal and collective benefits of values-based decision-making are thanks to values prioritisation and alignment between values and choices. While we can think of decision-making as all about the big stuff, it's often the small choices that accumulate and forge your version of a life well lived. Values-based decision-making is all about helping you harness your values to make more moves toward the life you seek, rather than being derailed by 'shoulds', 'not-enoughness', or the impostor experience. In Chapter Nine we take a closer look at values-based decision-making, but first, I want to get deeper into the impostor phenomenon from a more practical standpoint in the next chapter, followed by taking a closer look at your 'why'.

KEY TAKEAWAYS OF THIS CHAPTER:

* 'Shoulds' are expectations that you have of yourself or another, which are unmet.
* 'Should' language (e.g. 'I should have …') provides clues that there is a gap between how things 'are' and how you think things 'should' be.
* 'Shoulds' can indicate that there is a sense that reality is 'not enough' and can drive thoughts and feelings of 'not-enoughness'.
* The impostor experience is a specific form of 'not-enoughness'.
* Impostor thoughts help perpetuate, and are perpetuated by, a cycle of over-preparation, procrastination, and perfectionism. These behaviours, in conjunction with denial of ability and deflection of praise, can create short-term relief, but reinforce negative beliefs of enoughness over time.
* The impostor phenomenon is thought to affect up to 70 percent of adults.
* Impostor-driven actions can interfere with long-term growth and goals.
* Some aspects of the impostor phenomenon are worth keeping (e.g. humility and interpersonal effectiveness) and can positively impact teamwork and organisational performance.
* Self-compassion and intentional, core values–based actions can help reduce the self-limiting impact of the impostor phenomenon over time.
* Values-based decision-making and goal setting can help counteract the impostor cycle, not only improving alignment between your values and actions, but reducing the influence of 'shoulds' and perfectionism.
* Shame, silence, and judgement may amplify the impostor experience. Impostorness is a sign of caring rather than of deficiency.

CHAPTER 7
Values and the Client Experience with the Impostor Phenomenon

In the previous chapter, I described the impostor experience in detail. Here, I share more of my own experiences as a psychologist and propose ways to use your values to overcome the impostor experience. While the focus is on the professional work environment, I have also seen the impostor phenomenon arise in other areas of life, among parents – especially mothers who feel they're not living up to what a 'good mother' would do for their children. If you relate to the impostor experience, be it in the working world, parenting, education, or beyond, I hope you apply some of these insights in your own life.

Your Life as an Impostor

'I have written 11 books, but each time I think, "uh oh, they're going to find out now. I've run a game on everybody, and they're going to find me out".' – Maya Angelou

'The exaggerated esteem in which my lifework is held makes me very ill at ease. I feel compelled to think of myself as an involuntary swindler.' – Albert Einstein

Be it in high-performance coaching or clinical work, the impostor experience is prevalent and, importantly, highly treatable. Experiencing impostorness is not a sign of weakness nor does it reflect deficits. As we've discussed, you can view it as a demonstration of how deeply you care about what you're doing. Even procrastinators who shroud their care in an air of 'Oh I'll get to it later' are often driven by this depth of care.

I greatly admire clients who continue to show up for the work, despite thinking, 'I doubt I can be helped with this. No one else struggles the way I do.'

The impostor experience impacts people in varying ways. Some clients have shared how they feel persistently different or isolated from their peers or coworkers. Others describe an internalised sense of being different or not good enough. Although I differentiate between impostorness and not-enoughness, in my experience, they often overlap. Many clients describe both as stemming from the same underlying experience. Whether due to disconnection, impostorness, or a fundamental experience of not-enoughness, there is a gap between where someone sees themselves as being and where they feel they 'should' be. There's a gap between the actions they take, the actions they believe they 'should' take, and the values-aligned actions they could take that may alleviate some of their suffering.

A recurring theme I've heard from clients struggling with impostorness or not-enoughness is: 'In order to be enough, I should be / do / have more, or be / do better.' The issue with this mindset is that when not-enoughness is in play, 'more' is never enough. The solution is not to seek more, but to let go of the metaphorical rope between where you are, and where you 'should' be.[1] Letting go of the rope means accepting exactly where you are today. From there, you can begin to fully focus on what it is you need to do in order to move forward in ways that matter to you.

To move forward, you need to know what you want – and this requires identifying and reflecting on your core values. These values serve as the foundation on which you can start to build toward your unique version of a life well lived.

Getting Personal and Practical with the Impostor Experience

Cultivating a Curious Mind to Remedy the Impostor Experience

As a workshop facilitator, my impostor-related thoughts and feelings around presenting values workshops weighed me down for years. It didn't matter how many I presented or what positive feedback I received. My impostorness impacted who I'd offer to present workshops for, what I'd ask for fee-wise, and what I'd do in the workshops. I wouldn't just over-prepare; I'd demonstrate my over-preparation (and perfectionism) by getting too technical and 'under the hood' with folks who didn't need or want that level of nitty-gritty detail. I'd worry that I wasn't offering enough value without the detail. If I encouraged group discussions, I'd fear it was too surface-level and that I was wasting their learning. In my effort to prove I wasn't an impostor, I didn't make room for the messy potential of human experience in such gatherings.

Once I realised what was happening, I adapted Stephen Hayes' Relational Frame Theory[2] to help remedy the situation.

First, I considered the overall task of running a workshop. Initially, I broke it down into sub-areas like 'helping people identify their values', but after some experimentation I realised it was more useful to zoom out and focus on the workshop as a whole. That is, it wasn't a specific task but the entire workshop that triggered my impostor experience. This was driven by a sense of 'Who do you think you are?'

I wrote down: *'Running a values workshop for [Company name].'*

One by one, I wrote down and reflected on my core values. I asked myself, 'How does running this values workshop for X Company help me live in line with each of my values?'

For instance, for the value Achieve Together, I answered the question: 'How does running a values workshop for X Company help me live in line with my value of Achieve Together?'

I gave myself two minutes per value to dot point as many ways as possible in which running the workshop aligned with that value. The time limit was so that I didn't overthink it. It became challenging after the first four or five dot points, but I pressed on.

After the two minutes were up, I selected just one or two dot points per value to focus on and wrote about them in more detail. During this process, I remained intentional about my breathing. Why? Because I found this work somewhat stress-inducing and my breath anchored me and kept me intentional in my focus. Sometimes when we're under stress, we hold our breath, or breathe shallowly –

both of which can promote activation of the sympathetic nervous system or 'fight-or-flight' response – the last thing I needed while working through this exercise.

When thoughts surfaced like 'Yes, but I should demonstrate my knowledge because there'll be some people who need to go deeper', I allowed them to remain without hooking into them.

When my mind wandered, I gently noticed where it had wandered without judgement, thanked my mind for doing what it does best (it's my incredible thought machine), and then guided my attention back to my breath. From there, I would refocus on my values and the connection between them and the task I was seeking to make values connections with.

I did this for *all* of my values, even though really there were two – 'Achieve Together' and 'Contribution' – that proved most relevant to the workshop context. While you can go through this reflective process using all your values, it can be just as workable and far less taxing to focus on one or two of your values for the deeper reflection.

That said, it's worth remaining open when determining which of your values are relevant to your impostor experience. You may never have deeply considered how your values may help inform your experience of impostorness or motivate you to perform well when feeling like a fraud. I invite you to try this two-minute 'curious mind' exercise with each of your values, even if you only deep-dive with a couple of them.

Select One or Two Values

Now that you've done this work, focus in on one or two values. For me, I focused on Achieve Together, and Contribution. It's time to pair more closely the task and your focus values, one at a time.

My task: Values workshop
My focus values: Achieve Together; Contribution

I said to myself repeatedly for two minutes, slowly and in a whisper as was comfortable for me: 'Values workshop, Achieve Together.'

As I did so, I remained anchored to my measured, slow, and intentional breathing. My eyes were closed. I observed what thoughts came up without hooking into them. I gently forged a simple, light connection between 'values workshop' and 'Achieve Together'. I then did the same with my other focus value of 'Contribution'. I noticed any thoughts of impostorness without feeling the need to hook into them. My sole goal was to guide my attention back to the two concepts: 'values workshop' and my focus value. You might wish to try this for yourself, connecting a meaningful yet impostor-triggering task (i.e. your version of 'presenting a workshop') with a focus value of yours.

As I progressed with this exercise, I found myself discovering inspiring links between my focus values and the specific, task-related goal of running values workshops. I started reflecting on what Achieve Together really meant for the people in the room. Far from being just a 'values education' session, this was an opportunity for people to reach 'aha moments' together and unlock deep, personal insights for each other. This exercise helped me let go of the need to control every moment of the workshop and opened it up to being more emergent, allowing for unique moments of wonder and creation. More broadly, it can help you draw motivating connections between important impostor-triggering tasks in your life and your values.

Now, you can get more granular about the smaller actions you can take toward your task that align with your focus values.

You can continue doing this work over time, as often as you need. Remember, the objective is not to rid yourself of impostor-related thoughts or feelings but to become sufficiently anchored by and connected with your values that your 'why' fuels a level of performance that is not constrained by impostor-related safety behaviours. Over time, the impostor experience will lessen as you cease to engage in safety behaviours that have reinforced it and kept it going.

What I Learned from My Impostor Experience

A revelation for me in doing this values work around my impostor experience was that my inclination to include a lot of detail in the workshop was more about me trying to prove myself rather than what would best serve participants. My initial response to recognising this was to shame and blame myself: 'You're making it about yourself. You're trying to put all this detail in to prove you're worthy of being there. Why are you being so self-centred?' Implicit in this self-talk was 'You should not make it about you but you are.' If there's one thing I've learned it's that self-compassion is an important antidote to shame. So, instead of staying stuck in shame, first I intentionally offered myself compassion. Next, I intentionally reflected on how deeply I cared about delivering values workshops well and making a meaningful contribution. I recognised my attempt to shame myself as an act of caring, too – just another way my mind was trying to nudge me into action.

The thing with shame as a currency – when we use it to push ourselves around – we can find ourselves in a state of perceived threat. For me, I vividly recall the feeling in my body of sitting with that 'should': 'You shouldn't be making it about you but you are.' Taking this one step further, I was telling myself, 'This is not good enough; you are not enough.' Had I hooked into these thoughts I would have tried to control myself, and Perfectionism and Control may have come to the fore. In using self-compassion and values insights, it brought into sharp relief what mattered to me in this context. I could sit with the realisation that I didn't need to give so many details in workshops, not as a criticism but as an opportunity to level up my workshops and align them better in action with my values. Instead of over-preparing or over-compensating, I began to trust in values alignment and my desired outcome for each workshop – to connect people with their values and enable them to feel greater belonging and connection as a group.

At long last, I finished the final item on my list: to complete the statement, 'I care because …'

I care because my work has the potential to make a significant impact on the lives of others. I care because facilitating values workshops aligns with my core values of Collaboration, Achieve Together, and Connection. I care because helping others identify and act on their values brings out the best in them and elicits joy in me. I care because I believe in the power of values to transform people, teams, entire companies, and even countries. I care because I believe in the power of human values. As I write this book and reflect on my twisting and turning career journey so far, impostor feelings and thoughts are never far away. This statement of care lives with me daily, and provides me with the courage to vulnerably share my thoughts.

A sidenote. Impostorness and not-enoughness raise their heads at various times. Once you have your 'I care because' for an area of your impostor experience, don't lose it. Take it out and reflect on it every now and then. You'll find that it's inspiring and gives you energy and courage at times when you need to reconnect with your 'why'.

Chelsea, the Over-Prepared Presenter

Let's look at another example. Chelsea was a senior leader at an architectural firm, although her background was originally in planning law, not architecture. When she received a new brief, Chelsea would mean to get to it immediately, as she knew that if she didn't, avoidance would kick in. More often than not, however, she would find reasons to put it to the side for a few days. This stemmed from a doubt in her mind about her competency to complete the brief, even though she had completed many before. Finally, when she would pick it up, more often than not she'd realise she didn't have all the information she needed to make a start, and she needed to reach out to colleagues for that information. However, by this time, she worried that they would realise her questions meant she hadn't made a start, and they would judge her as an impostor and not good or diligent at her job.

Two of Chelsea's values that she identified as especially relevant were Collaboration and Humour.

Chelsea reflected that these values were important because they supported one another in her work. For her, collaboration made room for humour, and humour was part of collaborating. However, when Chelsea experienced impostorness, she wouldn't just avoid tasks; she would avoid collaborating with colleagues in the same way lest they discover her impostorness. Further, she would worry that her colleagues would view her well-known love of humour as indicative of her as an intellectual lightweight; that is, further evidence of her impostorness.

Chelsea also reflected that Avoidance and Perfectionism were key threat-based values for her. When under threat, she would prioritise these behaviours to keep her safe, including keeping her from being unmasked as an impostor.

From this process, Chelsea realised that the most important value to focus on actioning when experiencing impostorness was Collaboration and intentionally including some humour in this action. She reflected that at times when she was under threat, this felt unnatural, but in sticking at it, it started to feel more natural again.

Chelsea initially found acknowledging the universality of her experience quite challenging. She shared that none of her colleagues had similar experiences with this, especially as she was the only member of her team with no qualification in building or architecture. I asked her how she knew this, and she replied it was obvious that was the case. I encouraged her, and she agreed, to discuss this with one or two close and trusted colleagues to see whether her assumptions aligned with their experience.

On approaching Alice and Raphaël, Chelsea mused to them, 'I'm working on something and wonder if I can get your take. Sometimes, I feel like an impostor in this work. I don't imagine you feel the same but I wanted to ask you anyway whether this is relevant to you, too?' The floodgates opened! Chelsea quickly received the confirmation that she was not alone in her experience. Indeed, it was quite a relief for others she spoke with, who had also assumed their experience of impostorness was unique. This information helped Chelsea understand that there are *always* reasons for justifying impostorness if you go looking for them. From here, Chelsea could reflect on what she'd say to a friend experiencing such thoughts and feelings, and she practised these reflections on her coworkers who benefitted from them!

VALUES / CLIENT EXPERIENCE / IMPOSTOR PHENOMENON

Play and the Impostor Experience

For years, my primary income flowed from working as a professional classical singer, around Australia, the Asia Pacific, the UK, Europe, and into the USA. I would produce my own national tours across Australia, too, and I released four albums that all made it to #1 on the Australian charts. I was dedicated, and I can say, hand on heart, my values helped me give all I could to the audience, my colleagues, and the music – and this provided a buffer to the inevitable feelings from time to time of exquisite not-enoughness. As a performer, there was always the drive to prepare more. I assumed that giving 120 percent meant yielding 120 percent in return – the harder you work, the greater the outcome. But it's not that simple. Indeed, you can't put in more than 100 percent without it coming at a cost. The secret is working with people who can help you pinpoint what 100 percent means to you on any given day.

I work with athletes who have this same drive and who entrust their coach with the task of establishing what 100 percent effort looks like and working toward that. It's important because no matter your field of performance – whether in business, sports, the arts, or beyond – excessive practice can negatively impact performance over time, just as insufficient practice can.[3] There are many careers where it's a fine line between doing what it takes to succeed and grow, and doing more than it takes, so as to not be found out as an impostor yet at the expense of your longer-term performance over time.

If you find yourself over-preparing, procrastinating, or aiming for perfection, try this experiment. Find a way each day to incorporate play into moments of performance. For instance, select a song or piece of music that makes you feel good and playful, and listen to (or hum) it before making that presentation or running that race.

You might also inject humour into a presentation or high-pressure performance moment, not to reduce the significance of the moment but to ease the tension and help create a bond among those present. After all, humour has been identified as one of the key attributes of high-performing teams.[4]

Alongside humour and play, remind yourself that your area of performance is something that you do, rather than representing the entirety of who you are. Anchoring to your values while bringing play into the mix can serve to lighten the air and the sense of expectation around performance moments. Practise this consistently over time, rather than basing your assessment on just one or two performances (whether that's playing sport, performing on stage, or presenting at work). Periodically reflect on the effects: Has your performance experience or level changed at all? How about your overall enjoyment level? Do you feel less pressure or fewer concerns about falling short? Are you more plugged in to what matters most to you in such moments of performance?

Reducing Over-Preparation

Sam was an ambitious investment banker who came to me with a desire to 'learn how to better just be me', and a desire to overcome a pattern of 'crashing and burning' when making presentations to colleagues. 'I have all the knowledge and numbers to hand and in one-on-ones I'm fine, but I find presenting really confronting. I hope someday I'm in a position where I need to present to the board and right now I'd be shocking. I freeze up. If I didn't have my notes with me, I wouldn't be able to say a thing.'

For Sam, every meeting felt like her life depended on it. Her over-preparation included preparing detailed notes and reading from those notes through a presentation (aka performance instance).

We got into the nitty gritty of what these notes looked like and the level of preparation, and worked out what ten percent of that prep would amount to – Sam felt it was probably scripting to the point of having fully formed sentences with correct grammar that she would read. This over-preparation had become a safety behaviour, which Sam had internalised as keeping her safe from 'being found out' during presentations as less competent than she appeared. We began by trimming ten percent of her preparation time. She estimated she was still sitting at around 120 percent preparation (i.e. there was more trimming work to do). She focused on reducing word-for-word scripting to dot point notes. Over a few weeks, we cut back another ten percent, requiring her to recall more information from memory instead of relying on prepared material. All the numbers were still there just some of the rationale she'd need to bring to mind. She knew it all but accessing it when under pressure was a challenge. This is where play comes in.

One of the best things you can do for your performance is to detach from it and be in the moment. Bringing curiosity and a sense of play helps you to do that. A word of warning, however – it can feel dangerous to loosen the reins enough to do this. Instead of fixating on the outcome, your focus is on being present and approaching it with curiosity and a sense of play. Furthermore, curiosity and play can be injected into performance moments, but also into moments of downtime where you need to unhook and intentionally recall that you are so much more than your performance.

At the North-West University in South Africa, Master of Commerce student Liana Fourie was interested in the effect of play at work on the performance and engagement of employees.[5] After consulting with industrial psychologists, Liana and her supervisors selected 13 games that made room for different play-related interests, including foosball and darts, through Heads Up, Scrabble, Sudoku and Jenga. Fourie's research demonstrated that play that was suitably demanding – but not too much so – enabled employees to psychologically detach during their lunchbreak. This was associated with greater improvement in team performance over time. I introduced this research to Sam (who had been sceptical about deploying play at work), and we discussed what this could look like at her workplace.

At Sam's work, there was no foosball table or play-oriented resources to use at lunchtime so she decided to take a deck of Uno cards to work. This was confronting for Sam, who had always focused on being seen as relentlessly work-focused and professional. And here she was, committing to playing Uno for ten minutes in the middle of the day! She needed to rope in at least one colleague. She somewhat strategically chose a well-respected colleague, Jess, to join. After hearing about the rationale, Jess responded enthusiastically with 'I'm in!'

Before long, the word had spread and Sam had multiple Uno players, with others bringing Connect4 and playing cards. 'Lunchplay' had even started popping up as an entry in workers' calendars. Sam reported that Lunchplay helped her detach from her work, not only boosting her afternoon's performance but helping her approach colleagues and presentations differently. Others found it helpful, too. Play broadened to include other present-moment practices including mindfulness practice. Some folks played, some folks meditated, some even went for a silent walking mindfulness meditation. Increasingly, a culture developed of intentionally making time for a ten-minute present-moment unhook in the middle of the day. The unhook came to be understood as a performance tool, in what was a hypercompetitive environment.

When it comes to procrastination and perfectionism, play can serve a similar purpose. It enables you to detach from the task at hand sufficiently to approach it with less 'should'-based thoughts of 'what if' or 'if only'. Play can serve as an active form of mindfulness; dropping you into the present moment and into a sense of flow, where time can stand still and you can approach work with curiosity instead of impostor-related fear.[6]

What Doesn't Improve the Impostor Experience?

Sometimes, all this feels too hard. Why can't I just offer ways you can start thinking and feeling like *not* an impostor? As I've mentioned, we can't take thoughts away or divide them, we can only work with what we've got and guide our attention in constructive ways. Furthermore, as well as your mind being an incredible thought machine that aims to keep you safe from harm, it is also a natural sceptic.[7] When you are living the impostor experience and are told 'there's so much evidence to the contrary', my experience is that you *might* get some short-term relief, but the same issues can creep back. And, when they do return, they bring another layer of shame that you weren't 'strong enough' to overcome these 'silly' thoughts that are holding you back.

Given the way the impostor phenomenon manifests for so many, we know that all the evidence *against* you being an impostor mightn't be enough to overcome it. The issue is not one of finally mounting an argument to nip the impostor phenomenon in the bud through sheer bloody-minded logic. Instead of fighting impostor-related thoughts or feelings, refocus on what's meaningful to you in the present, guided by your values. Do more of what matters, even when it leaves you feeling like an impostor.

Overcoming the detrimental elements of the impostor experience involves time, acceptance, and anchoring to 'why' you're doing the thing that's leading to a sense of phoniness in the first place. That is, anchoring to your values, and enabling this deep sense of 'why' to provide you what you need to stick with it over time, and accept impostor feelings and thoughts while 'doing the thing' anyway. In accepting such thoughts and feelings, I am not suggesting you accept 'I am an impostor'. The goal is to get comfortable co-habiting with impostor thoughts and feelings, without feeling you need to do anything with them. Giving yourself permission to make room for them, without needing to do anything about them, can help them fade into the background. Ideally, you will reach a stage of saying to yourself, 'Whether or not this impostor thought is true, it's not working for me.' From this place, it's not about pushing the thoughts away or fighting with them any longer. It's about refocusing, in the present moment, on what is meaningful and workable for you now, guided by your values.

A Practical Approach

To close out this chapter on values and the impostor experience, I offer you two exercises to ease and manage the overwhelm of the impostor experience, using your values.

Using Values to Ease the Impostor Experience
Know Your Values
As always, ensure you've an up-to-date identification of your top five core values. That is, you feel aligned with their names and descriptions. You will never reach 'values perfection' and values work is an area where you're striving for workability and enabling values-

in-action rather than needing everything word perfect (although I know plenty of people who feel extremely satisfied and proud of their values array!).

You may also wish to identify your threat-based values, which can overlap with your impostor-related safety behaviours. For instance, if you identify Avoidance as one of your threat-based values, it is interesting to reflect on whether you also identify Procrastination as one of your impostor-related safety behaviours, as procrastination involves task avoidance.

Reflect, Non-Judgementally, on How Your Core Values Impact Your Impostor Experience
For each of your core values, how relevant is it to your impostor area? At first glance, for instance, Zoe's core value of Family may appear as less relevant to her impostor area around pursuing a career as a 'race car driver' than her value of Competitiveness. However, Zoe is motivated in part by her desire to help her family. They also support her no matter what she chooses. So, for Zoe, Family is an important purposeful energy resource when it comes to her performance on the track. I provide this example because sometimes it takes some thought around the relevance of your core values to your impostor areas. It can pay to get curious about this.

Write a brief reflection on why each of your core values is important to you in the area where you can feel like an impostor.

- **How are your values important? How can they show up at their best in this area?**
- **For each value: Is there a shadow side to this value that's in play? How might this value be adding to your sense of impostorness or not-enoughness, because you're failing to live up to your sense of what you 'should' be doing?**

- **Reflect on whether and how you may experience shame in failing to live up to this value in this area of your life? That is, shame at not being 'enough' or doing a good enough job?**
- **How can you acknowledge the universality of this experience of not-enoughness? That is, what can you say to yourself to remind you that you're not alone in this experience, and that it reflects how much you care?**
- **What would you say to a friend who was experiencing these thoughts and feelings, to provide them comfort and support?**
- **What have you learned about your experience, through working through these questions?**

Describe key tasks that are currently or have recently activated the impostor experience in you.

- **What is the task?**
- **What are some thoughts and feelings associated with your impostor experience?**

Have you:

- **Over-prepared?**
- **Procrastinated?**
- **Aimed for perfection?**

If so, how?

Afterwards, did you:

- **Deflect praise when someone offered it?**
- **Talk down your own ability?**

How does this task support your values, and which value is most important to this task?
- **Name the value**
- **How does this task help you live in line with this value?**
- **Why do you care about this task?**

Assuming that the task is values-aligned for you, we can assume that your impostor-related actions are *away* moves – they take you further away from the version of you that you wish to cultivate with the help of doing the task in question.

So – let's flip it, and look for *toward* moves you can take:
- **If you over-prepared, how can you do so 10 percent less?**
- **If you procrastinated, what would it look like to do that 10 percent less?**
- **If you aimed for perfection, how can you be 10 percent less perfect?**

When considering your initial actions, I invite you to think of each of these as an 'away' move – moving you 'away' from the version of yourself and your life that you wish to grow into, in the direction of the discomfort of the existence of a perceived impostor. My question for you is, what *toward* move could you make – toward discomfort, but also toward that version of your life you wish to cultivate for yourself?

In essence, I am asking you to move in the opposite direction of your impostor-related actions. If you routinely over-prepare consider this: How can you reduce your preparation by ten percent? This reduction in preparation should be enough that it feels uncomfortable without being so much that you feel completely overwhelmed. Start small. For instance, say you feel like an impostor when you give presentations and so you have adopted the habit of always scripting them. Over time, this has compounded your anxiety around people asking questions beyond what you've prepared. That is, you've internalised 'I need to script to stay safe'. So, you spend a lot of time preparing scripted answers 'just in case' for questions you may never field. Starting small might involve cutting out scripted preparation of these 'just in case' questions, and then working toward reducing and ultimately removing scripting altogether.

Don't base success or failure on a single instance; this is about creating value for you in the longer term. Initially, discomfort and perceived failures may arise. Stick with it for a period of time and allow your values to be your guide. It can help to let someone know that you're experimenting with this, too, such as your manager or a coworker you trust. Encourage them to give you positive feedback as well as constructive hints on what you can do to further build beyond your impostor experience.

Ask yourself:

- **What is my desired outcome: What am I trying to achieve by reducing actions related to my impostor experience? That is, what do I want to achieve and contribute to, beyond simply reducing discomfort?**
- **How do my values intersect with this: How does this goal align with my values?**

Managing Impostor Overwhelm in Performance Moments

When feeling overwhelmed during a performance moment, hook into your values to remind you of what matters most in the longer term. This is hard to do without some preparation for this moment, and that's what we're exploring in this exercise. A moment of performance is no time to focus on proving you're not an impostor;

it's a time simply to optimally bring what you have, whatever that might be, in that moment.

Let's look at an example. Charlotte was performing a principal role at an international opera house for the first time (Susanna in Mozart's opera, *The Marriage of Figaro*). She was confident of her singing ability but still experienced nerves and a sense of overwhelm around how she would stack up in this rarified environment. She knew this moment would impact her future trajectory at this house and other leading houses worldwide. She was so focused on proving herself that it was affecting her performance in rehearsal. In our session, she reflected that it was a sense of being an impostor that was driving her performance-related anxiety. She had wanted this her whole life, and she was having a hard time wrapping her head around the idea that she was here, and that she was 'enough' for this place. Alongside work identifying impostor-related safety behaviours and the above values work, Charlotte created a mantra that she could use come crunch time with impostor overwhelm during moments of performance (including rehearsals). Here's how to create a mantra for yourself.

Creating a Performance Mantra

1. **Create a short, memorable phrase (ideally three to five words) that you can say at times when you feel that sense of 'impostor overwhelm'.**
   - Keep it very simple. Consider integrating one of your values into this mantra. Charlotte identified Beauty as a focus value for the task of singing in this particular opera house, and coined 'Beauty is enough'.
   - **What does this mantra remind you of and connect you to?**
     - This mantra reminded Charlotte of what she was there to create – beauty.

Before each rehearsal and performance, Charlotte would do some controlled breathing that integrated this mantra. On the in-breath, she would focus on breathing in cool replenishing air. On the out-breath, she would breathe out her intention – 'Beauty is enough'.

> **2. Journal about this mantra.**
> - Journalling enables you to go deeper with 'why' this mantra symbolises what matters to you.
> - It allows you to get curious about 'how' you can use your mantra around moments of performance.
> - You can write about how this mantra connects to other values of yours, too. For Charlotte, the extended version of her mantra was:
>
> *'Beauty is enough to connect with those audience members who are here to be moved, who desire to be moved, who are rooting for me to move them. Vulnerability and commitment do that over striving for perfection. In my moment of performance, beauty is enough.'*

The process of journalling, including reaching a point where you have that extended version, enables you to understand your mantra more deeply so that those few words connect to a wealth of felt understanding for you.

> **3. Each morning for three days, sit with your mantra and journal about it. Collect up the most compelling 'why' statements from your journalling and allow them to inspire you and connect with your mantra.**
> - Begin these morning moments with three deep breaths to ground and focus on your intentionality.

> Breathe in through the nose, out through the mouth. Work on internalising the mantra. Say it, with curiosity and an openness to observe thoughts and feelings associated with it. When you are drawn back into impostor-related thoughts and feelings, allow this mantra, associated with a certain performance domain, to be your link back to your values.

Try this exercise for a month, to help you establish a pattern and simply observe any changes in your impostor experience. You can do this as a solo pursuit or, better still, include weekly discussions with a colleague or friend to share experiences and challenges. Sharing this work with another can help dispel feelings of shame or isolation in your impostor experience and provide additional perspectives on navigating impostor feelings.

* * *

Alongside capitalising on the power of the present moment, utilising your breath, your values, and a mantra or two, sometimes what's needed when you're faced with impostor-related thoughts or feelings is simply a statement to remind you that you're enough.

Sayings to Use in those Moments When You Need a Reminder that You're Enough

Here are some of my favourite pieces of impostor-related reflections, with a big thanks to my clients who have inspired them.

> *'It's natural to feel like an impostor at times like this; it's because you care about this work and want to do well.*

Doing values work around this has helped me "get" more deeply what it really means to say, "My impostor experience is a testament to how much I care".'
– Doug, full-stack developer

'Feeling like you're not good enough is something many people go through, especially high achievers. It doesn't reflect your actual abilities.'
– Tanja, university lecturer

'Everyone has moments of doubt, even those who seem the most confident. It's part of being human.'
– Ali, teacher

'Your unique background brings the team different perspectives. These differences bring unique value to the team; 'different' doesn't mean 'impostor' and hey, I actually wouldn't trade different for quids.
– Al, product manager

'I've learned that talking to others about how you're feeling is important. You might be surprised to learn how many peers have a similar impostor experience. This insight can lighten your load considerably.'
– Felix, volunteer

'Perfectionism is paralysing. Doing something well enough is better than not doing it at all because you're afraid it won't be perfect. Trust me, "well enough" gets you further in the long run.'
– Jo, CEO

'Avoidance only makes the task seem more daunting. Taking small steps aligned with what matters to you can help you build momentum and confidence.'
— Greta, author

'Reflect on the positive feedback you've received from colleagues and clients without trying to dismiss it. You can even link this through to your values-in-action. They see your value, even if you sometimes don't.'
— Sal, psychologist

'Impostor feelings often stem from comparing your insides to others' outsides. Everyone has their own struggles and insecurities, even if they don't show them.'
— Devon, doctor

Further Tips for Using Values to Reduce the Impostor Experience

- **Be patient and honest with yourself throughout the process. If you don't notice improvement in your experience, it doesn't mean your impostor experience cannot change. Modify the exercise to work for you.**
    - Try some different values-led actions.
    - Consider working with a psychologist skilled in third-wave cognitive behavioural therapies to help you work on your relationship with your thoughts and feelings. Values work is only a part of what you can do.
- **Reassess your values over time, as they will evolve.**
    - Use values-oriented impostor work as an opportunity to clarify what is important to you.

- Remember that there are no 'rights' or 'wrongs' – what you're looking to do is locate pools of motivation that help you take actions that lead to your personal success and fulfilment.
- **Celebrate small victories.**
  - Tiny steps aligned with your values have the greatest cumulative impact over time.
  - Don't wait for big breakthroughs or giant leaps – small values-led moves can help you shed the impostor skin and unapologetically embrace your path and potential.

Continual practice will help strengthen the alignment between your values and actions. While a month might not bring major shifts in your impostor experience, it can be long enough to notice increased fulfilment from values-aligned actions. Values-oriented impostor work can help you begin to equate 'success' with values alignment, regardless of short-term outcomes. From here, you can build toward a life that feels good, using values as your guide, rather than being derailed by 'shoulds' or impostor feelings.

In short, embrace the notion that you can live authentically while simultaneously experiencing impostorness. When you accept that your impostor-related discomfort comes from a drive to improve and a deep care for what you're doing, experiencing it can be met with vulnerability and curiosity rather than fear and doubt about whether you're enough.

By accepting rather than hooking into 'I risk being found out', you acknowledge it as part of your lived experience, rather than as an absolute truth. You no longer need to hide or fight it anymore; you can just allow the thought to be there. The commitment from this space is to vulnerability and values-led action, because this area of your life means a lot to you.

Next, let's explore how identifying your 'why' can further anchor to your values, help overcome your 'shoulds', and support your longer-term growth.

KEY TAKEAWAYS OF THIS CHAPTER:

* Impostor thoughts are normal and it's only necessary to tackle them if they impact your experience or actions.

* While the impostor experience was first investigated among academic women, it can arise in people of any gender and across various life domains, including work, parenting, and learning environments.

* Impostor thoughts and feelings can trigger safety behaviours like over-preparation, perfectionism, and avoidance / procrastination, which offer short-term relief but can reinforce the impostor cycle over time.

* The mindset of 'I should be / do / have more' can trap people in a loop of not-enoughness, where striving for more is never sufficient.

* Acceptance of what 'is', rather than focusing on what 'should' be, is key to values-aligned change and forward growth.

* Values-based exercises can provide a practical antidote to impostor thoughts.

* Integrating intentional breathing, mindfulness, and play into tasks can help you stay present and reduce anxiety, making space for curiosity and creativity rather than focusing on fear.

* Sharing impostor experiences with trusted colleagues can reduce feelings of isolation, or that you're the 'only one', or that your experience is different.

* Practical approaches, including reducing preparation by small increments rather than large leaps, and focusing on values-based goals, allows for gradual reduction of debilitating, impostor-related safety behaviours.

* During high-pressure moments where impostorness is high, anchor your actions to what matters most and personal meaning, rather than allowing your behaviours to be dictated by a fear of being unmasked.

* Values-based reflection encourages self-compassion by reframing impostor thoughts as evidence of caring, rather than being signs of inadequacy.

* Long-term fulfilment comes from aligning actions with your values, rather than from chasing external validation or trying to avoid impostor-related feelings.

CHAPTER 8
Connecting with Your 'Why'

> 'Everything can be taken from a man but one thing: the last of the human freedoms – to choose one's attitude in any given set of circumstances, to choose one's own way.'
> – Viktor E. Frankl [1]

Meaning and purpose help motivate us and enable us to flourish.[2,3] Furthermore, it takes practice to connect your actions with your 'why' and your values. In *Man's Search for Meaning*, psychiatrist Viktor Frankl describes humans as driven by a 'will to meaning'. In the book *Drive*, author Daniel Pink outlines how over and above basic rewards and punishments, humans are motivated by autonomy (the desire to direct our own lives), mastery (the urge to get better at something that matters), and purpose (the yearning to do what we do in service of something larger than ourselves).[4] When you align autonomy, mastery, and purpose with your core values, you find your own personal recipe for a fulfilling and successful life. And crafting your 'why' doesn't have to be in one grand statement; indeed you can create all number of 'whys' for activities or actions. Articulating 'why' helps you link your choices – big or small – to your values.

When you can articulate your 'why' around a specific decision, you're less likely to make excuses and avoid things that matter because they're hard. You're also less likely to do things that provide short-term validation or satisfaction at the expense of your longer-term growth. Your 'why' provides a bridge between knowing something matters to you and following through and doing it. It provides an ultimate expression of your values as a motivational compass, which unites multiple beliefs, needs, and goals in synchrony in a given context. This chapter explains why connecting with your 'why' is worth doing, even when it feels hard, for the sake of making decisions that feel great in the long run.

Chances are, at some point, you've struggled to make a decision. Perhaps the range of potential choices was so overwhelming you experienced 'paralysis by analysis'. Maybe the perceived size or importance of the decision caused you to feel overwhelmed, leading you to inaction. When facing indecision or being stuck in a cycle of inaction, it can feel tempting to believe that keeping things as they are allows you to put off making a choice until later. But in that moment, in doing 'nothing', you are making the *choice* to maintain the status quo. This choice comes with its own consequences and implications. The most insidious of status quo choices are those small, daily choices of inaction that seem so small that they don't matter but that take you away from where you want to go in life – in your character, career, relationships, or beyond. Even small choices contribute to your future, and you never know which decisions will turn out to be the big ones. Just as climbing the highest peak involves taking one small step after another in the right direction, your life is a tapestry made up of your choices.

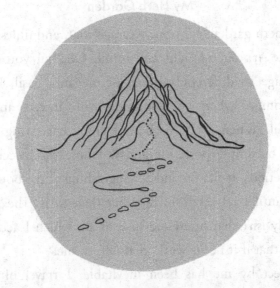

Whether a status-quo choice involves deferring your taxes to the point where you get a fine, staying in a relationship when you know you intend to leave, or consistently postponing exercise 'until tomorrow', it is remarkably easy to downplay the significance of maintaining the status quo on your growth and life trajectory. Now, what I don't want you doing as a result of me pointing this out is micromanaging every single choice – status quo or otherwise! Some actions in your day are far better automated rather than consciously chosen, and not all intentional, values-led choices will work out for the best. But often, when we're struggling to make a decision and perhaps facing paralysis by analysis, we become lost in the weeds and separated from what matters most to us. We've become focused on the minute detail rather than thinking about a longer-term, values-aligned 'why'. What I hope for you is that you can lift your head above the noise, and find greater clarity around where you want to spend your time and energy – more purposefully and intentionally – and make choices that enable that.

My Herb Garden

I love my herb garden. It's on my garage roof, and unless I actively go up there, it's out of sight and mind. Oh, but you should see it! From sage to different varieties of oregano, basil, lemongrass and chamomile, when it's humming with insects and flowers, it's beautiful. When it's at its best, I enjoy harvesting herbs and vegetables, or simply pottering and watching the insects. Yet, for extended periods, it sits untended, languishing at the bottom of my to-do list until I retreat from it rather than to it. The rest of my family really isn't that interested in it at all, which I accept, but it does mean that if it needs work, that falls to me.

Its neglect by me has been inevitable. I travel often, and I prioritise kids, work, loved ones, volunteer activities and exercise – basically everything trumps my herb garden. I lose touch with 'why' I have a herb garden, which is to feel connected to the food I serve people I love, and to have a peaceful space to sit in nature, replete with insects and sweet-smelling plants. It's as simple as that, but I overcomplicate it. I imagine my herb garden as if I have infinite time to spend on and in it. I get carried away with what I could do with it and how it should look. 'It must be the best herb garden I can create in the space,' I think to myself, before dreaming about what I could do, without doing a reality check. In anchoring to an impossible dream of what 'could' be, were I to devote far more resources to my little garden, rather than to my values-led 'why', the garden ends up falling short of where it could more realistically be. It took a long time for me to recognise I needed to meet myself halfway on this. That is, I needed to get real about what I need, when it comes to my rooftop garden, to fulfil its 'why' in the context of my busy life.

Not so long ago, after a period of inadvertent abandonment, I headed up to weed the garden. They had grown so tall, lush and thick I struggled to distinguish weed from herb. I stood there for a while, poking around, unsure where to start in the limited time I had. With furrowed brow I peered at the plants, wondering whether I should start pulling everything out or take just the most obvious suspects. Eventually, I did nothing. Paralysis by analysis set in.

When you focus on the details without understanding your 'why', you can become lost in the weeds – literally, in my case. Pulling out a few herbs along with the weeds would have at least let me use the herbs I'd intended to harvest while I was up there. But I didn't do that, and it was months before I finally ripped almost everything out. I had become so focused on what the herb garden 'should' be rather than on what I needed it to be, I found it an enduring source of guilt and a demonstration of my 'not-enoughness'.

Rather than focusing on the weeds as a sign of my shortcomings, I could have been making the most of the herbs for cooking. I could have been laughing at the weeds and celebrating them as a sign of an otherwise full life that takes me away from my herb garden. Yet, I paid attention to what it said about me that I hadn't done better with it, rather than paying attention to the positive side of what it said about me. I kid you not; it took a while for me to recognise that I was using my herb garden as evidence of my 'not-enoughness' and inability to prioritise. All that time, I could have been paying attention to how the herb garden's state was a testament to my prioritising things that really mattered to me – kids, loved ones, and so on!

Often, we delay choosing to change something because we fear the pain of what we will lose (in my case, the perfect herb garden) might outweigh what we will gain (a functioning herb garden albeit less fancy). We wait until the pain of maintaining the status quo becomes greater than the pain of making a change. But this waiting often comes at a cost.[5] Anchoring to your 'why' and using that and your values to guide your path can enable swifter, more effective decision-making, benefitting not just you, but your family and community.

By the time I finally got to weeding, I had to rip out pretty much the entire bed. The fear of what I'd cut off as a future option had held me back from taking action that, ironically, would have mitigated some of the loss. Because truth be told, the beds haven't been replanted with herbs and now (other than a few come-by-chance herbs) they're abundant only with regrown weeds! Rather than getting clear about my 'why' around the herb garden, I got bogged down in the small stuff as well as a grand vision that simply wasn't ever going to manifest as a reality.

Whether or not you care about herb gardens, you can apply the same logic to other areas of your life. If you're considering changing jobs, ending a relationship, buying running shoes or a new car, or fixing a leak in the roof – if it's a decision that comes with some pain, get clear on your values-led 'why'. Furthermore, intentionally go looking for what you might be afraid of losing in making this choice. As Marsha Linehan (and generations of Zen Buddhists) say, pain in life is inevitable, whereas suffering is optional – or put another way, suffering is pain without acceptance; that is, when we reject reality and the pain it involves, we suffer.[6] The gap between your actions and your values-based, 'why'-oriented choice represents your suffering because that gap represents a rejection of the reality that is. The larger the gap, the larger your suffering. Reduce the gap (either through moving closer to the desired state, or by letting go of it), and you reduce your suffering.

Core Values vs. Threat-Based Values

As we explored in Chapter Two, we can broadly categorise our personal values into core values and threat-based values, where TBVs reflect a subset of values that bubble to the top of our prioritisation when we feel our more basic survival needs are unmet. When connecting with your 'why', it's important to understand how your values influence your decision-making process. Again, this comes back to a general tenet in applied values work: action core values and *in*action threat-based values. In being avoidant with my herb garden, I was prioritising my threat-based value of Avoidance rather than noticing my inclination to do so, and reorienting to actions that would align with my core values around Connection and Family.

Core values align with your deepest aspirations and what you consider most important in life. They are the values that align with your self-determined 'authentic' self. They help underpin your long-term performance and wellbeing. When you connect with a values-led 'why', you're more likely to make decisions that enable lasting fulfilment and growth. Here, I'm not talking about one overarching 'why' but a smaller, more specific values-aligned 'why' that explains why you're motivated to take a specific action, or a group of actions toward a specific goal. The format of a 'why', big or small, is the same. It boils down to a simple statement of *'To ..., so that ...'*[7]

For example, if one of your core values is Creativity, your 'why' for taking on a challenging project might be: '*To* effectively convey my unique ideas, *so that* I can contribute meaningfully to my field.' Notice the first part of this statement describes the action, while the second part links to the prioritised values. This 'why' helps you connect with core values–oriented needs in ways that lead to longer-term satisfaction. But what about a 'why' that develops during a time of stress and threat? Without conscious thought, you might prioritise threat-based values that inform a surface-level 'why' that overestimates the importance of meeting short-term needs and underestimates the importance of considering a deeper, longer-term 'why'. For instance, my inadvertent threat-based 'why' was '*To* hold off on doing anything in my herb garden, *so that* I can try to find the time to do it properly.' It took values exploration for me to recognise this statement as a way of justifying maintaining the status quo – essentially out of avoidance.

The prioritisation of threat-based values is grounded in fear and insecurity, which are normal and natural responses, but this doesn't mean you need to focus on or action them. TBVs can be powerfully motivating toward actions that may appear to benefit us in the short term, but which run counter to the longer-term meaning-making we aspire to. For instance, Fred is a tennis player. As he has risen through the rankings and the stakes have become higher, increasingly he was driven to prioritise the threat-based value of Security around his game. His success was such that his family had come to financially rely on him playing well. He identified the 'why': '*To* play well and retain my ranking, *so that* I keep my sponsorship and earnings and can continue to support my family.'

While on the surface, the 'why' appears to be reasonable – to play well so that he can earn a decent living and support his family – on closer investigation with Fred, this 'why' linked to his TBV around Security, and it was having a detrimental impact on his game. Furthermore, because this 'why' also activated his values of Family and Achieve as a Team, the thought of not living up to it was met with a strong, negative emotional response. Fred had reached a point where he was playing fairly continuously under a veil of threat. It was little wonder his enjoyment had plummeted along with his consistency of performance.

Let's zoom out. What are the indicators for Fred that TBVs are driving this 'why'? Fred reports a sense of fear and concern around failure today. He is consumed by 'what ifs' that involve falling short of contributing on this day to his 'why'. He is not thinking about his 'why' in the broader context of his life and how his values of Family and Achieve as a Team are being more holistically served by his 'why.' Indeed, the Freds of the world (as Fred is, as you would expect, an exemplar of numerous clients I have had with similar experiences around this) report that there is a fixation on winning 'today'.

Connecting with Your 'Why' is Worth the Effort

Be it in sports or business or beyond, I see performers who reach this point harbouring so much attachment to the outcome today that there is no room for play, curiosity, or connecting with the present moment. Rather than an openness to and competitive hunger around the potential for success, the focus becomes on mitigating failure and the threat it brings. There is a focus on safety and security that adds a brittle, deathly serious component to the performance. This brittle seriousness not only erodes performance but sidelines values alignment and even acting in line with your version of an authentic self.

While Fred's thoughts, associated with his threat-oriented 'why', might have felt motivating in the moment as they pushed him to work hard, they were leading to stress, burnout, and preoccupation with 'what ifs'. His optimal performance in this state was far short of what it could be were he curious, present, and playful in spite of the stakes. And the thing is he knew he could do better – this compounded his suffering. The gap between his current performance and what he believed it could and should be was exquisitely frustrating; he knew there needn't be a gap but he didn't know how to close it.

In this example with Fred, and indeed when TBVs are in play, there is typically a focus on 'shoulds' – what you 'should' do or how the world 'should' be. There is little room for innovation, curiosity, and creativity in the present. The suffering associated with this 'should' compounds the sense of threat, which can serve to amplify the perceived 'should' even further. The beauty of intentionally inclining toward core values when considering your 'why' for a given situation is that your core values help you shift more readily into a mindset where you can hold space for what matters most to you in the long term. Sometimes, honouring what matters most in the long term necessitates taking a hit right now. Anchoring to your values enables you to weather such times.

When connecting with your 'why', it's worth pausing and reflecting:

- Is this motivation coming from my core values, or a threat-based value?
- Do I feel energised and positive, or agitated and fearful?
- Am I dreaming about what could be, or consumed by negative 'what ifs'?

Am I moving *toward* something that is driven by what matters most to me in the long term, or am I just trying to avoid a perceived threat?

Oftentimes, when threat-based values are in play and are infusing themselves into a 'why', this doesn't represent our complete abandonment of our core values. Rather, we're overlaying them with a need for safety or security, which is impacting on the nitty gritty of what we're focusing on, how we feel, and how we respond. One of the best things that you can do when formulating a 'why', that is one of the more important ones, is reflect on how your 'why' intersects with your core values. Ensure you have a values-based 'why' so that even when you're feeling threatened, you remain anchored to your 'why' from the perspective of your core values.

Let's recap on using values to ground your 'why' around a goal.

My statement of 'why':

'To ...   So that ...'

After your 'why' statement, consider the following:

- **How does this 'why' connect to each of my values?**
- **For each of your core values, reflect on how your 'why' helps you live in line with this value.**

For example, my singing-related 'why':

To uplift and move others through music, **so that** we can connect through meaningful experiences, fostering a sense of joy and achievement together.

How my values connect to my singing-related 'why':

Achieve Together: This is about collaborating with my fellow performers, tech workers, and the audience, to achieve the goal of making music, together. Making music takes a village and when the audience is moved and pleased, this is our moment of achievement, together.

Curiosity: My curiosity with the music keeps performances spontaneous and fresh, enabling both me and audience members to experience it for the first time, every time. The spontaneity and joy that flows from holding on to curiosity helps me move the audience.

Learning: My commitment to ongoing learning – moments in the practice room, researching works, learning them for the first time – is motivated by my desire to connect with and move people with music while maintaining a deep respect for the music and the rigour it requires.

Give without Expectation: I honour the music and my role as its conduit. I perform to the best of my ability, honouring authenticity over perfection for the sake of giving to the audience. I do so without preconceptions about the audience reaction, and without being derailed if the audience doesn't respond in the ways I hope for.

Gratitude: Being able to connect people with music that other people have written is something for which I'm deeply grateful.

Connecting your 'why' – whether big (why I sang for a living) or small (why I kiss and hug my sons goodbye when we part) – to your core values, can help you make decisions that align with the version of yourself you seek to grow into. The sorts of decisions that support your long-term growth and happiness. Connecting your 'why' with your core values does not stop you from taking into consideration practical concerns or threats that need attending to. Instead, it's about ensuring that more of your primary motivations come from a place of growth and authenticity rather than fear and avoidance.

Practical Exercise: Paying Attention to Develop a Values-Aligned 'Why'

Begin by taking three deep breaths, in through your nose, pause, and out through your mouth, and pause again. Please repeat this with two more breaths, nice and slowly, in and out, and include those pauses. Ensure that you breathe out fully, so that you're not banking air deep down low in your lungs (doing so can inadvertently support activation of the fight-or-flight response, which you don't need right now). Are you ready? Let's begin.

Bring to mind the area you wish to cultivate a 'why' for.

Remember that your actual 'why' will be quite simple: *'To ... So that ...'*

Consider a leadership position you hold, whether at home with another person or even a dog, in a community group, a classroom, workplace, or even a boardroom. In this leadership context: What do you pay attention to? What draws you to it? How do these two aspects align? Where do they diverge? Is there a way you can refocus your attention in this leadership role, to better prioritise what matters most to you? Your values can guide where your attention and priorities lie.

We can tend to prioritise surface-level 'shoulds' and filter for threats in areas we care about, which can lead to more 'shoulds': 'He shouldn't treat me that way' or 'She shouldn't have done that'. Prioritising short-term wins can undermine long-term, values-aligned actions that bring substance to our 'why'. Become intentional about where you direct your attention. With your values as your guide, reconnect with your 'why' in any given situation and reflect on how your values support it. If you find there is little alignment between your 'why' and your core values, reassess how this 'why' truly serves you.

What do you pay attention to?
What matters most?
What do you choose to prioritise?

Before moving into another case study, let's take a moment to recap on the invitation of this chapter.

Make an intentional practice of identifying your core values-oriented 'why' for goals that matter to you. It's natural for your focus to be pulled toward perceived threats, but hooking into associated thoughts and feelings can refocus you toward short-term survival at the expense of longer-term growth. Evaluate your 'why' through the lens of your values. Remember, a 'why' statement can comprise a 'to ...', which is action-focused, and a 'so that ...', which is values-oriented. Establishing a clear, simple, values-aligned 'why' you can return to repeatedly can help steady your course toward successfully completing a goal that matters to you.

Case Study: Jay's 'Big' Decision

Jay had had some success as a regular guest on a marketing-related television program. More recently, she had been offered a TV hosting role on a show related to her area. She came to me for help structuring her decision-making around whether to: (i) solely focus on growing her marketing and advertising company; (ii) grow her company alongside hosting the TV show; or (iii) fulfil a lifelong ambition of completing a PhD in an area of marketing and sport that was especially interesting right now.

While Jay needed to choose what to do, the three choices were interconnected in her mind. The television show might supercharge her current business if she could keep growing the business and still manage a gruelling TV schedule for nine months of the year. The promise and success of her business and her brand had landed her the TV offer in the first place. If she kept building this business, who knows where it might take her? If it went well, it would allow flexibility and autonomy of direction, alongside leaning into a growth strategy. She saw the research she was interested in undertaking as a game changer for her industry, bringing together new technology with existing methods that she might use to inform the trajectory of her business, leading to rapid growth down the track that might eclipse the growth strategy as it currently stood.

When Jay walked through my door, she appeared lost in the weeds. Each choice seemed abundant with possibility and fraught with downsides. She was considering each choice independently for its merits rather than all three against some higher benchmark of values alignment. She was focused on the pros and cons in general terms rather than digging deep and asking what matters to her, how her choices align with her values, and what her 'why' is in making the choice. She acknowledged that it was a terrific problem to have but that it was still a real problem for her as she was the one who would have to make the call on what would happen next.

Initially, when I suggested to Jay that we take a step back and consider her values, her look landed somewhere between dismay, horror, and frustration. She told me what she wanted was a roadmap to making a decision not a values map, and that she'd been to see other psychologists and coaches, and no one had provided that for her. She anticipated that delving into 'What is your North Star?' territory again was the last thing that was going to help her. I could understand this thinking because without a structured approach there can be a disconnect between values as ideals and values-in-action. This disconnect can lead to cynicism about the practical role and use of values. After hearing more about the process, however, Jay decided she was willing to give it a go.

It became evident that Jay believed that values were inherent, largely fixed once uncovered, and akin to personality traits – none of which are supported by the evidence base as I've discussed. Her attitude toward values-in-action was that there was a 'right' and a 'wrong' course of action, and that values alignment meant choosing the 'right' path. She also believed that such a path wasn't necessarily practical or pragmatic, and she assumed that it would fail to take broader life considerations into account. Additionally, she had assumed that somehow, she was simply meant to balance all her values at all times as best she could, rather than recognising that making trade-offs, and recognising values conflict as inevitable, is part of the work.

One of the benefits and necessities of core values work is that it pays to hold them lightly and flexibly, and they are what you make of them. It's important to recognise that values alignment is never going to be perfect, especially as you can't hold all values in equal priority; you need to make a choice as to which value(s) you prioritise in a given context. A values-led, goal-oriented 'why' can help inform and remind you of your values prioritisation.

The first thing to do when seeking to make a values-based decision is get clear on the broad decision you're looking to make. In the context of Jay, her question was: 'What am I going to concentrate on workwise?' Jay's decision is quite broad and that is how it often is. It is the choices that sit under the decision that will provide the substance and action potential. Choices offer alternative, optional pathways forward you can take for a given decision.

After identifying her broad decision, Jay needs to clearly identify the two or three choices that she is considering for this decision, which in this case she had already done:

1. **Focus solely on growing her marketing and advertising company.**
2. **Host a TV show while also growing her company.**
3. **Pursue a PhD in marketing.**

Then, she needs to ask herself: 'For this decision, how does each choice help me live in line with my values?' The task of working this through for each of your values is arduous but rewarding – the benefits outweigh the costs. Take the first choice, where Jay was focusing solely on growing her marketing and advertising company. Jay's core values included Achievement, Growth and Learning, Impact, Autonomy, and Curiosity. On rating each of her values against her choice to focus solely on growing her marketing and advertising company, she found that Autonomy was high, Growth and Learning was only so-so, Curiosity was so-so, Achievement was high, and Impact was moderately high. Trying to run her company alongside doing the TV show was high on Achievement but low on Autonomy, among other things. On the other hand, for 'pursue a PhD in marketing', Autonomy was moderately high, Impact was high, Growth and Learning was high, Achievement was so-so (which she justified on the basis of the timeline and opportunity cost of doing the PhD) and Curiosity was moderately high. As you're working through this exercise you can even jot down some notes about how it makes you feel.

As a sidenote, this is an example of how values truly are in the eyes of the beholder. I don't know about you, but I predicted different ratings for these value-choice combinations. Such is the individual nature of values and their meaning.

At this point, you might get a sense that it isn't just about the values ratings, but how you prioritise the values for the overarching decision, that makes the difference around what choice to make. And indeed, this is the next question to ask yourself during values-based decision-making: How will you prioritise your values for this overarching decision? Jay needed to decide whether Achievement was most important, or perhaps Curiosity, or Autonomy. Depending on how you've rated your values against each choice, plus how you have prioritised your values for the overarching decision you're looking to make, which choice comes out on top?

At this point, you might like to re-order (re-prioritise) your values to see how the order impacts on your decision. Place them in a different order. What happens? How does this affect which choice comes out on top? Quite often, the way you prioritise your values can have an impact on what the top choice is. That is, different values prioritisations elevate different choices to the fore.

In Jay's case, while Impact and Curiosity were important, Jay decided to prioritise Autonomy and Achievement in her decision-making. She was concerned about the impact of the TV show this soon on her company, and there were signs that the TV opportunity may still be there down the track. She also came to understand that her values made the PhD option really alluring, but in a finite universe where she couldn't do everything, it wasn't as much of a priority from a values perspective as creating a company with impact in the world more broadly.

This process of values-based decision-making provides you valuable reflection time and insight into how each of your core values will support those things that you hold most dear. Prioritising your values will likely help you identify and express your needs around relationships and goals, and how you wish to contribute to and achieve in the world.

I go into this process with this: when you live in line with your values, you are able to grow further into your authentic self. When these values are at their best – optimally guiding you toward areas that matter to you and that align with your capabilities – you may encounter less resistance to achieving meaningful goals. It won't always be easy, but it will feel right. This alignment fosters your version of a life well lived, though it takes time.

Prioritising values during decision-making helps you avoid choices based on 'shoulds'. Wherever possible, try operating from a place of what *is* by accepting the present, as well as focusing on what is most important to you in the long term, rather than getting caught up in 'should'-based fantasies that cause you suffering and keep you separated from the growth you seek. Values-based decision-making navigates you to what 'is' rather than what 'should' be, with a longer-term view of what to do. It can also help you step into the realm of discomfort and growth, with a clearer notion of 'why' you want to bother.

The Role of the Comfort Zone

When you feel this sort of psychological-meets-physical discomfort, consider what you want to do about it – not to stop or avoid it – but based on why you're stepping toward discomfort in the first place. Before turning away, ask yourself: What matters most to me here?

If you're like the rest of us, your first instinct is probably to avoid discomfort. We're wired to seek comfort and safety, and we live in a world where we are surrounded by systems and structures designed to minimise our discomfort – whether physical, cognitive, interpersonal, or psychological. From participation ribbons in school that reduce the sting of a perceived loss, to algorithms that curate our digital content and filter our opposing views online, we've created structures that shield us from discomfort. Yet, not all discomfort is 'bad'. In fact, some discomfort is essential for growth and transformation.

Note that I'm not talking about extreme situations – external or internal – that induce discomfort. I am not talking about the discomfort associated with a diagnosable mood or anxiety disorder. Such a level of 'discomfort' can be almost unbearable, is treatable, and if you are experiencing it please seek professional mental health support. Over recent decades among the general population, however, other milder forms of discomfort have been seen as inherently 'bad' or unacceptable – something we must avoid, shut down, escape, or mitigate. This avoidance can lead to the intensification of such feelings when we face a similar situation again. Not all discomfort should be avoided, especially when it is tied to personal growth or important values. Recognising this distinction can help shift your perception on discomfort from something to escape to something to engage with.

Maggie was afraid of flying. Each time she hopped on a plane for work, she would feel an overwhelming sense of panic and unease. She had even hopped off a plane feigning a tummy bug on one occasion, and had to catch a plane the next day. Yet when she flew with her family, she was okay. Upon reflection, Maggie realised that her strong sense of responsibility to her three kids was part of her response. When travelling with them, she would think, 'Well, we're all in this together no matter what happens to the plane,' but when flying alone, her fear was leaving them behind and something happening. Maggie's discomfort wasn't just about flying; it was about the deeper conflict between prioritising flying (with a low risk but with huge consequences for her kids) versus being with her kids. As well as systematic desensitisation and structured psychological work, it was important for Maggie to reframe the role of work travel as supporting her kids and their futures. This meaning-making enabled her to find the courage to travel for work as planned more often, and in so doing the symptoms of discomfort began to dissipate. Additionally, Maggie became more visible as a leader in her workplace and began to find herself fielding more opportunities there.

Discomfort often signals that you're stepping outside your comfort zone – and that can be a good thing. On the other hand, your comfort zone is where you feel competent and unthreatened and spending time there can be valuable, too. But here's the key: your comfort zone is dynamic. When you stop stretching beyond it, it shrinks. Mild discomfort is an opportunity to expand or at least maintain your comfort zone. To protect it over time and move in the direction you want, you need to persistently step into discomfort with activities that align with your values.

This brings us back to the idea of 'toward' moves. A toward move is a values-aligned action that takes you toward discomfort and toward the version of yourself you seek to cultivate. An 'away' move, by contrast, takes you away from discomfort but also away from the version of yourself you want to grow. Moving toward personal growth, contribution, and self-actualisation requires toward moves. And you can't move *toward* the version of yourself that you wish to become while avoiding all discomfort. You need to be the courageous hero of your own journey.

I have noticed a growing source of discomfort is answering phone calls – one I can relate to as I have already mentioned! Zoe, a client of mine, came to me initially for performance coaching involving her singing and speaking work. But as we worked together our work broadened into helping her become more comfortable with discomfort around perceived rejection, and also a fear that she might be seen to reject others. One area she wanted to address was taking phone calls. As a performer and speaker, Zoe received a lot of phone calls, including many unsolicited calls from people asking her to perform or speak, sometimes as a favour.

Previously, Zoe had tried to answer these calls and deal with the inquiries in real time. Over time, she had stopped answering calls from numbers she didn't recognise, and eventually she stopped answering calls from most friends, too. By not answering, her discomfort with phone calls grew, and her concern about not being able to handle any requests associated with those calls justified and exacerbated her sense of not being able to answer the calls. She reflected on missed calls from people she would have liked to speak to. Including opportunities she might have missed – opportunities to build relationships or take up work.

Noticing discomfort in an area that matters to you presents an opportunity. It's a chance to get clear on your 'why' – to identify which values are influencing your choices, how they're serving you, and whether they could serve you better. Zoe's 'why' for *not* answering the phone was: 'To avoid phone calls, so that I don't have to let anyone down by saying no to something, or so that I don't end up on the phone far longer than I have time for at that time.' Zoe reflected on this 'why' as a way of dealing with threats, and her values-based desire to be a collaborative and friendly person, who valued connection, too.

Zoe was very driven by connection. It showed up in her work as a performer and a speaker. Part of connecting with people was being accessible, and embracing serendipitous opportunities from which things could grow. She came to define her 'why' when it came to answering the phone as 'To be open to unlikely moments of serendipity and opportunity that come my way via my phone.' This was grounded in her values of Connection, Curiosity, and Equity.

What she needed alongside this 'why' were some strategies for triaging calls in a way that made answering her phone sustainable and manageable. She worked up a system. For unsolicited calls around singing or speaking work, as quickly as possible she'd say, 'Thanks so much for thinking of me. I can't talk right now but feel welcome to call my agent, Lisa, on …' She committed to ending these calls within five minutes, as previously she'd let them drag on. At first this was challenging but it got easier and left her feeling terrific. There were even a few unsolicited calls where it was fruitful workwise. For friends and colleagues, she would answer but also be realistic about how much time she had. Over time she shortened her 'why' to a mantra – 'serendipity and opportunity' – she'd remind herself of, in combination with taking a couple of deep breaths, before answering the phone.

Zoe had considered the choices she was making in not answering the phone as relatively inconsequential. It was only looking back over time that she realised her efforts to avoid challenging conversations were not only undermining the values she held as most important, including Connection, they were exacerbating her discomfort when faced with answering future calls. Her attempts to remain in the comfort zone had required her to retreat further and further to the middle, as the circle reduced around her. And her growth – in relationships and job opportunities – had suffered as a result of this. The realisation that the growth zone lay in the zone of discomfort was what she had needed to help her jumpstart her moves *toward* discomfort.

The Zones of (Dis)Comfort and Growth

Let's recap on the zones of (dis)comfort and growth again. I think of it like a bullseye, where your zone of comfort is in the middle. Remember that your zones of comfort and discomfort are dynamic, and they're constantly shrinking or expanding in proportion to one another (as comfort shrinks, discomfort expands, and vice versa). When you take steps outside of your comfort zone, into discomfort, you enter a band of growth potential. When you study for a test – and endure the discomfort of grappling with unfamiliar concepts – that is in the growth area. When you navigate a difficult conversation – that, too, is the growth area. When you do something new – growth area. And as always it's about pushing into that area – which is in the zone of discomfort – in ways that are meaningful to you and aligned with your values. As you push into your growth area, a subregion of your zone of discomfort, your comfort zone can expand and make room for some of what you have learned and experienced, as it's not so new and uncomfortable anymore.

As you keep travelling out from your comfort zone, through the area of growth and further into discomfort, your potential for growth initially gets larger before it gets smaller again. Once you are in the realm of deep discomfort where overwhelm and unmanageability come into play, it is no longer productive discomfort to engage with. It becomes hard to perform or function effectively. One of your tasks is to make calls on what values-aligned discomfort is manageable – what is still in your area of growth – while recognising that in order for you to grow, you need to push into your discomfort. Because ultimately, 'growth' is about expanding your comfort zone, not just by taking away any negative feelings or sensations, but by making sense of them and allowing them to be there in manageable ways.

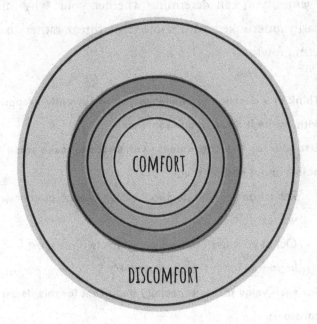

Connecting with your values and your 'why' can enable you to take a leap and make an action even when it's uncomfortable, in order to increasingly bring to life the version of yourself that you wish to cultivate. In Zoe's case, answering the phone only mattered because for Zoe it enabled her to better action her value of Connection – answering the phone meant she could forge genuine and valuable connections with more people. This doesn't mean there's a universal law around the benefits of answering the phone – only that for Zoe, it's a values-led action she identified as leaving her more values-aligned in life. Look for those small ways that you can take action to enhance values alignment in the small choices you make every day. Seek out toward moves and take them.

Practical Exercise: Identifying Your 'Why' for a Decision
This exercise helps you identify your 'why' for a current decision or challenge you're facing. By reflecting on how a decision relates to your values, you can determine whether your 'why' might be unnecessarily interlinked with short-term threat rather than your longer-term growth.

1. **Think of a decision or challenge you're currently grappling with. Write it down in one sentence.**
2. **List your top five core values, with space to make some dot points about each of them.**
   - Reflect on how this decision relates to each of your values.
   - Out of your five core values, which two are most important for this decision and why?
3. **For each value that is especially important for this decision, consider:**
   - If I were to prioritise this value above all other parameters for this decision, what is the values-led action I would take? Why? (Remembering this is hypothetical, and a way of getting to what values-led actions look like in the context of this decision; you're not yet making a decision on what to do. You're just getting to a 'why'.)

4. **Now, consider any threat-based values that might be influencing your thinking:**
   - Am I motivated by fear and avoidance in some way? If so, how?
   - What am I afraid might happen if I make this decision? To what extent do such consequences justify me prioritising threat mitigation over long-term growth? (There will be times when it is justified, but they will be in the minority.)
5. **Reflecting on your answers, write a 'why' statement for your decision / challenge that connects to your core values:**
   - *To ... so that ...*
6. **Review your 'why' statement:**
   - Does it feel authentic and motivating?
   - Does it support you for the longer term?

* * *

In the next chapter, we'll dive squarely into values-based decision-making as one of the most valuable resources you can bring into your life.

KEY TAKEAWAYS OF THIS CHAPTER:

* Purpose and meaning are important ingredients for motivation and flourishing.

* Values inform personal purpose and meaning.

* There is power in having clarity around a simple 'why' for a given moment or task.

* Crafting a simple 'why' statement can fuel your resolve at times when you need it. It can help align actions and decisions with values.

* Giving voice to what matters most regarding a situation or action can make it easier for you to follow through on it.

* *In*action does not delay the act of decision-making; *in*action is an action and is a choice. A choice to maintain the status quo.

* Choosing the status quo comes with consequences and implications, just like any other choice.

* 'Paralysis by analysis' can erode value and growth potential over time; values can help cut through the shiny stuff and the noise to help you make important decisions.

* Growth lies beyond the comfort zone, and expanding the comfort zone requires moving into and becoming more comfortable within the area of discomfort. Doing so makes more space for meaningful experiences and growth.

CHAPTER 9
Values-Based Decision-Making

There's a parable across multiple cultures that speaks to the multifaceted potential of how we can respond to any given choice, however small or large. The Cherokee parable involves a grandfather telling his grandchild about the two wolves that are waging a battle within each of us. The 'bad' wolf is driven by qualities such as envy, regret, greed, arrogance, self-pity, guilt, resentment, inferiority, dishonesty, false pride, superiority, and ego. The 'good' wolf is driven by peace, love, hope, serenity, humility, kindness, benevolence, empathy, generosity, truth, compassion, and faith. When the bad wolf has the upper hand, our actions are dictated by it, whereas when the good wolf has the upper hand, it guides our actions. The grandchild asks their grandfather, 'Which wolf wins?' The grandfather replies, 'The one you feed.'

The Power of Values-Based Decision-Making

Let's work with this metaphor in the 'Parable of Two Wolves' a while longer. Feeding one of your wolves is achieved whenever you hook into thoughts associated with it or follow through on actions that flow from its beliefs, needs and aspirations. The implication is that both wolves are an inevitable part of each of us. The thoughts and the desire to act in alignment with each of them are inevitable, too. But the desire to act does not necessitate that you take the action. The best you can do is let your values guide you, so you can grow into the version of yourself you are most proud of and fulfilled by over time. It is pointless to try to rid yourself of the 'bad wolf'; accept its presence and associated thoughts and seek to make space for them, while guiding your attention back to thoughts and desired actions that flow from your 'good wolf'.

When we consider qualities associated with our 'bad wolf' as strange, abnormal, or 'bad' we experience shame. When we feel shame, we can further focus on thoughts and aspirations that flow from our 'bad wolf'. Sure, we may focus on them to push them away, but we are still paying attention to the 'bad wolf' and inadvertently feed it. Your values-led growth necessitates you making room for both wolves and feeding your 'good wolf'. There is no need to feel shame over this proverbial bad wolf, given its inevitability in all of us. Shame can lead us to hyper-focus on the negative aspects of ourselves, inadvertently giving the 'bad wolf' more power and attention. Breaking this cycle involves practising self-compassion and recognising that experiencing negative or unhealthy thoughts or emotions is a natural part of being human.

Instead of fighting or denying the existence of the 'bad wolf', we can acknowledge its presence without judgement. This acceptance helps us redirect our focus and energy toward nurturing the qualities represented by the 'good wolf'. By aligning our actions with our core values, we feed the 'good wolf'. In turn, we foster qualities that are meaningful to us, including more universal qualities such as kindness, curiosity, and play. In practical terms, this means making conscious choices that reflect your core values. For example, if a situation triggers resentment (a 'bad wolf' quality), acknowledge these feelings without acting on them. I will soon stop with the wolf metaphor because I want to get back to talking about your mind. In reality, there are no 'two wolves' – your mind isn't separable into 'good' and 'bad'. Rather, your one incredible mind is doing what it can all the time to keep you alive, and for that you can be thankful. But the story highlights how sometimes, thinking in simple, binary terms can be helpful when deciding how to act. This is why thinking in terms of 'toward' and 'away' moves can be so helpful.

A simple question to ask yourself when considering which action to take is, 'Is this a toward move or an away move?' As discussed in Chapter Five, a 'toward' move takes you toward the version of yourself you're working to become – 'good wolf' territory. Toward moves align with what matters most to you; that is, they're aligned with your core values. Away moves take you further away from the version of yourself you seek to grow into over time. Away moves are often characterised by misalignment with your core values and tend to be rooted in threat-based thoughts and feelings. Quite often, away moves are attempts to escape discomfort, but in doing so, they also move you further away from the version of yourself you wish to grow into.

The problem with over-prioritising threat-based values and the decisions that follow is that they erode long-term value for the sake of short-term survival – often when survival mode wasn't even necessary. Growth typically benefits not just you but your broader community as well. By choosing away moves, you reduce the potential for that value to travel outward like ripples on a pond. Through values-based decision-making, you not only mitigate threats for yourself, you help inspire others toward their own growth-aligned core values. In today's world, the importance of values-based decision-making cannot be overstated. It is vital, for us as individuals and as a collective.

Habit-Based vs. Effortful Decision-Making

Human decision-making is impacting the trajectory of the planet more than ever before. Values-based decision-making is the process of applying growth-oriented values – specifically, your core values – to the decisions you make.

Many of our decisions are routinised and automated, managed by habits. This is incredibly useful for rinse-and-repeat decisions or those that are predictable and based on 'if, then' scenarios that help us maintain the status quo.[1] Habits also play a crucial role in managing cognitive load, freeing up our brain power so we can focus on challenges or novel situations that require effortful thought. But what about decisions that arise from new, unexpected situations, which cannot be automated and require careful consideration?

Values-based decision-making becomes especially relevant at times when effortful thought is required. It allows you to handle relatively novel scenarios with consistency and continuity. Before we dive deeper into values-based decision-making and its benefits, let's first contrast it with habits.

VALUES-BASED DECISION-MAKING

Barack Obama famously wore the same colour suit throughout his presidency. In an interview with *Vanity Fair* reporter Michael Lewis, Obama explained, 'You need to focus your decision-making energy. You need to routinize yourself. You can't be going through the day distracted by trivia.'[2] By 'routinising yourself,' Obama was referring to 'behavioural automaticity' – structuring your life in a way that reduces the number of trivial decisions you need to make, allowing you to focus your cognitive capacity on more important matters.

Behavioural automaticity helps increase the likelihood of you taking certain actions by structuring your environment accordingly. For example, stocking your fridge with healthy food rather than junk food increases your chances of eating healthily without needing to rely on willpower in a moment of hunger. Conversely, if your fridge is filled with cheesecake and hotdogs, you're more likely to eat them. We can build habits that support behavioural automaticity (such as consistently buying the same colour suit, or stocking healthy food), and in turn, behavioural automaticity can help forge new habits (like having healthy food on hand supporting healthy eating patterns). How we eat, exercise, socialise, and spend our time is impacted by our establishing and maintaining habits, good or bad.

You can think of habits as a type of behavioural automaticity. Habits involve patterns of behaviour (or thought) that run on autopilot, triggered by contextual cues in our environment. These cues prompt automatic responses based on our prior experiences.[3] Using the language of Thaler and Sunstein, whether we are 'nudged' by our environment's design or by habit triggers,[4] this process taps into our metaphorical 'default mode network' – also known as 'System 1 thinking'.[5] Here, decisions are made quickly and without much deliberate thought. We simply 'do' (through an action, thought, or emotion) based on prior instances of similar situations where we've habituated a specific response.

In contrast, values-based decision-making involves effortful, active thought – what we might call 'System 2 thinking'. This is reserved for decisions that we don't want to or can't automate, either because they occur infrequently, they're complex and require careful deliberation, or they involve a high level of ambiguity where we don't have all the facts. My invitation to you would be to complete a 'choice audit' where you review your habits and other choices you make using autopilot, and assess them for values alignment before further committing them to habit. In addition, I invite you to more systematically deploy values-based decision-making for choices that use more deliberate thought.

Values-based decision-making involves making choices that align with your core values and longer-term goals. It requires a deliberate and thoughtful process, where you take time (even if only briefly) to reflect on what matters to you and how each potential decision aligns with your fundamental beliefs and desired outcomes for the future. Values-based decision-making goes beyond habitual or automatic responses, instead focusing you on the underlying motivations and principles that guide your life. The 'why' behind a values-based decision can motivate you to follow through on the action or behaviour. Grounding decisions with your values provides the bridge that helps connect knowing something is good or right for you with actually following through and doing it. In other words, values form part of the motivational- and goal-oriented knowledge-action bridge.

Decision-Making and Choices

Values-led choices are the different values-led courses of action you might consider when making a decision. Rather than overwhelming yourself with numerous options, I recommend narrowing it down to two, or at most three, lead choices for a given decision. You can work through the values-based decision-making exercise later in this chapter (see page 267) for this.

Values-based choices that are committed to are the practical expressions of values-based decision-making. Each choice represents a tangible step toward living a life aligned with your core values and long-term goals. Your task is to determine which choices best support your longer-term version of a fulfilling life. Committing to a choice doesn't just involve weighing up your own long-term personal satisfaction or immediate pleasure; it's about considering what really matters to you. For instance, becoming more climate- or conservation-conscious may not necessarily improve your day-to-day comfort but might align with your values by contributing to a legacy that benefits future generations. Yet, the reality is that this long-term goal is achieved through making small, cumulative, impactful daily choices that align with this goal. Your values contribute to that aforementioned 'knowledge-action' bridge by providing you with the motivational impetus – the 'why' – to stick with such daily choices even if they come at the cost of convenience or expense.

Values-based decision-making is not independent of forming habits. When you start with a brand-new action that you wish to habituate, it can be highly motivating to be clear on 'why' it's meaningful for you, by connecting it to your values. That is, you can use values to help intrinsically motivate you to repeat an action until it becomes a habit.[6] Once a behaviour becomes habitual, the initial 'why' may fade into the background, as there is momentum in the habit. Take physical exercise, for example. Many of us have, at some point, aspired to be fitter, yet our motivations for wanting to do so can greatly vary. For instance, perhaps we're driven by shorter-term external rewards around aesthetics, or perhaps by longer-term longevity-related reasons. Getting clear on our values-aligned 'why' when establishing habits to support multi-step goals can provide us the motivational impetus we need to stick at it.

Decision-Making to Motivate Now: The Story of Jill and Terry

Jill had long-term fitness-related aspirations to help her lead a long and healthy life. She described her thoughts on fitness as 'too wishy-washy', adding, 'I really do care about my long-term health, but I struggle to come up with shorter-term goals that might get me moving more regularly.' She had a short-term goal of working out three times a week. She felt that focusing on long-term health benefits wasn't enough to drive her immediate actions. Jill also rejected extrinsic short-term motivators like appearance, dismissing them as 'superficial'. She was searching for a deeper, values-aligned source of motivation to create habits that would last.

I shared with Jill the story of Terry, who over the past seven years had been very effective at sustaining a high level of health and fitness. Terry had identified certain key ingredients that enabled him to follow through with regular exercise. These ingredients link to his values of Adventure, Achievement, and Connection.

Rather than focusing on his long-term goals as a rationale for daily practice, Terry found coordinated activities to sign up to, including fun runs and more recently even Iron Man competitions. Further, Terry always signs up with his friends rather than solo, and as a team they raise money for charity. The amount of money is not large, but the commitment to the team and the charity galvanises the follow-through and satisfies Terry's desire to contribute to causes he cares about. In taking this approach, Terry is satisfying his longer-term, values-led goals around health for life, but he does not have to bring that to mind regularly. Instead, he has found more frequent ways of building toward the longer-term goal in ways that incentivise him in the shorter term. In essence, he approaches these group activities as adventures, which enable him to connect more closely with friends, and provide him with a sense of achievement. He reflected that when he misses a training session these days (especially a group training), he experiences it as a values conflict, especially around his value of Connection. He has intentionally cultivated the association between his values and the daily and weekly activities so as to build that motivational knowledge-action bridge that values provide.

Over time, Terry's involvement in physical activity has become more habitual and momentum-based. He identifies as a 'fit guy'. He kicks the ball around with his kids at the local park and generally finds ways to be regularly active. He links his values of Adventure, Health, and Family to his fitness-related pursuits in ways that provide a 'why' to his actions and consistently motivate him to get up and move. Terry did not stop with exercise, though. He took a similar approach to behavioural automaticity and found ways to build motivation and habits around his dietary choices, too.

Terry works in consulting and finds himself eating out a fair amount. One day when RSVPing to a dinner invitation, in a moment of curiosity, he ticked the 'vegan' box on dietary requirements. Terry isn't a big meat eater, but he doesn't by any stretch consider himself 'vegan'. However, this simple act of ticking 'vegan' shifted Terry's thinking around eating out. He noticed something interesting about his vegan meal at the function, which was reinforced on subsequent outings thanks to his new tendency to tick the 'vegan' option. His meal appeared a lot more intentional. He mused to me later that there seem to be certain ingredients that are regularly paired together in standard meals; flour and butter, or egg and pastry, for instance.

Suddenly, unfettered from the typical animal–non-animal pairings in catering kitchens, he was experiencing different combinations including some he did not expect to enjoy (but often did). Quinoa and roasted vegetables, chickpea and avocado salad, baked cauliflower steak, black bean and corn-stuffed peppers.

He mused that he'd played around with 'vegetarian' before, but found that eggs, dairy, and often pastry, too, were regular stand-ins for meat, whereas 'vegan' meant that these weren't called on in the same way. By seeking to adhere to a vegan diet when out of the house, over time he lost several kilos, especially around his middle and he achieved a 'new normal' weight. He attributed this to the one tick-box exercise of 'choosing vegan', as other things by this stage were already being held constant. He found himself learning more about vegan meals and integrating them into his home life, too. He and his family began eating far more vegetable-based meals, albeit still with steak on the side for his meat-loving teenage kids.

A combination of starting with a 'why', integrating behavioural automaticity, and adopting habits over time, transformed not just Terry's approach to food and his longer-term personal health goals; they were starting to have an impact on his carbon footprint; on the packaged foods he no longer consumed, for instance. The momentum was still building, too, as he had more conversations with his family around packaging, rubbish, and what they consumed. Slowly but surely, this exercise of living more in line with his values for the sake of his longer-term health was seeping into other values that were important to him and his family, and indeed to shorter-term choices that he increasingly recognised as stepping stones to the version of himself he wanted to grow into.

As for Jill, I ended up setting up a call between Jill and Terry, so she could hear more from him directly about his trajectory to the present day. Around four months later, Jill completed her first fun run (with a combination of running and walking), recommended by Terry. She did so with a small group of friends who decided to raise money for a foundation that supports breast cancer treatment, as a member of the group had gone through treatment several years prior. The process of doing so had Jill training several times a week with her teammates, meeting at a local park at 6 am. In further 'tweaks' inspired by Terry's unapologetic values-first mentality that questioned and sought to remove barriers to values-led actions, Jill had started sleeping in her workout gear, popping her trainers on and getting out the door in record time to make training.

The group now have their sights set on another fun run. They consider themselves a team, working together toward a series of achievements or short-term goals, with a collective longer-term goal of building togetherness, memories, and good health for life. They've even given themselves a nickname – the 'lifers' – which is not only a nod toward their health goals but to their commitment to one another these days. In turn, Jill has found her longer-term goal of longevity and good health was more multifaceted than she first thought. The social component has taken on a new dimension of meaning, both enabling physical activity for longer-term health, and contributing to longer-term health through its direct contribution to her improved sense of belonging and mental health.

The Importance of 'Why' in Decision-Making

When you can clearly articulate the values-based 'why' that makes sense of the goals you seek to achieve, you can better grow purposeful energy, or motivation, to help you achieve your goals. The motivation you unlock can help you automate values and goal-aligned actions that are repeated actions. But what about the actions that are, quite simply, really hard to turn into habits, or to relegate to your autopilot?

If you conduct a values audit of your habitual behaviours and thoughts, keeping those that align with where you want to go and gently over time letting go of those that don't serve you, you'll free up more space for deliberate thinking that is necessary for other, more deliberate, choices. Harvard University physician and psychologist Professor William James said in the late 1800s, 'The more of the details of our daily life we can hand over to the effortless custody of automatism, the more our higher powers of mind will be set free for their own proper work.'[7] I suggest values-based decision-making is the 'proper work' that Professor James referred to.

In the case of Jill and Terry, the more they managed to automate behaviours that supported their health and wellbeing, the more satisfied they felt *and* the more mental capacity they had for personal and professional growth. When we can automate more of our basic needs, we create greater bandwidth to pay attention to needs associated with what Maslow called self-actualisation and self-esteem. These higher-level needs are almost impossible to automate, even with an abundance of resources. Returning to Professor James, we free up the mind to get down to its 'proper work' of what matters most.

Pay Attention Where It Matters

William James also observed, '*Voluntary attention is always derived*; we never make an *effort* to attend to an object except for the sake of some *remote* interest which the effort will serve.'[8]

In other words, at times when we purposefully guide our attention in one way or another – whether it's to perceived criticism, capsicum, or the temperature of the water we're drinking, it's because we believe doing so is valuable. And given our mind is an incredible judgement machine whose primary job is to keep us alive, it is less effortful to guide our attention to short-term gains that provide for our survival, comfort, and pleasure, than it is to guide our attention to longer-term yet less clear-cut gains that benefit our growth – even when those rewards tend to be larger.

What would you choose – eating your favourite sweet treat today or working toward a healthier body in a month's time starting now? If you're like me and the majority of our fellow humans, you'll be drawn toward the sweet treat today. If you choose the sweet treat, you might have an inner dialogue of something like, 'Tomorrow, I'll start eating healthier.' Furthermore, if you chose the sweet treat yesterday (or chose not to exercise yesterday, to continue health-related behaviours), you're more likely to repeat the behaviour today.

There are times, however, when we consciously choose to resist the sweet treat in favour of future health benefits, or we hold back from outwardly expressing our frustration at our child or coworker in favour of preserving the relationship or maintaining our sense of self. In these moments, we resist acting on short-term rewards, even though it involves some discomfort now, prioritising our future self and choosing the relative present pain that comes with it.[9] So – it's *possible* to do. But to sustain this, it helps to be clear on that 'future interest' – our 'why' – which is served by actions that support the long term. It can also help to remember that you're essentially choosing a smaller amount of short-term pain to avoid the longer-term, more enduring suffering that arises when you widen the gap between where you are and where you want to be. When you focus on your values-aligned, goal-oriented 'why' in the moment of choice, it strengthens your ability to make the hard choice of growth and fulfilment. In doing so, you choose to minimise the longer-term gap over immediate gratification.

When we remain unclear on a values-based, growth-oriented 'why', we are more likely to keep choosing the status quo until the pain of staying the same becomes greater than the pain of change. If you've ever been in a relationship that you knew needed to end, or a job – even a career – that was making you miserable, and you put off the decision to leave but eventually did, you know this dynamic. Often, we wait until the pain of staying outweighs the pain of making the hard call.[10] This comes with an opportunity cost – the cost of the opportunities missed by being tied to people, places, and things that no longer serve you. This cost means losing out on the values-aligned growth and fulfilment you might otherwise have fostered.

How we motivate ourselves – how we incentivise ourselves and direct our attention when making choices – affects our likelihood of reaching our goals. It's essential to build a motivational bridge across the knowledge-action gap; that is, between knowing something is important, and actually *doing* it.[11] And while individually oriented goals such as personal fitness are more tangible for their long-term returns, it can be more difficult to pin down the specifics – such as the 'what, how, when' – of collectively oriented goals. The bigger the collective goal, the more ambiguous and uncertain it can seem, making it easier for us to underestimate the impact of our individual contributions.

Yet, our decisions around how we interact with one another, how we care for the environment, or how we think about the bigger picture have an impact on collective outcomes – not just for the direct contributions we make, but also by nudging the collective mindset in one direction or another. When we repeatedly make choices that don't align with our core values, we miss opportunities not only for personal growth but for collective progress. I am not trying to promote any particular course of action here, but rather, to invite you to consider this question: 'Are my choices contributing to a threat-based trajectory built around short-term survival at the expense of the longer term, or a growth-oriented trajectory for myself and my community more broadly?' My premise is that in focusing on identifying what matters to you, and living more in line with your values with that in mind, this takes you and indeed us all further in the direction of growth.

Values-Based Motivation to Achieve Your Goals

It's especially important to find a sticky, meaningful 'why' behind decisions that involve short-term pain for long-term gain. Let's explore how you can motivate yourself to achieve goals in a way that goes beyond relying on fleeting inspiration or enthusiasm. Rather than focusing on superficial results – like the fitter body in the example above for instance – I encourage you to dig deeper. Ask yourself: Why is this goal truly important? For an athlete, for example, rather than just focusing on winning that gold medal, focus on what the act of transcending your potential will mean to you in the longer term, and given that, how you need to act each and every day starting today. It's extraordinary how fleeting even the greatest accomplishments become in retrospect. Who you want to become, not just what you want to achieve, tends to increase in importance as the years go by. In turn, who you are becoming has an impact on what you can achieve.

Big Decisions Need Effortful, Values-Based Decision-Making

As we've already discussed, the current interest in how we can build good habits in our daily life is vital for managing life and decision-making so that we can reduce cognitive load and deal with the challenges of a volatile, uncertain, complex, and ambiguous world. Good habits free up our cognitive capital that we can put toward matters requiring deeper, deliberate thought. But good habits alone are just the beginning. Many of the world's greatest challenges that impact us as individuals and as a species need collective choice and collective action to effect the necessary, coordinated response required.

Values offer an exciting avenue for future research and applications to close the gap between what an individual claims is important to them (environmental sustainability, for instance) and actions that would bear out this importance. It appears that values-based decision-making may hold the key to training our brains' reward systems to feel satisfaction from making choices aligned with our core values, even when those choices offer no immediate external reward.[12] This is especially important given that it may be impossible to adequately habituate or nudge entire populations to the sorts of behaviours that are necessary to mitigate threats emerging in the modern world.

It will be essential to constructively utilise media and algorithms as part of motivating groups of people toward values-oriented 'whys' associated with constructive collective action, but in ways that afford the individual agency through assigning a layer of their values atop the decisions they make and the reinforcement they receive. For this, we must get better at values-led thinking that helps foster positive emotional responses that provide motivational impetus to values-aligned actions that benefit us all with larger, later rewards. This involves getting clearer on our values and on the assumptions that keep us making the same choices that fail to serve us or reflect how we seek to grow and develop over time. It's time to think more laterally about how our values operate in our lives, and how we can use them more actively to help us grow.

Values and Functional Fixedness

The next time someone has a strong, emotionally charged response to something, dig a little deeper into what values might be in play for them. In my experience, when someone presents a strong argument around a particular belief, it's often rooted in a fixed notion of how that belief, and the actions associated with it, support a value that is especially important to them. The challenge is that when high conviction accompanies a belief – driven by a felt sense of that conviction rather than rational argument – trying to argue against it rarely yields progress. Instead, it can be more effective to explore the values driving the emotional response, which may be leading to a certain belief being surfaced and reinforced through the loop of belief activation, going looking for evidence that supports that belief, emotional reinforcement of the validity of the belief, triggering further evidence gathering, and so on.

I find common ground can be sought more readily when we focus on values rather than beliefs. In fact, values can provide the lens through which someone might re-evaluate a belief in a given situation – not by abandoning it, but rather by modifying the assumptions they have about the relevance of a belief in that situation. Before I provide a direct client example to illustrate this, allow me to detour briefly (but relatedly) into 'the candle problem'.

Have you ever marvelled at a child's ability to find new uses for everyday objects? My son Cas came home from school one day and told me, 'Mum, there's a nice fish tank in the hard rubbish down the street. Can I bring it home and use it?' My first thought was 'Oh no, another responsibility – fish!' I was already imagining the feeding, cleaning, and ethical concerns of keeping fish in a small bowl. Thankfully I didn't say this aloud. Sensing my hesitation, Cas explained, 'I want to make another terrarium, it's the perfect size, and I can use the plants growing outside.' As we walked to retrieve the fish tank, I smiled at my assumption that a fish tank must mean fish. Cas reminded me of our 'functional fixedness' as we grow older (and my determination to fight the good fight against it over and above what's useful!).

The Candle Problem

Functional fixedness involves our assumptions or biases about how to use objects and concepts. It's a tendency that increases as we age, where we view things for their specific, known functions or uses at the expense of seeing other functions (or solutions) they might offer us. Psychologist Karl Duncker's famous 'candle problem' illustrates this. The test involves a challenge: You're given a candle, a box of thumbtacks, and matches, and asked to fix a candle onto the wall (a corkboard) and light it without letting any wax drip onto the table below. If you're unfamiliar with the problem, think about how you'd go ahead and solve the problem before continuing to read.

The solution is to think differently about how you might use the materials, perhaps even about the wall you're affixing things to. Consider all parts beyond the constraints initially presented to you or the assumptions they might conjure for you. From a different vantage point, the thumbtack box becomes your candle holder; the thumbtacks can affix it rather than the candle (with the candle inside) to the corkboard wall, thereby suspending the candle on the wall and catching any dripping wax.

As we age, our tendency toward functional fixedness increases, along with our propensity for cognitive biases.[13] We become more likely to make systematic, personalised assumptions about situations due to our past experiences and learnings. Psychologists Daniel Kahneman and Amos Tversky might refer to these as 'prediction errors' because they explain the difference between our expectations or evaluation and 'reality'.[14] Interestingly, emerging research suggests that human values may predict – dare I say even present a personally calibrated understanding of – individuals' cognitive biases.[15]

This is in part why I argue elsewhere that personal values can help explain the differences between how different people make decisions and evaluate the world. Values have the capacity to explain individual-level prediction errors, which is what makes them so powerful when it comes to embedding human-like qualities (including our best bits!) into human-like artificial intelligence (AI). Together, values and actions enable personalised predictions not just about *how* but *why* you or I might interpret the same situation differently. Values wouldn't have this explanatory and predictive power without their role as schemas, their impact on our biases, or their connection through to our actions and emotions.

Returning to the candle problem, it's a great example of 'functional fixedness' during problem-solving – but this concept isn't confined to inanimate objects. We often make assumptions about what someone else means or feels based on their actions or expressions, with our values and broader biases shaping how we interpret these cues. We view the motivations and intentions of another person through our own lens of what 'that' action or expression most likely signifies.

Similarly, someone who holds the belief that 'family' involves a woman caring for her children may experience functional fixedness around this idea. As a mother, when travelling for work I reliably field the question: 'Who is looking after your children?'; my husband, Didier, is yet to be asked this question. Rather than hooking into the 'belief' that this question came from narrow-mindedness or signified something negative about the asker, I found it helpful to remember the role of functional fixedness. And from here, these days I think of Darryl – a client I'm about to introduce you to.

Darryl's story reminds me that people can experience functional fixedness around the concept of 'family'. A person may feel a values conflict when confronted with a family structure that varies from their own assumptions or beliefs about what 'family' means, but that does not mean they're not amenable to this changing over time. Assumptions and beliefs about what a complex concept like 'family' signifies can be reshaped by cross-referencing them against our values, getting to the root of what really matters to us from the vantage point of those values, and taking actions that align with our intentional, needs-based change in perspective. When we appreciate a values-aligned rationale for shifting our assumptions, this provides motivation and a 'why' around going to the effort of doing so.

Darryl's Story: Moving Beyond Values as Assumptions

Darryl was about to become a grandfather and he was at a loss as to what to do. All his life, he'd held the belief not only that a 'family' consisted of a husband and wife, but that the husband was the breadwinner and the wife cared for the children. In Darryl's eyes, the security and sustainability of the family unit relied upon these roles remaining strong and intact. Already, perhaps you can see the link here for Darryl between his value of Family, and the assumptions he is making from a security-oriented perspective about what 'family' necessarily constitutes. The first challenge for Darryl had been that his daughter, Trish, had married the love of her life – Tanya. Darryl had prioritised threat-based values involving Control, Avoidance, and Moral Vigilance around this union. He hadn't attended the wedding and had effectively become estranged from his daughter and daughter-in-law.

Before seeing me, Darryl hadn't explored his rationale for his discomfort. He had held tight to his belief that a family 'should' consist of a man and a woman coming together to raise children. However, the news of a grandchild on the way had stirred things up for Darryl, and he was motivated to find a way of 'handling' the situation with his daughter in order to have a relationship with his grandchild, who he considered an 'innocent' in the situation. In time, the irony was not lost on Darryl that the motivation to make a change came when his value of Family was activated by the news of imminent grandparenthood. He was motivated to live out his value of Family as a grandfather and father of a daughter who was about to become a mother.

When Darryl came to me, he came to 'Learn some ways of coping with my daughter being in a gay relationship and having a child, as I want to be in my grandchild's life.' Initially, when I asked, 'How would you like things to be different?' (I'm paraphrasing there), he replied, 'Well, that's no use as I can't rewind the clock. She's married to a woman, pregnant; she's having a child. There's nothing I can do about any of it.' On probing his thoughts about same-sex marriage, it became apparent that his concern was for his daughter not having a 'proper family' and that this might involve financial and social instability.

It's worth remembering that Darryl's complex concepts around family had been shaped over a lifetime. His functional fixedness around family roles stemmed from the importance of those roles in his own family during challenging times earlier in life. However, with the arrival of a grandchild coming, Darryl was motivated to find another way. Over time, he adjusted his outward responses based on intentional, values-based decisions about how he wanted to show up for his daughter and her family. Eventually, as his perceived sense of threat diminished, his internal beliefs shifted, too, and he came to find enjoyment and delight in his expanding family.

When Darryl first came to see me, he believed his daughter's choices were the source of his pain, rather than his own frame of reference. And I can guarantee it would not have helped if I had said to him, 'Well, it's your thinking that needs to change.' Darryl needed to take his own journey, not only to reach the right destination for him but to experience the relief that a reframe can provide. Simply telling him to reframe would not have worked.

We began by exploring what 'family' meant to Darryl and how this concept had developed. Initially, Darryl associated family with distinct, traditional roles as I've mentioned. He attached feelings of security and stability to these roles and associated them with feeling loved, protective, and protected. He described a sense of comfort and 'rightness' about the world when returning home to his family when he was a younger father, especially when his kids were small. He approached these roles a bit like a 'rudder' for the family; without them he felt a sense of uncertainty and extreme discomfort and unease. He had interpreted these feelings as reflecting some 'truth' about his beliefs, and from here he brought in further evidence to support the importance of maintaining traditional roles in a family.

Through our work, Darryl came to recognise that his discomfort was not necessarily a reflection of reality but a result of his own experience, programming, and values activation. Further, he realised that his desire to have a positive relationship with his daughter, daughter-in-law and grandchild was sufficiently strong as to enable him to move *toward* the discomfort and the version of his life he wished to grow into. He stopped avoiding his daughter and daughter-in-law, and perhaps most importantly began letting go of the 'shoulds' around what a family unit must look like.

To get to this point, Darryl had spoken at length about housing prices, the influence of social media these days, and the relentless connectivity for kids once they reach their teen years. He lamented how hard it was for any young family these days, let alone one that was 'different' and how much he worried for his daughter. We gradually broke down 'roles', which he had initially anchored to quite rigidly, into underlying 'needs' of love, financial security, support around identity formation, and ensuring kids had time with parents.

During the fourth session, Darryl turned to me and said, 'You know, Greta, it's suddenly occurred to me. It doesn't matter whether my daughter works or is gay; she has everything to be a great mum, and so does her partner. Thinking about all the ingredients of Family we've talked about, they have them.' His shoulders dropped, the creases around his eyes loosened, and it looked like a weight had lifted. To his surprise, his discomfort had diminished over time, his concern for his daughter's financial and social security had, too, and ultimately he was left wondering, 'I don't know what all the fuss was about. What was I thinking making a mountain out of a molehill? Imagine what I could have missed out on.'

After that, we had another two sessions to wrap up and work through how he was managing the repair work needed with his daughter and daughter-in-law (in his words, he'd been 'a bit of an ass' with them). He took a values-led approach, recounted our work to them and his realisation, and took time to work through some specific areas of hurt including his absence at their wedding. He was prepared for resistance from them, but to his delight, they welcomed him back into their lives and, when the time came, the life of his grandchild.

Breaking values down into beliefs (Darryl's past experiences), current needs (to have a relationship with his daughter and her family), and future goals (being part of his grandchild's life) can be a valuable way to gain insight and grow. This process helps personalise values and update them, unearthing unhelpful assumptions that may drive a shadow side to one's values or lead to a perceived values conflict. It can make them more flexible, resilient, and aligned with our goals. It motivates us to question assumptions and find ways of living more purposefully as individuals and as social beings.

Darryl's story exemplifies how breaking down ideological differences through a values lens can shift the dialogue beyond polarisation, making room for negotiation and mutual understanding. In a world filled with complexity and ambiguity, we need to accept the worthy role of functional flexibility while also challenging our assumptions where they are not serving us in moving forward constructively.

The candle problem and Darryl's family dilemma highlight how assumptions, if left unchecked, can create decision-making constraints that don't serve us. These examples show how, when we perceive discomfort ostensibly around beliefs, it's worth digging deeper to find potential values conflicts. From there, we can explore our deeper needs that are in play. For Darryl, his care for his daughter was tied to a need of security and safety, associated with unchallenged assumptions about his value of Family. In prioritising what mattered most to Darryl when it came to Family, he was able to challenge those assumptions that were causing him personal and relational pain, and intentionally choose other values-based actions that aligned with longer-term goals around Family.

Applying Values to Small Choices

When it comes to values-based choices, there is a tendency to apply this just to the big stuff: for instance, whether to buy a house, move city, take a certain job. After all, these are the decisions that are especially novel, where we have particularly limited information about the implications of one choice over another, and the 'leap of faith' is especially large given the level of 'known' and 'unknown' unknowns. But there are little choices, which involve decision-making, that we make every day, which impact on the trajectory of our self-development and our life. A big one is how we respond to other people and treat them. More often than not, we don't think about how our behaviour not only impacts others but sets us up to respond next time. I suggest values-based decision-making to take you in the direction of the version of yourself you seek to grow into over time.

Another area where we can apply values-based decision-making to our daily practice is around behaviours that we seek to ingrain and habituate to. That is, where you want to make a conscious decision to make a change that sticks rather than maintain the status quo. It might be a context where at some point you can use behavioural automaticity and rely on habit to make something happen, but right now you need to anchor to and use your 'why' to establish a pattern of behaviour.

Let's revisit a theme we touched on earlier, featuring Jill and her desire to start exercising, but this time, I'll use myself as the example. A while back I decided to get back into running three times a week for at least 40 minutes per run. I'd selected my route, chosen the time of day, and even purchased new running shoes. I was all in! My first run was set for Sunday morning at 7 o'clock, leaving me enough time to get home, shower, and have breakfast with my family before the day gets underway. But I woke that Sunday feeling unusually tired, so I hit the snooze button. Suddenly, it was ten past seven. 'If I get up now, I'll only get in a 30-minute run.' I hesitated – will it even be worth it? As I mused on this, the minutes ticked by. Now I had 25 minutes. Should I still go? I don't know. 20 minutes. 15 minutes ... It doesn't feel worth it now; 'I'll try again next time,' I told myself. The same thing happened again the next time, and so on, until occasionally I'd run, but not three times a week as I had planned. On reflection, what mattered most was not the amount of time I ran but getting out the door at all and setting up momentum to form that routine.

This is an example of self-imposed constraints, where we can unintentionally create mental barriers to success by narrowly defining what success looks like.[16] I set myself up in a way where smaller, but what turned out to be important steps, felt insufficient or like a failure. If my goal had simply been making it out the door *at all* – any time between 7 and 7.40 that morning – and running *at all* while I was out there, I probably would have made it. In this case, even one minute would have been a win and something to build on.

These constraints on success didn't just undermine my habit formation; they reduced my chances of doing something I'd identified as important for my longer-term wellbeing. Beyond that, I internalised my failure, turning it into a small but cumulatively impactful part of a narrative about my inability to follow through: 'See, you won't stick to this. Why bother setting an exercise goal? And you wasted all that money on new shoes.'

If you, like me and many others, struggle to consistently make it out the door in the first place to exercise, then your first goal could be just that: making it out the door and exercising for at least a minute at the times you commit to. The 'why' behind 'just getting out the door for a minute' is likely to differ from your larger goal of 'running for 40 minutes' (and that aspiration is still in the picture, just not active yet). And instead of a perfectly acceptable 'why' like, 'To run for at least a minute when I say I will, so that I build a regular running habit,' you can create a values-based 'why' that taps into your deeper motivations. For instance, 'To run for at least a minute at these times, so I can create a practice that energises me, and helps build my confidence and momentum for lasting change.' Your 'why' behind these micro-goals can remind you of why even a seemingly small action, like running for just a minute, is important for your long-term growth.

Your values-based 'why' helps build the motivational bridge between *knowing* something is good for you, like exercise, and *doing* it (bridging the 'knowledge-action' gap).[17] To build this motivational bridge, you need two things: a clear 'why' and a manageable gap between what you 'know' and what you intend to 'do'. While I had high conviction about the benefits of a 40-minute run (the 'knowledge'), the gap between this knowledge and my ability to act on it proved too wide. I needed to start with a smaller action (and a commensurately smaller gap).

I also could have tried to create a stronger motivational bridge by making my 'why' even more values-oriented. But in my case, the real issue was I needed to reduce the size of the gap between knowledge and action, not strengthen the 'why'. In other cases, however, like studying for a test that will arrive one way or another, it pays to focus on building a strong motivational bridge with a well-defined, values-based 'why'. The stronger the 'why', the easier it will be to take action, even when a task feels overwhelming.

Doing anything – especially when it's uncomfortable – becomes easier when you feel compelled by a motivational force beyond just a 'should'. Having a reason to do something involves articulating why you 'want' or 'need' to do it. Simply saying 'I should do this' won't provide the motivation or sufficiently connect the act back to your values. Furthermore, as we humans are contrarian creatures, we can find ourselves mounting resistance against a 'should'.[18] And unless your goals align with values that are important to you, you won't feel that sense of drive that can stand in for habits until they're formed.

Let's recap what we've discussed. Decisions you make today involve you making a choice that typically involves future action or a goal – whether it's doing the dishes in 30 seconds time, calling your mum on Wednesday, or climbing Mount Kilimanjaro in a year. The key is to ensure that your choice aligns with your values, you build a solid 'why', and make sure the 'what' is manageable and doesn't involve constraints that overly limit your chances of success. Not every action needs to be consciously considered for its values alignment – it's unlikely that doing the dishes will get this sort of treatment, but if you *were* to think about it, chances are doing the dishes would in fact link back to what's important to you and your values. This is where functional *flexibility* comes in – an ability to look beyond the narrow-use cases we typically ascribe to our values, in order to recognise their deep involvement across our lives.

The candle problem as an example of functional fixedness demonstrates the assumption-based constraints we can place around decision-making or problem-solving. We can make unconscious assumptions that limit the values-led choices we make. We can build in functional flexibility by using our values more adaptively to guide our actions. It is worth examining the choices you're considering through the lens of what is most important to you. Look closely at the top two or three choices and consider why they're in the mix. If

'Do nothing' is one of the options, it deserves to be scrutinised for its pros and cons just as much as the others – it's a choice in itself. And where there is a choice, either that you want to make but know that you're not going to, or a decision to make where you're unsure which way to go, it helps to get clear about and connect with your 'why'.

Practical Exercise: Implementing Values-Based Decision-Making

This exercise becomes easier with practice. Over time, it will feel increasingly intuitive and less effortful. To integrate it into your routine, consider spending some time each week (on a Sunday, for instance) identifying several hypothetical decisions you may face and establish values-based choices around them. Having a repertoire of these scenarios under your belt can be useful when you're faced with real-time dilemmas that require quick, values-based thinking.

The process starts by clearly identifying the decision you're looking to make and then identifying two or three lead choices you're choosing between. Once you've made a decision and one choice is committed to as the course of action, it becomes a values-based goal. Keep in mind that you know the least about how well a goal fits you at the time you set it. So, evaluating and readjusting it along the way is perfectly fine. Indeed, I'd go so far as to say, part of values-based decision-making is remaining open to changing or abandoning goals where closer scrutiny or more information reveals their values alignment is not what you thought it would be. Let's begin.[19]

1. Identify a Decision
- Write down a decision you're currently facing. It could be a major life choice or a smaller, everyday decision. Keep it broad, simple, and brief at this stage.

2. Identify Lead Choices
- List two or three potential choices. If 'doing nothing' is one of the options be sure to include it.

3. Rate Your Core Values Against Each of Your Lead Choices
- To prepare for this step, first list your values names and your one-line definition of each, so that you can keep referring back to them easily.
- When you're ready, consider how well each of your lead choices aligns with each of your core values.

4. Prioritise Your Values for the Overarching Decision
- You need to prioritise your values in order of importance for this decision. Which value will you identify as highest priority? Which is second-highest priority?

5. Assess Your Responses
- Given how you've rated the alignment between your values and your choices, and how you've prioritised your choices, which is your most values-led choice?

6. Reflect on Your Values-Led Choice
Write down your reflections. For instance:
- How does your final choice resonate with you?
- Are you ready to commit to the choice? If not, what is holding you back, or what other information do you need?
- Does it feel like an authentic, growth-oriented choice that meets your needs now and in the future?

VALUES-BASED DECISION-MAKING

If you're not ready to make a decision, that's absolutely fine. You can try changing the way you prioritise your values to see how that impacts on what emerges as your values-aligned choice if you wish. However, be clear with yourself on your commitment. For instance, if 'doing nothing for now' is your commitment, then be clear with yourself about that and the implications that will flow from it.

Once you have committed to an action, be clear on the goal associated with this choice:

> How long will it take to achieve?
> When will you check in so as to re-evaluate and make any necessary adjustments along the way? Weekly, monthly, quarterly – it's up to you.

There are some further questions you might want to consider – but if you're inclined to overthink things to the point of inaction, can I suggest treading lightly with these. For some people, the most important thing is breathing, connecting to the present moment, and really working to focus in on what needs doing right now rather than zooming out and becoming overwhelmed by the enormity that is a reality of any audacious goal if you choose to see it that way. With that disclaimer out of the way, here are some further questions some people find helpful.

> If this is a multi-step goal, what is one small action you can take today in service of your values-led choice?
> Is this a one-off action, or something you will be repeating? If it's a repeatable action, how often and for how long? Diarise this now – with a brief note: 'in service of ...' and include your highest prioritised values in the diary entry.

- Are there other small upcoming actions you wish to diarise now?
- Is the gap between knowing you want to do this, and the action itself, able to be bridged successfully? How can you strengthen this bridge, for instance by enlisting the support of friends, tweaking your environment to nudge you in the right direction, and getting clear on your 'why' in order to boost your motivation and resolve.

7. Compose Your 'Why'

- Informed by the values you're prioritising as part of this decision-making process, compose a concise, simple 'why' that is short, memorable, and feels authentic for you. This 'why' is something you can come back to at times when you need to remember why making this choice matters to you. It's the backbone of that motivational bridge that connects 'knowing' and 'doing'.

8. Reflect and Adjust

Once you're underway with actioning a choice, you can reflect on how it's going. This can be after completing the goal, or partway through.

- How has working toward this goal made you feel?
- How is it enabling you to grow into your values-aligned, authentic self?[20]
  - Has it supported *consistency* of your values-in-action?
  - Has it supported your *conformity* to that best version of yourself you seek to action (not a version based on 'shoulds' or others' expectations)?
  - Has it enabled you to forge genuine *connections*?

- Has it provided you *continuity* – that is, does it honour your goal of 'becoming' more aligned with your values-led self over time?
- What adjustments would you like to make?
- If relevant: What would need to be true for you to abandon this goal altogether?
- What (if any) timelines would you like to assign to secondary choices you're thinking about in relation to this goal?

* * *

Values-Based Decision-Making is Worth the Effort

Values-based decision-making gets easier with time, practice, and patience. Using a structured approach, especially in the early days, helps you bypass the 'shoulds' of modern life and connect with what matters most to you. It provides clarity on how your values translate into actions. I can pretty much guarantee that early on you'll be applying this approach to 'big' decisions, like where to go on a holiday, whether to take a job or even whether to start a family. But as you practise, you'll begin to recognise its utility in everyday life.

Over time, you may become more intuitive with applying your values in one moment to the next, thinking, 'Ah, in this moment I want to prioritise Achievement and work late tonight.' Your intuitive grasp of values prioritisation and alignment will begin to provide you the courage of your convictions to make such decisions with greater clarity and unapologetically. Instead of working through the full values-based decision-making exercise using all your values, you'll zero in on which ones are most relevant (i.e. highest in priority) for the current context. Values-based decision-making provides a powerful framework for navigating the multitude of decisions we face daily – those that aren't yet on autopilot or can't be. It helps unearth assumptions we might be carrying, and opens the door to recognising biases that influence not just our own decision-making, but also our expectations about how others 'should' be making decisions.

By aligning your decisions with your core values, you can create a life that feels more authentic and fulfilling. This approach helps you move beyond the immediate pull of threat-based values and short-term gratification, allowing you to focus on the 'larger, later' rewards that truly matter to you and foster the growth you've been seeking.

The journey to mastering values-based decision-making is ongoing and relies on your willingness to reflect on and sometimes challenge your assumptions. Each decision of yours, big or small, presents an opportunity to strengthen your connection to your values and grow into the version of yourself you aspire to. I encourage you to consider how you can bring your values closer to the forefront of your daily choices. In doing so, you won't just be making decisions that feel good, you'll be crafting a life that deeply resonates with who you know yourself to be.

KEY TAKEAWAYS OF THIS CHAPTER:

* The 'Parable of the Two Wolves' offers a reminder that we become what we pay attention to and action over time.
* Values-based decision-making can help bridge the gap between habitual responses and deliberate thinking and action.
* Functional fixedness can limit creative problem-solving and decision-making.
* Exploring the role of values can help reduce rigid thinking associated with tightly held beliefs.
* Applying values to daily decisions (like how you treat others) can help shape long-term growth that feels right.
* Values-based decisions don't need to be limited to big life choices; values-based responses can be applied to smaller, everyday decisions.
* Some practical tools for values-based decision-making include choice audits to help identify how well current actions align with values, engaging in 'small steps' to reduce overwhelm and build momentum, and use of mantras and clear 'why' statements to support motivation in challenging moments.
* With practice, values-based decision-making can become more intuitive and less effortful.
* Over time, values-in-action can support the development of an 'authentic' self and reduce the pull of external 'shoulds' or short-term shiny stuff.

CHAPTER 10
The Worthy Role of Values at Work

In this chapter, the focus turns to applying values in a work context. We will start exploring the role of organisational or company values and how this role has evolved over the last decade. In addition we'll look at the relationship between individual and company values.

Company Values Humanise the Organisation

The values of a company enable its people, customers, and broader stakeholders to understand what it stands for – its priorities and expected behaviours[1] – and be inspired by them.[2] They help define the core of 'who' the organisation is by humanising it and enabling connections with others. Company values provide the blueprint for action and decision-making, giving everyone a common understanding of the organisation's identity and the attitudes, appetites, intentions, and behaviours that flow from it.

Company values guide the communication style of those who act on its behalf and signal to those who come into its orbit, 'This is who I am.' In turn, people can judge whether they wish to connect more closely. Because values transcend day-to-day similarities and differences, they can offer an inclusive 'cultural campfire' for gathering around. These values act as a compass, providing guidance and identity. They inform what constitutes aligned actions or decisions both short term and for the longer-term strategy, and they help attract the right people.

Having clearly articulated values is informed by and helps guide the organisation's risk appetite, helping determine which opportunities the business should pursue. This is vital when signalling to prospective employees or customers, 'These are our values, and this is the level of risk you can infer from our values.' In essence, a well-articulated set of values says on its behalf, 'This is who we are, and these are our priorities now and over time. Do they align with yours?'

Case Study: Sazzamply and Attracting the Right Talent

Sazzamply is a fictional SaaS-based software company.[3] After a decade, it is still growing rapidly. With around 1,500 employees and a global footprint, it offers sustainable resource-management tools that help companies reduce their environmental footprint through efficient resource management. Using machine learning, it provides data-driven insights into their current footprint and suggests actionable steps that facilitate long-term reduction along with cost reduction.

Sazzamply's employees bring a diverse array of values and interests, which enable the company to function cohesively while benefitting from the innovation and critical thinking that different perspectives allow. This diversity of thought helps protect Sazzamply from 'groupthink', where people too readily agree, and encourages healthy debate and the exchange of ideas.

Alongside this values diversity, Sazzamply's people share common ground via their shared commitment to the company values. Their appetite for uncertainty and associated risk aligns with Sazzamply's industry, life stage, and mission (although it varies internally – with those in finance being less risk tolerant than those in sales). More broadly, Sazzamply's values signal to its people what is needed to thrive at the company, including a willingness to work fast while recognising that change happens incrementally, not all at once.

Sazzamply's Values

Earn Trust Every Day	Trust isn't simply given; it's earned in every interaction, decision, and action. We act with integrity and transparency as part of our daily practice, ensuring we can stand by our data, research and product. This enables us to build strong, lasting relationships with customers whose trust provides us the freedom to innovate.
Sustainable by Design	Sustainability is a foundational principle that informs everything we do. From eco-friendly remote workspaces to product development, we embed sustainable practices deeply and creatively into our operations.
Supporting People, Together	When people come together, they can create magic. We recognise collaboration, understanding one another, and care for the whole person as parts of an intentional practice, not something that 'just happens'.

We Move Fast, With Alignment	In our world, speed matters – but so does direction. Staying flexible, responsive, and values-aligned, enables us to adapt to change and seize opportunities swiftly while remaining aligned with who we are at our best.
Small Steps and Giant Leaps	Our future is shaped by our actions today. Innovation is equal parts creativity, rigour, and questioning the status quo. We balance small steps to improvement with paradigm-shifting leaps. Both are necessary for innovation.

Now over a decade old, Sazzamply's tween self in some ways resembles a mature company, yet still has many of the hallmarks of a young company, too. While product market fit was established years ago, it continues to evolve and Sazzamply's growth trajectory hasn't yet stabilised.

Sazzamply's needs around systems and processes, and the right personnel for its current maturity, continue to evolve, too. Early on, like many new companies, its values had focused on developing and shipping product over people matters. Values like Agile Minded and Ship Fast were prioritised to maintain a focus on iterating quickly and making sales. More recently, Agile Minded was changed to *We Move Fast, With Alignment.* Further, *Supporting People, Together* was added to address the importance of culture and collaboration. These adjustments also came from a need to mitigate an emerging unspoken value of 'Work and ship at any cost', which had led to unsustainably long work hours, the loss of top talent, erosion of quality control, and ultimately, the beginnings of associated customer churn.

Initially, Sazzamply's values helped attract the right talent for a high-growth startup. As the company became (relatively) more stable and mature, it began attracting a more diverse group of talent including those who valued (and therefore need) structure and security. This cultural inflection point can be a rough ride, as scaleups like Sazzamply increasingly need people who appreciate structure and early employees can begin to struggle with the new systems and processes coming in. Yet early on in this phase of tightening up systems and processes, the new hires at Sazzamply who needed more structure found themselves struggling with the relatively high level of uncertainty and the growing pains inherent in a fast-growing startup, which aren't apparent from the outside but become visible once you're in the (metaphorical) building.

However, on closer inspection, there were hires in this group who worked out extremely well. Specifically, people who held values around structure / security, teamwork, *and* creativity tended to thrive in certain teams. It was apparent that the managers of those teams personally held these values and brought out these values-in-action among their team members. They were adept at taking their teams through tasks in ways that served these values. For instance, one manager, Sue, had developed a system of 'micro milestones'.

Sue encouraged her team to break down projects into smaller, achievable milestones (goals). Structured feedback on these milestones provided a good sense of the team members' progress and direction while allowing them to creatively refine and iterate as needed prior to the next milestone. Sue also shielded her team from the potential negative impact of uncertainty associated with Sazzamply's rapid growth. Similarly, another manager, Jason, developed his team identity and purpose by taking time to establish their shared vision and contingency plans, helping his team feel more prepared for changes.

These supportive practices that involved fostering a sense of trust, accountability, agency, and creative problem-solving, turned out to work for everyone in the team not just newbies with needs around security. It became apparent that the solution to navigating the people needs of Sazzamply would not be solved by screening out people who highly valued Security, but rather looking at a potential new hire's values in combination with one another. As Sazzamply discovered, everyone has security-related needs to some extent, and going some way to meeting these needs is beneficial. What proved important for the Sazzamply culture was ensuring that such people also held 'social' values around Care for Others or Teamwork ideally, as well as individual, growth-oriented values around creativity.

Sazzamply recognised a need to signal to the market not just what the company *does* but who Sazzamply *is* at its core. This shift was crucial for attracting the right people and to enable those people once they were 'in the building' both around expected behaviours and decision-making. Over time, Sazzamply improved its ability to signal its values to the market, assess alignment during recruitment, and cultivate that alignment across the employment lifecycle, especially in the early weeks and months.

* * *

On the one hand, companies like Sazzamply strive to embed and action their company values in ways that enhance performance. But what happens when a company lacks clearly defined or actively implemented values? One thing is for sure; even in the absence of regularly articulated and enacted values, there will never be a true absence of values. Values always exist, even if unspoken. They are inferred through actions, and whatever is understood as the most important or 'true' values of an organisation will ultimately guide its behaviour.

The Problem with a Values Vacuum at Work

You can probably think of companies with two sets of values; one set is stated and the other set is practised. The stated set is displayed on the wall and the other is understood through what is prioritised when the rubber hits the road. This duality is deeply divisive. At best, it breeds cynicism, and at worst a tendency for employees to adopt a *further* shadow value; one of 'appearances matter more than substance'. Over time, this state of play can undermine the fabric and integrity of the organisation.

I have never encountered a company that intentionally set out to have two divergent sets of values. This divergence seems to occur when leaders underestimate the relevance and role of values both day to day and over time, not just as stated but baked into practice.

When initially establishing values, it's important to avoid taking a siloed approach where a single department or level is wholly tasked with identifying and defining the company values. And while leadership involvement in values identification is key, ultimately everyone in the organisation needs to be brought on board, no matter the company size. Further, values identification and refinement is the 'easy part'; the more arduous and important part of values practice is connecting values not only to strategic pillars but all the way down to individuals' daily decisions and ways of working. This requires a deep embedding of the importance of values in company culture. It necessitates buy-in and demonstrative action from the top down, and belief in management's commitment to values activation from the bottom up.

Identify the Company's Needs for Values

The process of identifying and refining values should be holistic and take into account internal and external needs, based on the company's lifecycle stage and market conditions. Ideally, the executive team owns this process with the CEO playing a leading role in executing the values plan. This helps ensure a broad understanding of the company's needs when developing values, signals commitment from the CEO (which serves as powerful social proof internally that values matter), and helps bake in a connection between values, strategy, and action.

Sarah Rushworth, in her doctoral thesis on values within fast-growing, founder-led Australian companies in the mid-2000s, distilled company values into three areas of utility for the organisation. That is, businesses tend to consider the benefits of values across one or more of three overlapping areas: strategic, enabling, or tactical.[4] She linked them to the 'how', 'what', 'why', and 'who' behind business operations.

Assessing Values Fit for the Organisation

BENEFIT	HOW, WHAT, WHY, OR WHO	QUESTIONS & DESIRED OUTCOMES
STRATEGIC	A long-term view on *what* and *why* an organisation formulates its strategy.	Do our values help us: • Generate trust (internal, external) • Grow / retain reputation • Forge integrity • Retain a focus on what matters • Prioritise effectively • Make decisions

ENABLING	Identifying *who* the right people are: workers, customers / clients, other stakeholders.	Communicate & embed 'this is who we are'
		• Align the workforce
		    Attract the right talent
		    Hire for alignment
		    Grow alignment over time
		• Signal to external stakeholders
		• Maintain identity during expansion & under remote working conditions

TACTICAL	A guide to action: *how* to do things.	Expected behaviours: • 'What we do' • 'What we don't do'

Interestingly, Rushworth's research showed that most companies at that time initially introduced values for strategic and / or enabling reasons. Few did so for tactical reasons (i.e. helping employees understand expected behaviours) or reported that tactical benefits had been gained from rolling out values. From my own values work with organisations, today there is ample interest in using values as a means of guiding behaviour, as well as their utility in offering strategic and enabling benefits.

Until recently, adopting values-in-action was more the exception than the rule across many industries. The process of developing organisational values was often treated superficially; formulate some values that might appeal to the market, announce them, display them on the wall and in the annual report, and expect the workforce to pick them up largely by osmosis. These values were often treated as vague principles that either stated the obvious without being backed up by a compelling 'why' that justified the use of generic language (e.g. integrity, be 'good'), or which sounded fine but became impractical or unfit for purpose when it came to making decisions with them – that is, when it came to truly acting on them, especially under pressing conditions.

The evolution of values has seen them shift from principles on a page, to values that are made real and demonstrated through actions. Increasingly, you will find businesses that:

- **List the names of their company values.**
- **Describe each value in a way that grounds it in the specific context of the business.**
- **Provide specific examples of behaviours that align with each value (often tied to interpersonal dynamics or decision-making).**

- **Create hyperlinks to projects or initiatives within the business that demonstrate a value in action.**
- **Use hashtags and iconography that stand for a value and are used when calling out a value-in-action or the need to prioritise a value in a certain situation.**

Historically, values were often adopted because a senior leader – perhaps a founder, CEO, or influential people leader – recognised the benefits of doing so. These benefits might have stemmed from a broad-based belief in the power of values, or from observing specific situations where values could help. Today, values are increasingly expected – required, even – by the workforce, or might be adopted due to external pressures from stakeholders, or as a way to signal 'this is who we are' to the broader community and for the sake of attracting the right workforce.

Ultimately, it doesn't matter *why* values are rolled out or refined so much as *how* this is done. Consider a company where the culture has gone sideways and inappropriate behaviours, specifically problematic interpersonal dynamics, have taken hold. These behaviours may not be illegal, but they are certainly damaging. In such cases, it can be tempting to roll out values to 'fix' current problems, as opposed to guiding the company's very identity over time, and gradually aligning behaviours to those values.

The beliefs, needs, and long-term goals of an organisation – its values – require continuity and a holistic focus. It's not just about addressing immediate communication or cultural needs. However, values can help inform systems and processes that provide support for people matters from a more organisation-specific lens. Values provide a 360 degree inside-out and outside-in view of the company.

Values Personify Your Company and Make It Real (and Loveable)

This might sound very dry but stay with me. A business is a 'legal person', with the same rights and responsibilities as a natural person like you and me. It can enter into contracts, own assets, is subject to taxes, and can do other things that a 'natural person' can do – even have children! In the values context, thinking of an organisation as a 'person' is particularly helpful, because it clarifies why it's so important for the company to foster an authentic identity to be seen as a 'whole' and to be understood for what it's likely to do and why. Just as with people, organisations come with beliefs shaped by past experiences, current needs, and future goals and aspirations. And, just as with 'natural' people, businesses face trade-offs between values and must prioritise them for a given situation. An organisation's agents – its owners, employees, contractors, and so on – are there as its representatives and guardians, and when operating in these roles must align their actions with its interests and values.

In this sense, if an organisation's activities define its structure and form, its values personify it. Values give stakeholders – from employees to customers, shareholders, and other interested parties – the chance to know, understand, and even trust and love the business. Organisational values do not just point vaguely in the direction of where a business needs to go, then; they provide context for where it has been and where it needs to go moving forward.

An organisation's values can unlock for it the '4Cs' of authenticity:[5]

- **Consistency in behaviours, decisions, and communication style helps drive an understanding of the expectations others can have of the business.**

- *Conformity* is then necessary, not to 'conform to social expectations' but rather, to conform to the expectations it has established for itself through its preferred behaviours to date.
- Genuine *Connections* with its people and other stakeholders, again contributing to trust and predictability.
- *Continuity* is key. The mindset needs to be, 'We are only ever becoming authentic, and becoming more values-aligned' rather than 'We've achieved it! Job done!'. Authenticity in values alignment is an ongoing process, rather than a static state that can be ticked off a list. A business (or indeed a human) is only ever becoming 'authentic' rather than *achieving* authenticity.

In recognising that authenticity is worked up over time, and, further, involves 'conforming to expectations' that others have about us and that we seek others to have about us, we must be considerate of how we hold ourselves in any given moment and how that aligns with how we want and need to be held up over time. In an organisational setting it is especially important that we don't inadvertently hide behind the claim of 'authenticity' when there is poor behaviour in play. Nothing undermines engagement and loyalty like unspoken values that are calling the shots, especially when they are threat-based. Values misalignment at work undermines the company's 'sense of self' in the eyes of its beholders. A company, just like a person, needs to show up as they seek to show up over the long term rather than getting sidetracked by short-term threats. The organisation must use its values as a guide to becoming that version of itself it strives to be understood as.

While achieving greater values alignment (and related value creation) between an organisation and its values takes time, sabotaging perceived authenticity of values can happen in the blink of an eye. One decision that fundamentally breaks values alignment via consistency, conformity, connection, and continuity. Oftentimes, these existential breaks that profoundly impact a company seem patently obvious in retrospect – prompting comments from stakeholders along the lines of 'How could management (or the board) have been so shortsighted?!' Yet at the time it was judged unlikely to have devastating consequences. At the moment, the risk that comes from fundamental breaks in values alignment are considered at best part of 'reputational risk'; it will be interesting to see how this expands into other areas of risk over the next decade.

I make this reflection because broken trust represents a seismic event of values erosion for the business, which triggers a values conflict in stakeholders that can be hard to overcome. The company's stocks on multiple fronts can take a hit; quite literally share price where that is relevant, and also more insidious 'stocks' can decline in materially meaningful ways. Its attractiveness to top talent. Its capacity to direct its attention on value-creating activities rather than storm mop-up. The engagement and performance of its people. In *becoming* more aligned with its values through the actions and decisions of its people, the organisation is becoming more valuable, and vice versa.

Furthermore, alignment between the company's values and the values of its people is not unchanging. It is a dynamic relationship, which can change – for better or worse – over time. Additionally, values diversity at work offers a remedy for groupthink; you're bound to get a convenient divergence of vantage points thanks to the individual values lenses people bring to their workplace.

The Importance of Individual Values Diversity at Work

I've already touched on the inevitability and worth of values diversity in general. Values diversity among people at work is one of the more underappreciated areas of human diversity. Unlike many areas of diversity it is one that is dynamic and can shift and change over time, as individuals' needs and goals change. Bringing people together who have different values and associated interests in the organisational context is necessary – and valuable.

When you think about what values are at their most basic – complex concepts or 'schemas' that help us make sense of the world – it becomes clear that values diversity is inevitable. Take Roy and Lila. They both value Contribution and Collaboration, and love working at one of Australia's most successful companies. They're both great leaders and generally get on well, yet reliably can be found at loggerheads when it comes to making decisions around new products. The conversation tends to centre around return on investment. Lila points to the future potential should everything work out. Roy tends to focus on the risks of things not working out. The discussion, in the moment it occurs, *sounds* like a rational, logical conversation about financials, risk, and return. Indeed, it is a terrific conversation to have.

In our values work together, it became clear that one of Lila's other values is Adventure and one of Roy's other values is Accountability. When looking at how Lila and Roy described these values, it emerged that Lila thrives on the uncertainty and the twists and turns that emerge as part of getting a new product line up and out the door. Roy, on the other hand, prioritised actions that have a lower level of risk and require a higher level of certainty in order to sit comfortably with what accountability means to him. That is, a level of accountability that manifests as being able to maintain control of factors as they unfold, even if this means having less 'epic wins' along the way.

Let me zoom out and tell you what I saw. Lila and Roy were in a stalemate. Both were receiving messages from their emotion network[6] that was prompting them to retrofit evidence and reasoning to their vantage point, rather than recognising that in fact what was driving their perspective were beliefs grounded in deeper-seated values concepts and predispositions toward Adventure versus Accountability. On coming to appreciate the influence of their values on their evaluations, interpretations, and responses, they were able to shift their perspective and their conversation to one where they focused their attention on prioritising the company's values in a given situation, over and above their own.

This new vantage point enabled them to think about what organisational values they needed to be prioritising, and how this prioritisation would inform the choice they would land on. All of a sudden, Adventure and Accountability were considered mutually available resources that could in and of themselves be prioritised and applied where appropriate, in service of the organisation. From here, a greater appreciation of these components was gained. As my work with the organisation broadened out, its leaders began to change their thinking around individual values.

While maintaining some necessary parameters around values alignment (such as not hiring for values that fundamentally would lead to entirely inappropriate prioritised actions for the company), they started thinking about values alignment as a team sport. What values did they need in a given team? Akin to an orchestra where the conductor had been looking for a bunch of violinists to play the lines of the woodwinds and the brass, too, all of a sudden, they recognised the need to look at individual values with a systems lens. 'Aha! We need to consider values alignment not just between one person and the organisation, but from a team-based perspective. What do we need in this team in order to complement its values lineup?'

The unique values that each of us brings to the workplace has an impact on how we make sense of and action the organisational values. It's up to the organisation to enable any individual who starts with them the best chance of growing values alignment with the company and its values over time. The onus is on the business to help each person with values onboarding, and achieve optimal alignment with company values in the precious first year. We must get past the days when values alignment is considered the responsibility of the individual. It is not a happenstance that occurs when a small set of 'right values' is hired in an attempt to values match. Values alignment is dynamic and takes ongoing work on the part of the company and its people.

KEY TAKEAWAYS OF THIS CHAPTER:

* Company values help define the identity of an organisation, and help forge connections, both internal and external.
* They provide a blueprint for action and decision-making.
* They signal to stakeholders including employees, customers, owners, and shareholders, what the company stands for and help establish and align expectations and behaviours.
* Values humanise organisations and create a 'cultural campfire' – a gathering place for connection, belonging, and shared purpose.
* A company's values will evolve as a company moves through different stages of its lifecycle and its needs and goals change accordingly.
* In the absence of clearly articulated and actioned company values, a 'values vacuum' will be filled with unspoken values, which can be counterproductive.
* Company values must be embedded in day-to-day operations, from leadership to front-line employees.
* Modern company values frameworks link statements to specific behaviours, decision-making examples, and even iconography and hashtags to link actions with values.
* Values play an important role in fostering organisational authenticity per the '4 Cs': consistency, conformity, connection, and continuity.
* Individual values diversity in the workplace reduces groupthink and promotes innovative problem-solving.
* Diverse individual values can be intentionally balanced and cultivated within a team environment.

* The relationship between an employee's personal values and the company's values is dynamic and can be nurtured to enhance values congruence and alignment.

* Values alignment at work can improve decision-making and foster loyalty, and provide a competitive advantage when attracting top talent.

* Values alignment at work is a team sport, up to 'we' not 'me'.

CHAPTER 11
Conclusion

Values Matter

Values are the drivers, the 'positive schemas' that bring your beliefs from past experiences together with your current needs and future desires and aspirations. They help you evaluate, interpret, and respond to the world around you. Throughout this book, we've explored how values can inform, shape, and make sense of your experience, all the while with a focus on your long-term growth. Whether you view this growth as becoming more of who you want to be, or letting go of what you are not, doesn't matter so much as taking the small steps in the right direction, which enable you to get where you want to go.

Individual Values and Collective Impact

Focusing on your core values is far from a self-centred exercise. Over and above benefitting your long-term path and fulfilment, their impact flows outward into your relationships, community, and the world you live in. Cumulatively, personal alignment to core values can lead to broader positive change not just for you and me as individuals, but at the level of company, community, and society. By focusing on personal values alignment, you not only improve your own life but also contribute to a more values-driven world.

Your individual values influence your evaluations, interpretations, and responses whether you're aware of them or not. Gaining insight into your values is key to having agency over your decisions from an angle other than 'shoulds'. Personal values insight, including into our core and our threat-based values, provides a means of weighing up choices not just based on their short-term allure, but on the basis of how they align with what really matters to us over time.

Values-Based Decision-Making

Values-based decision-making can provide you a clear framework for action, where you understand your no-go zones even when their pull for short-term gratification is strong. At first it can feel exhausting and intense, but over time as you become more intuitive about what constitutes a values-led choice, it is freeing. Leading with values-led actions enables you to show up with consistency, conform to the version of you that you seek to recognise in the mirror, foster genuine connection with others, and continue this process moving forward as an act of *becoming* rather than *being* you. And it's never too early or late to start.

CONCLUSION

Values work provides a pathway for growth and development regardless of your age, stage, background, level of success, or area of pursuits. Your values are the ultimate democratisers because they enable you to lead at your best, no matter your circumstances, instead of waiting for things to improve first. No matter your life so far, success can be marked by the small steps you take in the direction you seek to grow into, rather than by some externally imposed version of what it entails. After all, there's enough pain in life already without adding more suffering by gazing longingly over the horizon at what ought to be rather than focusing our attention on what 'is' and building from there. As hard as acceptance of what 'is' can be, especially in the midst of situations that are inherently unfair, meeting your life where it's at is not about accepting less than you aspire to. It's about facing where things are so as to genuinely ask, 'What does it look like for me to build forward from here, aligned with me at my best?' When you feel lost or out of touch with yourself, or you want to unlock and elevate your performance, start now with small, manageable, values-led choices. There is no such thing as too small a values-led choice.

Applying Values in Daily Life

You can prime yourself for daily values-based living by making time for regular reflection on your values and how they're guiding your actions. As you sip a morning coffee (or tea, or water!), a quick reflection on one of your values that you seek to bring into your day, and how you might action it in some teeny way as soon as you put down your cup, can prime you to notice it throughout the morning.

Have you heard of the 'red car' effect where when you talk about red cars, you notice them more? When you bring to mind core values, say, of Achievement and Family and take time to journal about how they do or could show up in your life together at home, you can start to better consider how you can action them together in that context. You will find more instances where your values are applicable. You can more intentionally find common ground that caters for several of your seemingly less congruent values, as well as noticing the pang of values conflict at inflection points where prioritising one negates adequately actioning the other for a moment.

Remember that values conflicts are inevitable and the goal is not to strive for perfect values alignment at all times. Rather, you can get better at noticing conflict, weighing up whether you need to overcome it, and if you conclude that the conflict is inevitable then you can build your ability to sit with the discomfort of this conflict and understand that you can allow it rather than feeling like you need to do something about it.

Navigating the Impostor Within

Throughout *What Matters to You*, we've explored ways values can inform and shape your life and your relationships, including how they can help navigate challenges associated with the impostor phenomenon or straight-up perfectionism. These experiences involve sitting with the deep discomfort of the gap between your performance as it is and as you think it should be to be 'enough'. Understanding your core values can help you acknowledge what matters most to you, and why a role (as a student, parent, or at work, for instance) can matter so much that you deem yourself unworthy or incapable of living up to what it means to be enough in that role.

This shift in perspective, not where you seek to remove this sense of unworthiness but where you make room for it as a symbol of how much you care and, grounded in your values, you stick at a pursuit anyway, allows you to embrace the hard things that matter. You can lean into the vulnerability and discomfort required for personal growth and associated achievements to occur, rather than seeing feeling 'not enough' as evidence of shortcomings.

Furthermore, as much as I talk about the importance of accepting these feelings of discomfort, by understanding and aligning with your core values, you can more effectively combat feelings of fraudulence and self-doubt. Values alignment in the choices you make can bring you courage and conviction even when you feel you're moving against the social tide of what's expected of you. You suffer less from falling into the trap of comparing yourself to others or feeling inadequate. You better recognise your achievements and contributions on the basis of their alignment with your core values rather than on the basis of their alignment with others' perceptions of enoughness, and this enables you to build a stronger sense of self and values-led purpose. You're left more resilient to impostor feelings and better equipped to pursue goals that are personally meaningful.

Values, Decision-Making 'Noise', and Predicting Human Behaviour

Our values bias us toward ways of approaching people, problems, and situations. Implicit in my perspective of values as schemas and their uniqueness to the individual (given the differences between your beliefs, needs, and goals, and mine or anyone else's) is the idea that values explain some variation in how we, respectively, evaluate and interpret situations. Taking this one step further, values may help explain not only why we prioritise things differently but why we *value* things differently. For instance, why one person is willing to pay more to purchase biodegradable bin liners whereas another person is not. Traditionally, differences in willingness to pay for such goods were treated as 'noise' that was too complex to be explained and too insignificant to bother. However, in understanding values as schemas that can be mapped in a predictable albeit individually nuanced way, we can approach 'noise' as a reflection of underlying values that shape individual preferences and decisions, beyond short-term or transitory ambitions or desires.

Values and Value

In time, I believe we will become better equipped to map out the relationships between people's values and how we value things – goods and services from washing machines and cars to shares to psychological services. We've already seen economists start talking about the role of values in social agreements, like fiat money,[1] and their impact on and importance to society. This will increase further, out of navel-gazing territory and into practical applications.

I have high conviction that values can help explain the 'noise' in how people value things; the individual-level variation between how people behave or ascribe value to things that appears to defy logic or 'rational' thought. Values provide a bridge between 'rational' and 'irrational' thought, bringing together thoughts, behaviours and emotions, and paving our way to understanding individual logic as a combination of shared and unique components influenced by our values.

We are approaching a time when it will not just be insufficient, it will be deeply ill-advised to crudely categorise people's decisions as rational or irrational based on their alignment with a predetermined 'best outcome' and its assumptions. Why do I say this? Because in a landscape of increasing automation of decision-making with AI, if we leave it up to 'rationality' of action, this could have dire consequences for the decisions made. Acting 'rationally' is subjective; the rationality of an action depends on the time horizon we consider. Moreover, rationality can involve dualities where two incongruent actions are both rational and yet determine two very different courses of action.

As an example, take 'rational' financial decisions that often focus on maximising relatively short-term gains, neglecting longer-term, systemic impacts. In 1900 when drilling for oil, had someone said 'Hang on a minute, what are the ramifications and implications for people who'll be here in the year 2050?' this probably would have sounded bizarre and an unnecessary consideration. At the time, the 'larger, later' gains would have involved the monetary gain to be had from investing in the short-term capital costs of setting up the drilling equipment and infrastructure. Now, we can at one level understand these gains as 'smaller, sooner,' compared to the larger, later gains of systems-level planetary integrity.

In 1900 the global impact of human decision-making on the trajectory of the planet was not fully recognised. Now, we know better but we are still working with the same amazing and ancient operating system that is our mind. As we move forward, it will be crucial to embed human values in our decision-making, including in the algorithms that increasingly have a role to play either in the decisions we make or those that are made for us.

Human Values and Artificial Intelligence

Whatever your personal thoughts about artificial intelligence (AI), it is now an inevitable part of our world, including generative AI (GAI), which is maturing rapidly. This growth, along with automated, human-like decisions becoming more common, offers both an opportunity and a need to incorporate the best of humanity –

our values – into AI systems. Achieving this requires a focus on individual values, rather than broad categorisations that oversimplify human complexity. Relying on crude, outdated categorisations that bucket people's values into broad dimensions, is grounded in assumptions that stem from 20th-century computational power and statistical techniques. It limits AI's ability to truly reflect human values and renders it less likely that we will solve one of the greatest challenges of our time: the 'alignment challenge'.

The 'alignment challenge' involves ensuring that AI systems' goals and behaviours align with human values and ethical standards. Individual-level values, which act as a motivational bridge between thoughts and actions, offer a unique opportunity to humanise AI. Further, in an era marked by volatility and uncertainty and the threat that brings, overcoming the alignment challenge is an important part of ensuring that human-like decision-making systematically includes the best of us. The horizon looms closer than ever and what lies beyond it is daunting, complex, and unclear, including the role of AI and its role to help or hinder. It is imperative that we become more intentional about the values we prioritise both in daily life and at the point of training and application of human-like AI.

The depth and predictive as well as prescriptive power of human values reflects the opportunity and peril they present. Human values are not just 'nice-to-haves'; they are fundamental drivers of our experience. Individual values reflect our humanity, differentiating us from other species and enabling us to contribute to something greater than ourselves.

Future Directions

I hope that future research and practice on human values embraces methods and technology that makes way for the individual experience. In using modern technology to help people identify their core values, we can move beyond the constraints of survey-based approaches that limit our understanding of values to the group level. Conversely, I hope that research and applications that use (or will use) artificial intelligence with embeddings provides for complex modelling of values, paving the way for human nature at its best to be characterised, catalogued, and brought to life in vibrant and individual detail.

Values-based work also has a deeper role to play in coaching and clinical settings. It is already a central part of therapeutic modalities like Acceptance and Commitment Therapy, but there remains opportunity to broaden the role of values further still in these domains. Values can elevate the experience of people who want help with decision-making and matters of identity to delve more deeply into their drivers and how they want to grow.

As we've discussed, values also allow us to make generous assumptions about the motivations and intentions of others, which can be particularly useful in challenging situations. While maintaining clear boundaries with others is sometimes important, understanding their values can help us cope and foster greater resilience in the face of relationship difficulties. Furthermore, values work can help nurture your relationships with those you care about. By intentionally seeking out areas of alignment between what matters to you and what matters to them, you can grow areas of compatibility and shared understanding in what you do and say. Engaging in values work together can help foster a deeper sense of connection, shared goals, and mutual respect, while allowing space for your differences.

Values are incredibly helpful for optimising performance, too, and this is an area that continues to evolve. When we focus on aligning our performance goals with what truly matters, we become more willing to embrace the discomfort of pushing ourselves in the present without succumbing to the fear of failure. Values-enhanced performance promotes growth that allows us to excel over the longer term without being constrained by self-limiting beliefs.

An Invitation

Having a grandfather who regularly talked about his own values (Modesty, Integrity, Family, Dignity, and Courage) and how they guided him through life no doubt contributed to my interest in values. Grandpa passed down his commitment to values-based living to his family members, in moments of challenge and opportunity. He taught me about the fundamental role that values can play in helping cultivate wellbeing and performance with the longer term in mind. It wasn't until I was through my postgraduate psychology training, however, that I started to look into the reaches of their potential.

The Role of Values in Understanding Self and Others – My Story in Brief

I really wasn't sure whether it was appropriate to put this personal note in here about my experience. Largely because values are far more interesting than me and, frankly, I'm tired of talking about myself after my singing career. But I've been convinced it might be of use to someone, somewhere, and in that spirit, here I go. I have always struggled with my social battery – I know I am far from alone in doing so. After starting to talk at around nine months, I had stopped talking by eighteen months and didn't talk again until I was three when I started talking in sentences. At school I was

CONCLUSION

teased for my quirks and special interests in different breeds of cow, horse, and chicken, and my fascination with patterns (basically, I love categorising things). I went to an audiologist for investigations into why percussive noises were painful for me, a particular shade of purple still makes me puke, I struggled with interpreting others' intentions and motivations, and as I've always put it, 'My facial recognition software is on the blink.' That is, I struggle to recognise faces. I have always been deeply empathetic, and the combination of deep empathy coupled with always taking people at face value has left me in some challenging situations over the years. Added to this, I spent years feeling like a 'chameleon in every room', unsure about who or where I was underneath the people-pleasing and projection of an image of me that aligned with what people wanted to see.

Throughout this time, it didn't occur to me that I might have a quirky operating system; indeed I felt quite 'normal' in the context of my family, who are loving, empathetic, and quirky. But I longed for an external system to help me better make sense of my inner experience and other people. Values provided that to me. I learned more about my own values and realised everyone has their own unique values prioritisations. I started to inquire after or simply infer other people's values; their core values and in time, as I read more into the evidence base, their threat-based values, too.

I sought to make generous assumptions not just on the basis of what people said to me but what mattered most to them. When people showed up as tense or threatened, I made sense of this experience through the lens of threat-based values. I saw people not as 'good' or 'bad' but complex, multifaceted, and needs-based. I inferred emotion states based on the values inferences I drew. It coloured my empathy with a solution-focused lens. Not only that, values provided me a way of standing up for myself and making some hard decisions, while remaining anchored to what matters most to me and who I seek to grow into.

My eventual diagnosis of Autism Spectrum Disorder (ASD) was not just a broad relief. It came with a musing that values might offer a level of granularity that helps make sense of the human experience. Post-diagnosis, I spent time with an incredible occupational therapist who helped me understand my experience with language and processing better. I made peace with my quirks and leaned into values prioritisation as a way of more formally approaching how I wanted to show up in any given room. I replaced people-pleasing with values alignment. It enabled me to increasingly walk into any space as myself, and be okay if folks don't understand what they're getting. It also helped me meet other people where they are at, too. I must admit this took time, and I have been 'over trusting' on occasion, but I refuse to allow my tendency to trust to be dampened by one or two bad experiences. I have now seen how values can help make sense of my own motivations and emotions as well as those of others. This approach to values-aligned empathy and self-compassion can support a diverse array of people to build identity and sense of self, even after a lifetime of masking as in my case.

If you long for a simpler inner life and an exterior that aligns better with what matters most to you, know your values and commit to actioning them more often, over and above ego-oriented 'shoulds' or actions that flow from short-term desires. Make values-based, generous assumptions about the intentions and emotion states of others, and while standing your values-based ground, respond as best you can with empathy and grace.

I hope that moving forward, you can better notice threat-based responses and recognise the natural tendency to prioritise threat-related actions with an understanding that, even amidst uncertainty and turmoil, you can still choose to align your behaviour with your core values. Steer clear of avoidance and seek to make 'toward' moves in the direction of the version of yourself you aspire to grow into longer term, even if it involves short-term discomfort. Core values alignment is possible, even at times when you notice a tendency to hook into threat-related thoughts that seek to justify threat-based responses. Harness your newfound understanding of values during times of negotiation and seek to understand another's behaviours not through 'walking in their shoes' but by seeking to occupy their heart — by way of their core values.

Aligning more of your actions with your highest values enables you to stand for something meaningful. Even as one of ~8 billion people globally, your life and your contribution matters, not just to you or those who love you, but to us all. A values-aligned life honours the opportunity you have to elevate your existence for yourself, your family, and well beyond. So, what is one small, values-led choice you can make today? Live boldly in line with your values, let what matters most to you be your legacy to the world.

ACKNOWLEDGEMENTS

Writing *What Matters to You* would never have happened without the influence and inspiration of so many people over many years. As I reflected on who to thank, the list kept growing, making it clear that acknowledging everyone individually would be impossible.

In that spirit, to anyone reading this who senses they may have played a role – you probably did. Thank you. There are, however, several groups of people I would like to recognise explicitly.

To my mentors, friends, and colleagues – the brilliant minds who challenge me, hold me accountable, and inspire me – your commitment to understanding what matters most in life has been a continuous source of encouragement through every season of my life.

To my clients, workshop participants, and everyone who has shared their stories and values with me, thank you for trusting me with your experiences. This book simply wouldn't exist without your openness and generosity.

To my editor and publishing team at HarperCollins Publishers, my heartfelt thanks for your thoughtful guidance and steadfast support in bringing this book to life. The fact that you do this over and over is extraordinary.

WHAT MATTERS TO YOU

To my family, thank you for your love, patience, and belief in me. You've encouraged me to follow my curiosity and trust in the power of ideas and values to change lives.

And finally, to you, the reader. Thank you for your curiosity and willingness to explore what truly matters. I hope this book meets you where you are and helps you find what you need.

With gratitude,
Greta

APPENDIX

Some Common (Generic) Core Values

Here are some values names and descriptions that might help get you started with thinking about what values are most important to you.

Acceptance	Willingness to accept other views
Accountability	Taking responsibility for your actions and being answerable to others for the outcomes of those actions
Achievement	Success in the form of reaching (achieving) a goal or desired outcome
Adaptability	Capacity to adjust to new conditions such as changes in your circumstances or your environment
Adventure	To undertake unusual, new, exciting or daring experiences
Altruism	Overarching concern for the happiness and wellbeing of others, over and above yourself
Authenticity	To communicate in a genuine way that is in line with your personality and beliefs
Awareness	To directly take note and be aware of a situation in the moment, as it occurs

Balance	An appreciation of a situation, event, array of elements or objects being in steady and correct proportions
Beauty	An appreciation for pleasing or positive and meaningful visually aesthetic qualities, which can range from a beautiful object or painting, to a sunset, to your grandmother's wrinkles
Collaboration	To work together with others toward a common goal
Communication	To share and exchange information by speaking, writing, and via non-verbal means
Community	To identify with and contribute to a group of people unified by common interests or place
Compassion	To be caring and compassionate to others and yourself
Connection	To connect to people, place and community
Contribution	To contribute and add to the world you live in
Courage	From the root word 'cor' (Latin for 'heart'), a willingness to go forth and do or deal with something that needs to be done, even though it frightens you or you find it unpleasant
Creativity	To use imagination and original ideas to create something new or unique
Curiosity	To be inquisitive and interested in something; to explore, discover, or learn something
Dignity	Recognising and respecting the inherent worth and rights of all individuals
Empathy	The ability to understand and share the feelings of another, fostering emotional connection and compassion
Equity	Striving for fairness and justice by recognising and addressing the different needs and circumstances of individuals and groups
Excellence	Striving to do something to the best of your ability
Fairness	To maintain balance and fairness ('give and take') with others
Family	To appreciate a group of people often related by blood or marriage, or associated by background

SOME COMMON (GENERIC) CORE VALUES

Freedom	To have the freedom to act, speak or think in order to be yourself and to allow others to be themselves
Generosity	Willingness to give time, energy, or resources to others without expecting anything in return
Gratitude	Being thankful and appreciative for what you receive, including expressing your appreciation where appropriate
Health	Caring for and taking care of your mental and physical health
Humility	To be modest and humble, free from arrogance or vanity
Humour	To appreciate amusing or comic content in speech, writing, or non-verbal communication
Inclusivity	Embracing diversity and ensuring that everyone feels welcome and valued, regardless of differences
Independence	To be free to make your own decisions and chart your own course of action without obligation to others
Influence	To have a great influence or impact on someone or something
Innovation	Encouraging and embracing new ideas, methods, and technologies to improve processes and outcomes
Integrity	Intentionally consistent and honest in your words and actions and in your approach to others
Intelligence	To appreciate reflective thought and mental computation to inform decision-making and problem-solving
Justice	Commitment to fairness and equality, ensuring that people are treated justly and without bias
Leadership	To be a leader and role model to people including community groups and organisations
Learning	To continue to develop knowledge or skill, either through formal study or informal learning
Legacy	To leave something of value or importance for those who come after you
Love	Warm, personal attachment or affection as for a close family member or friend

Loyalty	To be trustworthy, committed and reliable to others
Mastery	To strive for a comprehensive and excellent knowledge or skill in a particular domain
Novelty	To appreciate the unique, original, unusual or new qualities of an object or event
Openness	A willingness to be open with your thoughts and feelings
Optimism	Intentionally taking a positive, constructive attitude toward situations and / or people; past, present, and / or future
Persistence	To continue your course of action or in your opinion in spite of obstacles or opposition
Pleasure	Deriving enjoyment or happiness from experiences
Prudence	Exercising caution, foresight, and good judgement in decision-making and actions
Respect	To show respect and regard to yourself, others and your surrounds
Responsibility	To take responsibility for your actions
Security	Being free from care, danger or threat
Spirituality	Connecting with things bigger than yourself and beyond the material or physical world
Sustainability	A commitment to making choices and taking actions that ensure the long-term health and viability of systems such as the environment, society, and the economy
Wealth	Appreciating an abundant supply of material resources such as money or valuable possessions
Wisdom	To be knowledgeable, reflective and experienced and to draw on these qualities when making decisions or casting judgements
Work Ethic	Approaching tasks with industriousness, commitment and dedication

NOTES

Introduction
1. Gottman, J. M. (2011). *The Science of Trust: Emotional Attunement for Couples.* W. W. Norton & Company.
2. Hardy, D. (2020). *The Compound Effect: Jumpstart your income, your life, your success.* John Murray Press: London.

Chapter 1. Understanding Values
1. Atzil, S., Gao, W., Fradkin, I., & Barrett, L. F. (2018). Growing a social brain. *Nature Human Behaviour*, 2, pp.624-636. https://doi.org/10.1038/s41562-018-0384-6.
2. Colombo, S. L., Chiarella, S. G., Lefrançois, C., Fradin, J., Raffone, A., & Simione, L. (2023). Why knowing about Climate Change is not enough to change: A perspective paper on the factors explaining the environmental knowledge-action gap. *Sustainability*, 15(20). 14859. https://doi.org/10.3390/su152014859.
3. Gouveia, V. V. (2003). The motivational nature of human values: Evidence of a new typology. *Estudos de Psicologia* (Natal), 8(3), pp.431-443. https://www.researchgate.net/publication/262626789_The_motivational_nature_of_human_values_evidence_of_a_new_typology.
4. Schwartz, S. H. (2012). An overview of the Schwartz theory of basic values. *Online Readings in Psychology and Culture*, 2(1). https://doi.org/10.9707/2307-0919.1116.
5. Feldman, R. (2012). Oxytocin and social affiliation in humans. *Hormones and Behavior*, 61(3), pp.380-391. https://doi.org/10.1016/j.yhbeh.2012.01.008
6. Brosch, T., Coppin, G., Scherer, K. R., Schwartz, S., & Sander, D. (2010). Generating value(s): Psychological value hierarchies reflect context-dependent sensitivity of the reward system. *Social Neuroscience*, 6(2), pp.198-208. https://doi.org/10.1080/17470919.2010.506754.
7. Schwartz, S. H. (2012). An overview of the Schwartz theory of basic values. *Online Readings in Psychology and Culture*, 2(1). https://doi.org/10.9707/2307-0919.1116.
8. Rokeach, M. (1979). *Understanding Human Values.* Free Press: New York.
9. Rothgerber, H. (2020). Meat-related cognitive dissonance: A conceptual framework for understanding how meat eaters reduce negative arousal from eating animals. *Appetite*, 146. https://doi.org/10.1016/j.appet.2019.104511.

10 Saucier, G. (2018). Culture, morality and individual differences: Comparability and incomparability across species. *Philosophical Transactions of the Royal Society of London*, 373(1744). https://doi.org/10.1098/rstb.2017.0170.
11 Schwartz, S. H. (1992). Universals in the content and structure of values: Theoretical advances and empirical tests in 20 countries. *Advances in Experimental Social Psychology*, 25, pp.1-65. https://doi.org/10.1016/S0065-2601(08)60281-6.
12 Seligman, M. (2004). Can happiness be taught? *Daedalus*, 133(2), pp.80-87. https://www.jstor.org/stable/20027916.
13 Pankin, J. (2013). Schema theory and concept formation. Massachusetts Institute of Technology. https://web.mit.edu/pankin/www/Schema_Theory_and_Concept_Formation.pdf.
14 de Jong, T., & Ferguson-Hessler, M. G. M. (1996). Types and qualities of knowledge. *Educational Psychologist*, 31(2), pp.105-113. https://doi.org/10.1207/s15326985ep3102_2.
15 Neisser, U. (1976). *Cognition and Reality: Principles and Implications of Cognitive Psychology*. San Francisco: W.H. Freeman.
16 Anderson, J. R. (1983). *The Architecture of Cognition*. Harvard University Press: Chicago.
17 Schank, R. C., & Abelson, R. P. (2013). *Scripts, Plans, Goals, and Understanding: An Inquiry into Human Knowledge Structures*. Psychology Press.
18 Widmayer, S. A. (2002). Schema theory: An introduction. https://api.semanticscholar.org/CorpusID:30998082.
19 Bartlett, F. C. (1932). *Remembering: A Study in Experimental and Social Psychology*. Cambridge University Press.
20 Piaget, J. (1954). *Construction of Reality in the Child*. London: Routledge & Kegan Paul.
21 Young, J. E., Klosko, J. S., & Weishaar, M. E. (2003). *Schema Therapy: A Practitioner's Guide*. Guilford Press, p.7.
22 Psychologist Jeffrey Young developed Schema Therapy to help people identify and change deep-seated and self-defeating patterns of thinking and behaviour rooted in childhood experiences. Often in psychology, schemas are discussed in the context of people's suffering when negative or 'maladaptive' schemas are overactivated. This has led to a misapprehension that schemas are necessarily negative when they can be negative, positive, or neutral. It is in the context of 20th-century psychology where maladaptive schemas tended to be the focus. Take the very helpful client guide to Schema Therapy by David Bricker with Jeffrey Young: 'A schema is an extremely stable, enduring negative pattern that develops during childhood or adolescence and is elaborated throughout an individual's life. We view the world through our schemas.' This guide implies that all schemas are negative but, to labour the point, they can be positive, neutral or negative. In Young's Schema Therapy, he identifies specific maladaptive schemas that he believes are at the core of many psychological problems laid down early in life, which he calls 'Early Maladaptive Schemas' (EMSs). EMSs are amenable to change, and that's where Schema Therapy comes in, to shift and change EMSs in the context of treating personality disorders and complex

psychological difficulties despite EMS's roots in early childhood experiences and unmet emotional needs.

Psychologist Adrian Wells also deals with (negative) schemas in Metacognitive Therapy (MCT). Wells developed MCT to address the underlying cognitive processes that contribute to the maintenance of psychological issues, including anxiety and depression. From his perspective, schemas are relevant because they influence how people manage their thinking and emotional responses. Unlike Schema Therapy, the aim of MCT is not to work on schemas directly. Instead, MCT points out and targets their malleability and our capacity to change them – with hard work, we can dial them up or down. From Wells' perspective, as detailed in his book *Metacognitive Therapy for Anxiety and Depression* (Guilford Press, 2009), schemas aren't 'stable entities that should be erased but instead are seen as the products of thinking processes'. Wells explains how schemas are self-perpetuating through the mechanisms outlined in his 'self-regulatory executive function model' (S-REF): We filter for information and stimuli in ways that support our worldview (even when our worldview isn't working for us). In so doing, this filtered information feeds into and reinforces our existing schemas. The extent to which schemas are reinforced depends on how they're prioritised. Prioritisation is not about which schemas are triggered or activated – we cannot control that – but rather, the amount of attention we give them and the actions we take once they are activated. To reiterate – we can't control which schemas are activated, but we can impact where we pay attention and how we respond through our actions. This is especially important to remember when it comes to discussing threat-based values (the values we tend to prioritise when we're under threat). We can't control them being triggered but we can control whether we act on this trigger. More on that in Chapters Two and Four.

23   Schwartz, S. H. (1992). Universals in the content and structure of values: Theoretical advances and empirical tests in 20 countries. *Advances in experimental social psychology*, 25, pp.1–65. https://doi.org/10.1016/S0065-2601(08)60281-6.

24   Schwartz, M. S. (2015). Ethical decision-making theory: An integrated approach. *Journal of Business Ethics*, 139, pp.755–776. https://doi.org/10.1007/s10551-015-2886-8.

25   Gouveia, V., Chaves, S. S. da S., Oliveira, I. C. P. de, Dias, M. R., Gouveia, R. S. V., & Andrade, P. R. de. (2003). The use of the GHQ-12 in a general population: A study of its construct validity. *Psicologia: Teoria e Pesquisa*, 19, pp.241–248. https://doi.org/10.1590/S0102-37722003000300006.

26   Schwartz, S. H. (2016). Basic individual values: Sources and consequences. In T. Brosch & D. Sander (eds), *Handbook of Value: Perspectives from Economics, Neuroscience, Philosophy, Psychology and Sociology*, pp.63–84. Oxford University Press.

27   Lee, J., Evers, U., Sneddon, J., Rahn, O., & Schwartz, S. (2019). What do we value? How our values influence everyday behaviour. The Centre for Human and Cultural Values, University of Western Australia.

28   Rokeach, M. (1973). *The nature of human values*. Free Press.

Chapter 2. Two Sets of Values

1. Gouveia, V. V., Milfont, T. L., Vione, K. C., & Santos, W. S. (2015). Guiding actions and expressing needs: On the psychological functions of values. *Psykhe: Revista de la Escuela de Psicología*, 24(2), pp.1–14. https://doi.org/10.7764/psykhe.24.2.884.
2. Harris, R. (2009). *ACT made simple: An easy-to-read primer on acceptance and commitment therapy*. New Harbinger Publications.
3. David, S. (2016). *Emotional Agility: Get Unstuck, Embrace Change, and Thrive in Work and Life*. New York: Avery/ Penguin Random House.
4. Harrison, D. A., & Klein, K. J. (2007). What's the difference? Diversity constructs as separation, variety, or disparity in organisations. *The Academy of Management Review*, 32(4), pp.1199-1228. https://doi.org/10.2307/20159363.
5. Schwartz, S. H. (2012). An overview of the Schwartz theory of basic values. *Online Readings in Psychology and Culture*, 2(1). https://doi.org/10.9707/2307-0919.1116.
6. Gouveia, V. V. (2003). The motivational nature of human values: Evidence of a new typology. *Estudos de Psicologia* (Natal), 8(3), pp.431-443. https://www.researchgate.net/publication/262626789_The_motivational_nature_of_human_values_evidence_of_a_new_typology.
7. Shalom Schwartz and Valdiney Gouveia are two leading and competing values researchers who both present survival values in their models of and research on human values.
8. Porges, S. W. (2011). *The Polyvagal Theory: Neurophysiological Foundations of Emotions, Attachment, Communication, and Self-Regulation*. W.W. Norton & Company.
9. All names in *What Matters to You* are pseudonyms, and the scenarios presented are composites, drawing from the experiences of many individuals rather than representing any one person's story. Any similarity to a specific individual is purely coincidental.
10. Hayes, S. C., Strosahl, K. D., & Wilson, K. G. (1999). *Acceptance and Commitment Therapy: An Experiential Approach to Behavior Change*. Guilford Press. Wells, A. (2009). *Metacognitive Therapy for Anxiety and Depression*. Guilford Press.
11. Harris, R. (2009). *ACT Made Simple: An Easy-to-Read Primer on Acceptance and Commitment Therapy*. Oakland, CA: New Harbinger Publications.

Chapter 3. Know Your Core Values

1. A sidenote about core values identification. Values take time to uncover. Using a quick psychological inventory fails to get down to an individualised level of values definition or usage. A population-level values questionnaire such as Schwartz's Portrait Values Questionnaire helps assess where people sit, relative to one another, on the relevance of broad values domains in their lives. This doesn't get down to a level of values identification that enables nuanced, values-based decision-making.

    In the real world, values are hypothesised, tested and iterated over time. Values are repeatedly uncovered and tested in action for their fit; we evaluate and readjust until we refine our values to a point where we're happy with them, at least for this chapter of life. We must choose them and refine them, not have them allocated to us from a constrained list of dimensions from a questionnaire. Even though they represent relatively stable positive schemas that impact how we interpret the world and we can call upon them to guide our decisions, the top five values we prioritise currently depend on our life stage and what is around us. Our values prioritisation can change following a major life event.

2. Schwartz, S. H. (1992). Universals in the content and structure of values: Theoretical advances and empirical tests in 20 countries. In M. P. Zanna (ed.), *Advances in experimental social psychology*, 25, pp.1–65. https://doi.org/10.1016/S0065-2601(08)60281-6.

3. Schwartz, S. H. (2012). An overview of the Schwartz theory of basic values. *Online Readings in Psychology and Culture*, 2(1). https://doi.org/10.9707/2307-0919.1116.

4. Rokeach, M. (1973). *The Nature of Human Values*. Free Press.

5. Ryan, R. M., & Deci, E. L. (2000). Self-determination theory and the facilitation of intrinsic motivation, social development, and well-being. *American Psychologist*, 55(1), pp.68-78. https://doi.org/10.1037/0003-066X.55.1.68.

6. Kashdan, T. B., & McKnight, P. E. (2009). Origins of purpose in life: Refining our understanding of a life well lived. *Psychological Topics*, 18(2), pp.303-316. https://www.researchgate.net/publication/43170672_Origins_of_Purpose_in_Life_Refining_our_Understanding_of_a_Life_Well_Lived.

7. Steger, M. F., & Kashdan, T. B. (2007). Stability and specificity of meaning in life and life satisfaction over one year. *Journal of Happiness Studies*, 8(2), pp.161-179. https://doi.org/10.1007/s10902-006-9011-8.

8. Özer, D., Altun, S. A., Kayaoğlu, K., & Tanrikulu, A. B. (2023). Evaluation of the relationship between values and psychological resilience of individuals diagnosed with substance use disorder: A cross-sectional study. *Archives of Psychiatric Nursing*, 44(6), pp.101-106. https://doi.org/10.1016/j.apnu.2023.04.023.

9. Harrison, D. A., & Klein, K. J. (2007). What's the difference? Diversity constructs as separation, variety, or disparity in organisations. *Academy of Management Review*, 32(4), pp.1199-1228. https://doi.org/10.5465/amr.2007.26586096.
Schwartz, S. H. (2012). An overview of the Schwartz theory of basic values. *Online Readings in Psychology and Culture*, 2(1). doi:10.9707/2307-0919.1116.

10. Schwartz, S. H. (1994). Are there universal aspects in the structure and contents of human values? *Journal of Social Issues*, 50(4), pp.19-45. https://doi.org/10.1111/j.1540-4560.1994.tb01196.x.

11. Chopra, D. (2014). Being judgmental. https://www.deepakchopra.com/articles/being-judgmental/.

12. Bazerman, M. H., & Neale, M. A. (1992). *Negotiating Rationally*. New York: Free Press.
Fisher, R., Ury, W., & Patton, B. (2011). *Getting to Yes: Negotiating Agreement Without Giving In*. Penguin Books.
Harris, R. (2009). *ACT Made Simple: An Easy-to-Read Primer on Acceptance and Commitment Therapy*. New Harbinger Publications.
Shell, G. R. (2006). *Bargaining for Advantage: Negotiation Strategies for Reasonable People*. Penguin Books.
Thompson, L.L (2012). *The Mind and Heart of the Negotiator*. Pearson Education.

13   Dammann, O., Friederichs, K. M., Lebedinski, S., & Liesenfeld, K. M. (2021). The essence of authenticity. *Frontiers in Psychology*, 11(1), pp.1-6. https://doi.org/10.3389/fpsyg.2020.629654.

14   Fisher, R., Ury, W., & Patton, B. (2011). *Getting to Yes: Negotiating Agreement Without Giving In*. Penguin Books.

15   Thompson, L. (2012). *The Mind and Heart of the Negotiator*. Pearson Education.

16   Fisher, R., Ury, W., & Patton, B. (2011). *Getting to Yes: Negotiating Agreement Without Giving In*. Penguin Books.

17   David, S. (2016). *Emotional Agility: Get Unstuck, Embrace Change, and Thrive in Work and Life*. New York: Avery/Penguin Random House.

Chapter 4. Know Your Threat-Based Values

1   It is important to note that the names used for threat-based values can be used in many other contexts as well. The definitions provided here are specifically given in the context of threat-based values.

2   Kabat-Zinn, J. (1994). *Wherever You Go, There You Are: Mindfulness Meditation in Everyday Life*. New York: Hyperion. https://mbsrtraining.com/mindfulness-exercises-by-jon-kabat-zinn/walking-meditation-by-jon-kabat.

3   Harris, R. (2009). *ACT Made Simple: An Easy-to-Read Primer on Acceptance and Commitment Therapy*. New Harbinger Publications.

4   Hayes, S. C., Strosahl, K. D., & Wilson, K. G. (2016). *Acceptance and Commitment Therapy: The Process and Practice of Mindful Change*. Guilford Press.

5   Deci, E. L., & Ryan, R. M. (2000). The 'what' and 'why' of goal pursuits: Human needs and the self-determination of behavior. *Psychological Inquiry*, 11(4), pp.227-268.

6   Tang, Y. Y., Holzel, B. K., & Posner, M. I. (2015). The neuroscience of mindfulness meditation. *Nature Reviews Neuroscience*, 16(4), pp.213-225. https://doi.org/10.1038/nrn3916.

7   Karpman, S. B. (1968). Fairy tales and script drama analysis. *Transactional Analysis Bulletin*, 7(26), pp.39-43.

8   If you're interested in reading further about how the Drama Triangle can be used to conceptualise a threat-based values response, visit my blog at gretajbradman.com.

9   Ibid.

Chapter 5. The Power of Meaning in an Uncertain World

1   Maslow, A. H. (1970). *Motivation and Personality* (2nd ed.). New York: Harper & Row. p.159.

2   Ibid.

3   Frankl, V. E. (1992). *Man's Search for Meaning: An Introduction to Logotherapy* (4th ed.) (I. Lasch, Trans.). Beacon Press. (Original work published 1946.)

4   Freud, S. (1923). *The Ego and the Id*. London: Hogarth Press.

5   Hoffman, E. (1994). *The Drive for Self: Alfred Adler and the Founding of Individual Psychology*. Addison Wesley.

6   Brosch, T., & Sander, D. (eds). (2015). *Handbook of Value: Perspectives from Economics, Neuroscience, Philosophy, Psychology, and Sociology*. Oxford University Press.

NOTES

7   Harris, R. (2009). *ACT Made Simple: An Easy-to-Read Primer on Acceptance and Commitment Therapy*. New Harbinger Publications.

8   Tseng, J., & Poppenk, J. (2020). Brain meta-state transitions demarcate thoughts across task contexts exposing the mental noise of trait neuroticism. *Nature Communications*, 11, 3480. https://doi.org/10.1038/s41467-020-17255-9.

9   Hayes, S. C., & Lillis, J. (2012). *Acceptance and Commitment Therapy*. American Psychological Association. https://doi.org/10.1037/17335-000.

10   Tyng, C. M., Amin, H. U., Saad, N. M., & Malik, A. S. (2017). The influences of emotion on learning and memory. *Frontiers in Psychology*, 8, pp.1454. https://doi.org/10.3389/fpsyg.2017.01454.

11   Ekman, P. (2003). *Emotions Revealed: Recognizing Faces and Feelings to Improve Communication and Emotional Life*. New York: Times Books.

12   For an account of this more recent research, see neuroscientist Lisa Feldman Barrett's 2017 book *How Emotions Are Made: The Secret Life of the Brain*. Available at lisafeldmanbarrett.com.

13   Gendron, M., Roberson, D., van der Vyver, J. M., & Barrett, L. F. (2014). Perceptions of emotion from facial expressions are not culturally universal: Evidence from a remote culture. *Emotion*, 14(2). pp.251-262. https://doi.org/10.1037/a0036052.

14   Tyng, C. M., Amin, H. U., Saad, N. M., & Malik, A. S. (2017). The influences of emotion on learning and memory. *Frontiers in Psychology*, 8, p.1454. https://doi.org/10.3389/fpsyg.2017.01454.

15   Mohammadi, G., Van de Ville, D., & Vuilleumier, P. (2023). Brain networks subserving functional core processes of emotions identified with componential modeling. *Cerebral Cortex*, 33(12). doi.org/10.3389/fpsyg.2017.01454.

16   Lindquist, K. A., Wager, T. D., Kober, H., Bliss-Moreau, E., & Barrett, L. F. (2012). The brain basis of emotion: A meta-analytic review. *Behavioral and Brain Sciences*, 35(3), pp.121-143.

17   Kassam, K. S., Markey, A. R., Cherkassky, V. L., Loewenstein, G., & Just, M. A. (2013). Identifying emotions on the basis of neural activation. *PLOS One*. https://doi.org/10.1371/journal.pone.0066032.

18   Barrett, L. F. (2009). The future of psychology: Connecting mind to brain. *Perspectives on Psychological Science*, 4(4), pp.326-339. https://doi.org/10.1111/j.1745-6924.2009.01134.x.

19   Craig, A. D. (2002). How do you feel? Interoception: The sense of the physiological condition of the body. *Nature Reviews Neuroscience*, 3(8), pp.655-666. https://doi.org/10.1038/nrn894.

Chapter 6. 'Shoulds', Being Enough, and the Impostor Experience

1   Miller, W. R., & Rollnick, S. (2023). *Motivational Interviewing: Helping People Change and Grow*. (4th ed.) New York: Guilford Press.

2   Higgins, E. T. (1987). Self-discrepancy: A theory relating self and affect. *Psychological Review*, 94(3), pp.319-340. https://doi.org/10.1037/0033-295X.94.3.319.

3   If you're wanting to go deeper on the impostor phenomenon, I highly recommend psychologist Cassandra Dunn's 2023 audiobook, *The Imposter Solution: Back yourself. Believe. Achieve.*, published by Audible.

4   Clance, P. R., & Imes, S. A. (1978). The imposter phenomenon in high achieving women: Dynamics and therapeutic intervention. *Psychotherapy: Theory, Research, and Practice*, 15(3), pp.241-247. https://doi.org/10.1037/h0086006.

5   Ibid., p.241.

6   Sakulku, J., & Alexander, J. (2011). The impostor phenomenon. *International Journal of Behavioral Science*, 6(1), pp.73-92. https://www.researchgate.net/publication/265147816_The_Impostor_Phenomenon.

7   Thompson, T., Foreman, P., & Martin, F. (2000). Imposter fears and perfectionistic concern over mistakes. *Personality and Individual Differences*, 29(4), pp.629-647. https://doi.org/10.1016/S0191-8869(99)00218-4.

8   Clance, P. R., & O'Toole, M. A. (1987). The impostor phenomenon: An internal barrier to empowerment and achievement. *Women and Therapy*, 6(3), pp.51-64. https://doi.org/10.1300/J015V06N03_05.

9   Thompson, T., Davis, H., & Davidson, J. (1998). Attributional and affective responses of impostors to academic success and failure outcomes. *Personality and Individual Differences*, 25(2), pp.381-396. https://doi.org/10.1016/S0191-8869(98)00065-8.

10 Thompson, T., Foreman, P., & Martin, F. (2000). Imposter fears and perfectionistic concern over mistakes. *Personality and Individual Differences*, 29(4), pp.629-647. https://doi.org/10.1016/S0191-8869(99)00218-4.

11 Clance, P. R., & O'Toole, M. A., op cit.

12 Zanchetta, M., Junker, S., Wolf, A., & Traut-Mattausch, E. (2020). 'Overcoming the fear that haunts your success' – The effectiveness of interventions for reducing the impostor phenomenon. *Frontiers in Psychology*, 11. https://doi.org/10.3389/fpsyg.2020.00405.

13 Bravata, D. M., Watts, S. A., Keefer, A. L., Madhusudhan, D. K., Taylor, K. T., Clark, D. M., Nelson, R. S., Cokley, K. O., & Hagg, H. K. (2020). Prevalence, predictors, and treatment of impostor syndrome: A systematic review. *Journal of General Internal Medicine*, 35(4), pp.1252-1275. https://doi.org/10.1007/s11606-019-05364-1.

14 Ibid., p. 1273.

15 Tewfik, B. A., (2022). The impostor phenomenon revisited: Examining the relationship between workplace impostor thoughts and interpersonal effectiveness at work. *Academy of Management Journal*, 65(3), pp.988-1018. https://doi.org/10.5465/amj.2020.1627.

16 Satell, G., & Windschitl, C. (2021). High-performing teams start with a culture of shared values. *Harvard Business Review* (May). https://hbr.org/2021/05/high-performing-teams-start-with-a-culture-of-shared-values.

17 Gómez-Jorge, F., & Díaz-Garrido, E. (2023). The relation between self-esteem and productivity: An analysis in higher education institutions. *Sec. Organizational Psychology*, 13. https://doi.org/10.3389/fpsyg.2022.1112437.

18 Pierce, J. L., & Gardner, D. G. (2004). Self-esteem within the work and organiZational context: A review of the organiZation-based self-esteem literature. *Journal of Management*, 30(5), pp.591-622. https://doi.org/10.1016/j.jm.2003.10.001.
19 Johnson, A. R., Jayappa, R., James, M., Kulnu, A., Kovayil, R., & Joseph, B. (2020). Do low self-esteem and high stress lead to burnout among health-care workers? Evidence from a tertiary hospital in Bangalore, India. *Safety and Health at Work*, 11(3), pp.347-352. https://doi.org/10.1016/j.shaw.2020.05.009.
20 Brown, B. (March, 2012). Listening to shame [video]. www.ted.com/talks/brene_brown_listening_to_shame.
21 Brown, B. (2012). *Daring Greatly: How the Courage to Be Vulnerable Transforms the Way We Live, Love, Parent and Lead*. Gotham Books.

Chapter 7. Values and the Client Experience with the Impostor Phenomenon

1 Hayes, S. C. (2005). *Get Out of Your Mind and Into Your Life: The New Acceptance and Commitment Therapy*. New Harbinger Publications.
2 Hayes, S. C., Barnes-Holmes, D., & Roche, B. (eds) (2001). *Relational Frame Theory: A Post-Skinnerian Account of Human Language and Cognition*. Kluwer Academic/Plenum Publishers.
3 Flegl, M., Depoo, L., & Alcázar, M. (2022). The impact of employees' training on their performance improvements. *Quality Innovation Prosperity*, 26(1), pp.70-89. https://doi.org/10.12776/qip.v26i1.1665.
4 Diviney, R. (2021). *The Attributes: 25 Hidden Drivers of Optimal Performance*. Penguin Random House: London.
5 Fourie, L., Els, C., & de Beer, L. T. (2020). A play-at-work intervention: What are the benefits? *South African Journal of Economic and Management Sciences*, 23(1). A2815. https://doi.org/10.4102/sajems.v23i1.2815.
6 Csikszentmihalyi, M. (1990). *Flow: The Psychology of Optimal Experience*. Harper & Row.
7 Miller, W. R., & Rollnick, S. (2012). *Motivational Interviewing: Helping People Change* (3rd ed.). Guilford Press.

Chapter 8. Connecting with Your 'Why'

1 Frankl, V. E. (1992). *Man's Search for Meaning: An Introduction to Logotherapy* (4th ed.) (I. Lasch, Trans.). Beacon Press.
2 Deci, E. L., & Ryan, R. M. (2000). The 'what' and 'why' of goal pursuits: Human needs and the self-determination of behavior. *Psychological Inquiry*, 11(4), pp.227-268. https://doi.org/10.1207/S15327965PLI1104_01.
3 Seligman, M. E. P. (2011). *Flourish: A Visionary New Understanding of Happiness and Well-being*. New York: Free Press.
4 Pink, D. H. (2011). *Drive: The Surprising Truth About What Motivates Us*. Canongate Press.
5 Duke, A. (2022). *Quit: The Power of Knowing When to Walk Away*. New York: Portfolio/Penguin.
6 Linehan, M. M. (2014). *DBT® Skills Training Handouts and Worksheets* (2nd ed.). Guilford Press.

7   If you're interested in getting into the nitty gritty of 'why' formulation and activation, you might consider pairing what you learn with the following reference: Sinek, S., Mead, D., & Docker, P. (2017). *Find Your Why: A Practical Guide to Discovering Purpose for You and Your Team*. Portfolio/Penguin Random House.

Chapter 9. Values-Based Decision-Making

1   Wood, W., & Neal, D. T. (2007). A new look at habits and the habit-goal interface. *Psychological Review*, 114(4), pp.843-863. https://doi.org/10.1037/0033-295X.114.4.843.

2   Lewis, M. (2012). Obama's Way. *Vanity Fair* (October). https://www.vanityfair.com/news/2012/10/michael-lewis-profile-barack-obama.

3   Wood, W. (2019). *Good Habits, Bad Habits: The Science of Making Positive Changes that Stick*. Picador/Macmillan.

4   Thaler, R. H., & Sunstein, C. R. (2008). *Nudge: Improving Decisions About Health, Wealth, and Happiness*. Yale University Press.

5   Kahneman, D. (2011). *Thinking, Fast and Slow*. Farrar, Straus and Giroux.

6   Neal, D. T., Wood, W., & Quinn, J. M. (2006). Habits—A repeat performance. *Current Directions in Psychological Science*, 15(4), pp.198-202. https://doi.org/10.1111/j.1467-8721.2006.00435.x.

7   James, W. (1890). *The Principles of Psychology*, volume 1. New York: Henry Holt, p.122.

8   Ibid., p.416. (Italics in original.)

9   Hofmann, W., Baumeister, R. F., Förster, G., & Vohs, K. D. (2012). Everyday temptations: An experience sampling study of desire, conflict, and self-control. *Journal of Personality and Social Psychology*, 102(6), pp.1318-1335. https://doi.org/10.1037/a0026545.

10 Prochaska, J. O., & DiClemente, C. C. (1982). Transtheoretical therapy: Toward a more integrative model of change. *Psychotherapy: Theory, Research & Practice*, 19(3), pp.276-288. https://doi.org/10.1037/h0088437.

11 Ryan, R. M., & Deci, E. L. (2000). Self-determination theory and the facilitation of intrinsic motivation, social development, and well-being. *American Psychologist*, 55(1), pp.68-78.

12 Cutler, J., & Campbell-Meiklejohn, A. (2018). A comparative fMRI meta-analysis of altruistic and strategic decisions to give. *NeuroImage*, 184, pp.227-241. https://doi.org/10.1016/j.neuroimage.2018.09.009.

13 Stanovich, K. E., & West, R. F. (2000). Individual differences in reasoning: Implications for the rationality debate? *Behavioral and Brain Sciences*, 23(5), pp.645-665. https://doi.org/10.1017/S0140525X00003435.

14 Tversky, A., & Kahneman, D. (1974). Judgment under uncertainty: Heuristics and biases. *Science*, 185(4157), pp.1124-1131. https://doi.org/10.1126/science.185.4157.1124.

15 Kakinohana, R. K., & Ronaldo, P. (2023). Differences in decisions affected by cognitive biases: Examining human values, need for cognition, and numeracy. *Psicologia*, 36(26), pp.1-14. https://doi.org/10.1186/s41155-023-00265-z.

NOTES

16 Wood, W., & Neal, D. T. (2007). A new look at habits and the habit-goal interface. *Psychological Review*, 114(4), pp.843–863. https://doi.org/10.1037/0033-295X.114.4.843.
17 Ryan, R. M., & Deci, E. L. (2000). Self-determination theory and the facilitation of intrinsic motivation, social development, and well-being. *American Psychologist*, 55(1), pp.68-78. https://doi.org/10.1037/0003-066X.55.1.68.
18 Miller, W. R. & Rollnick, S. (2023). *Motivational Interviewing: Helping People Change and Grow*. (4th ed.) New York: Guilford Press.
19 I standardised this values-based decision-making exercise while in the Decision Neuroscience Lab at the University of Melbourne around 2018, and in 2019–2020, with the help of the incredible developer Bill Malkin who brought my wireframes to life, it was built into a tool called Eiris.
20 Dammann, O., Friederichs, K. M., Lebedinski, S., & Liesenfeld, K.M. (2021). The essence of authenticity. *Frontiers in Psychology*, 11. https://doi.org/10.3389/fpsyg.2020.629654.

Chapter 10. The Worthy Role of Values at Work

1 Tessema, M., Dhumal, P., Sauers, D., Tewolde, S., & Teckle, P. (2019). Analysis of corporate value statements: An empirical study. *International Journal of Corporate Governance*, 10(2), pp.149-164. https://doi.org/10.1504/IJCG.2019.101522.
2 Gorenak, M., & Košir, S. (2012). The importance of organizational values for organization. *Management, Knowledge and Learning International Conference 2012*, pp. 563-569.
3 Sazzamply is a fictional company and any likeness to a real company is purely coincidental. This example brings together common features I have seen across multiple companies and industries.
4 Rushworth, S. (2008). The what, why and how of organisational values: A study of the interpretation and implementation of organisational values within fast-growing Australian companies. PhD Thesis. Australian Graduate School of Entrepreneurship: Swinburne University of Technology. https://doi.org/10.25916/sut.26273254.v1.
5 Dammann, O., Friederichs, K. M., Lebedinski, S., Liesenfeld, K. M. (2021). The essence of authenticity. *Frontiers in Psychology*, 11. https://doi.org/10.3389/fpsyg.2020.629654.
6 'Emotion network' is shorthand for a distributed network of processes that impact on our affective state. I am not meaning to refer to a literal and singular 'emotion system' that has some sort of discrete entity or fingerprint in the brain.

Chapter 11. Conclusion

1 Fiat money has value because a government declares it as legal tender, but it lacks the inherent worth of physical commodities like gold or silver, or even a cow. It allows us, among other things, to exchange pieces of paper or plastic ('cash') for goods or services, such as a new car, or to deduct points from a digital ledger (like money from a debit or credit card) to pay for tangible items, like a loaf of bread or an educational course.